How to tell if your
cat
is plotting to
kill you

Also by The Oatmeal

5 VERY GOOD REASONS TO PUNCH A DOLPHIN IN THE MOUTH (AND OTHER USEFUL GUIDES)

How to tell if your
cat
is plotting to
kill you

The Oatmeal

**Andrews McMeel
Publishing, LLC**
Kansas City · Sydney · London

HOW TO TELL IF YOUR CAT IS PLOTTING TO KILL YOU

Andrews McMeel Publishing, LLC
an Andrews McMeel Universal company
1130 Walnut Street, Kansas City, Missouri 64106

www.andrewsmcmeel.com

13 14 15 16 17 TEN 15 14 13

ISBN: 978-1-4494-1024-7

Library of Congress Control Number: 2012935506

ATTENTION: SCHOOLS AND BUSINESSES
Andrews McMeel books are available at quantity discounts with bulk purchase for educational, business, or sales promotional use. For information, please e-mail the Andrews McMeel Publishing Special Sales Department: specialsales@amuniversal.com

Contents

6
ways
to tell if your
cat thinks it's a
mountain lion

1. Disappearing outdoors for days at a time,
returning looking like he just finished a fourth tour of Vietnam.

(These are kitty "Vision quests.")

2. Constantly attempting to take down animals much larger than himself.

3. Eating dog food.

Your cat is trying to bulk up by taking in excess protein.

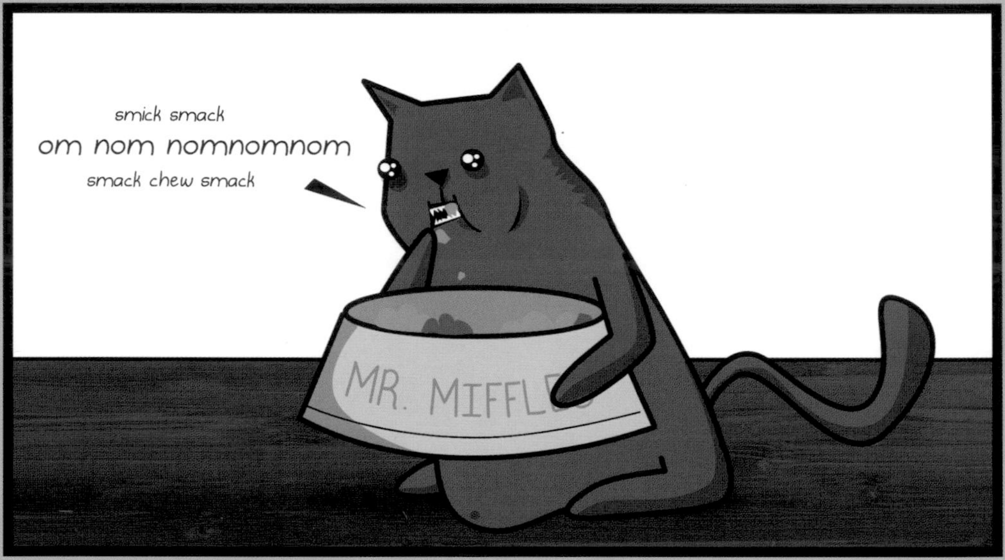
smick smack
om nom nomnomnom
smack chew smack
MR. MIFFL

4. Showing no fear of large predators.

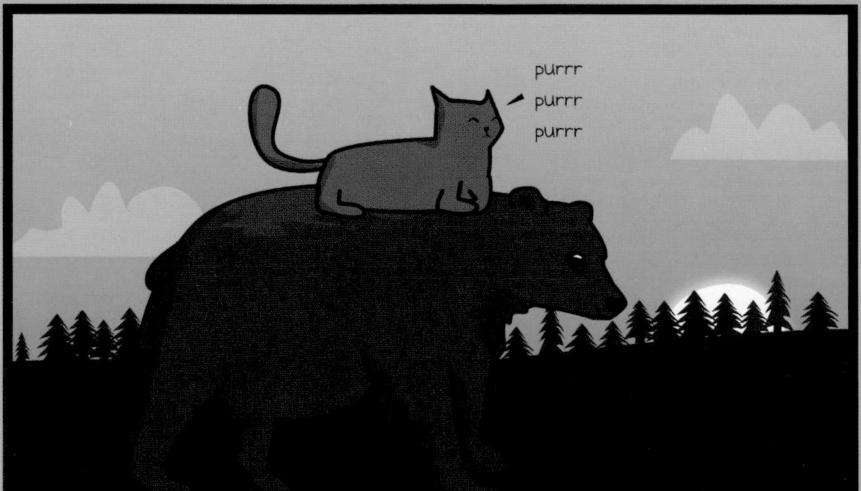
purrr
purrr
purrr

5. Sneaking up on large, inanimate objects.

This is caribou hunting practice.

6. Being overly vocal.

Your cat thinks these are terrifying roars of awesomeness.

MROOWWWWRR
MRAWMARMM MROW
OWRR MROPOWMRRRRR

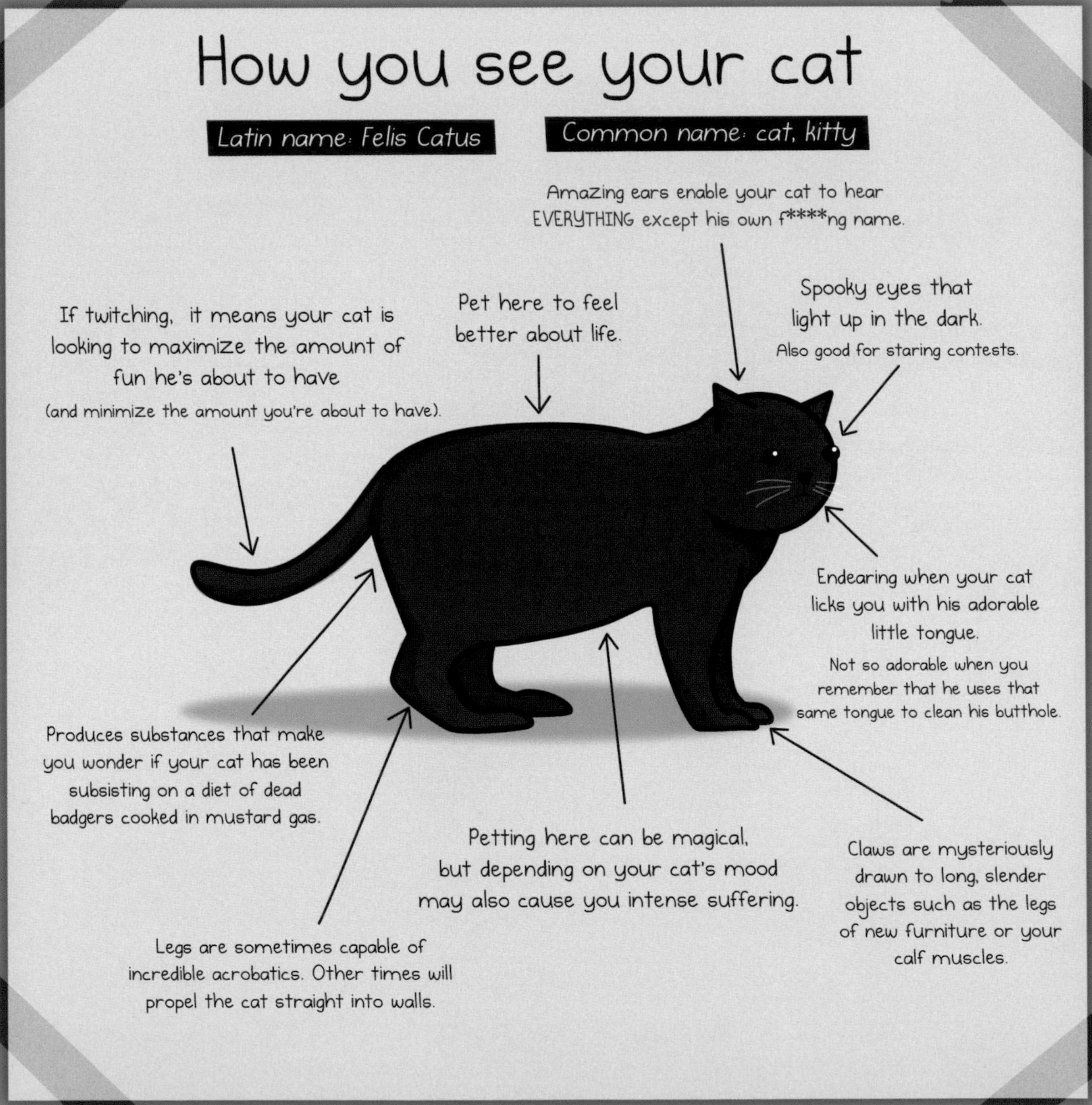
How you see your cat
Latin name: Felis Catus
Common name: cat, kitty
Amazing ears enable your cat to hear EVERYTHING except his own f****ng name.
Pet here to feel better about life.
If twitching, it means your cat is looking to maximize the amount of fun he's about to have (and minimize the amount you're about to have).
Spooky eyes that light up in the dark. Also good for staring contests.
Endearing when your cat licks you with his adorable little tongue. Not so adorable when you remember that he uses that same tongue to clean his butthole.
Produces substances that make you wonder if your cat has been subsisting on a diet of dead badgers cooked in mustard gas.
Petting here can be magical, but depending on your cat's mood may also cause you intense suffering.
Claws are mysteriously drawn to long, slender objects such as the legs of new furniture or your calf muscles.
Legs are sometimes capable of incredible acrobatics. Other times will propel the cat straight into walls.

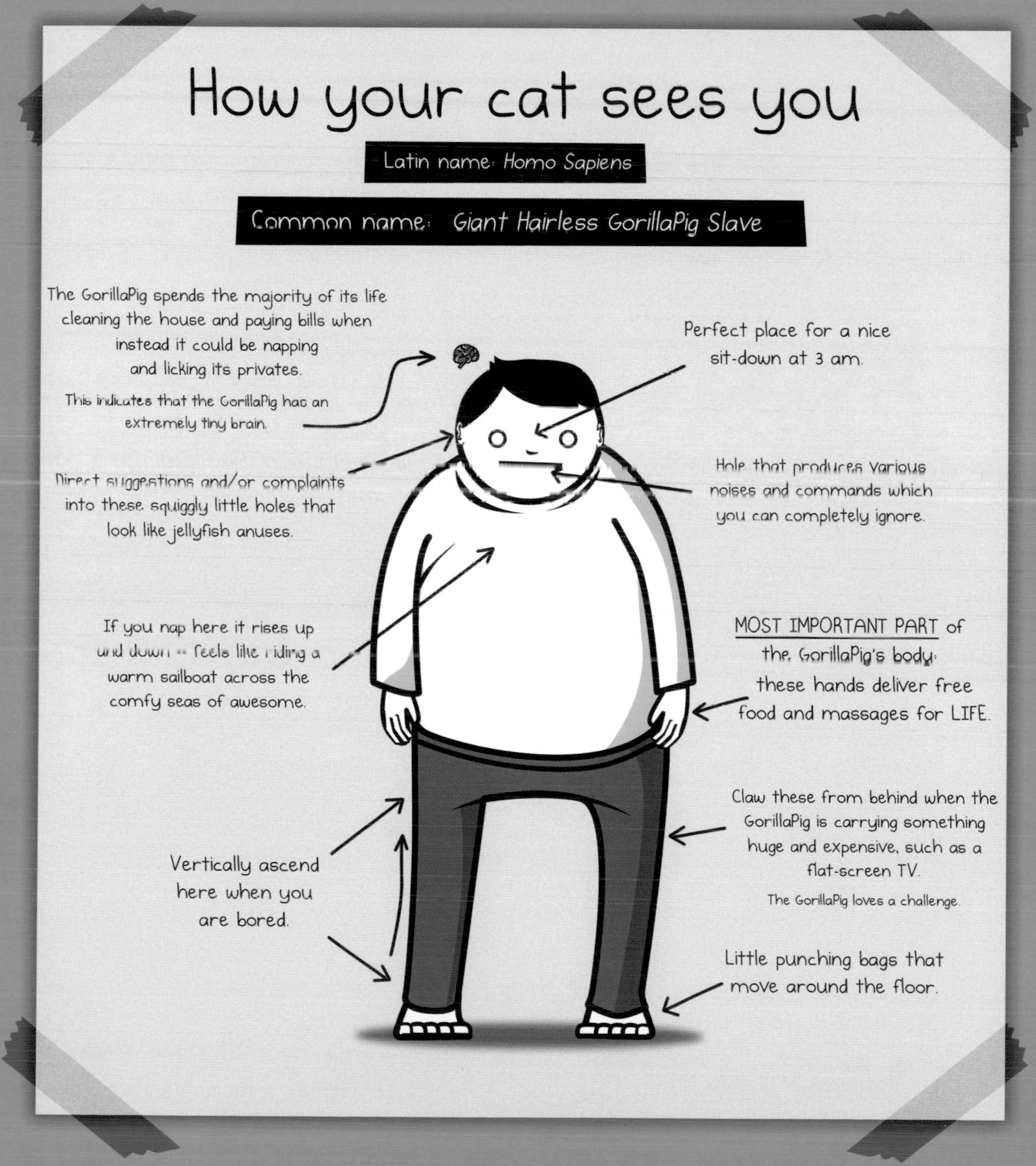
How your cat sees you
Latin name: Homo Sapiens
Common name: Giant Hairless GorillaPig Slave
The GorillaPig spends the majority of its life cleaning the house and paying bills when instead it could be napping and licking its privates.
This indicates that the GorillaPig has an extremely tiny brain.
Perfect place for a nice sit-down at 3 am.
Direct suggestions and/or complaints into these squiggly little holes that look like jellyfish anuses.
Hole that produces various noises and commands which you can completely ignore.
If you nap here it rises up and down -- feels like riding a warm sailboat across the comfy seas of awesome.
MOST IMPORTANT PART of the GorillaPig's body: these hands deliver free food and massages for LIFE.
Claw these from behind when the GorillaPig is carrying something huge and expensive, such as a flat-screen TV.
The GorillaPig loves a challenge.
Vertically ascend here when you are bored.
Little punching bags that move around the floor.

How to pet a kitty

1 The kitty decides when it's petting time.

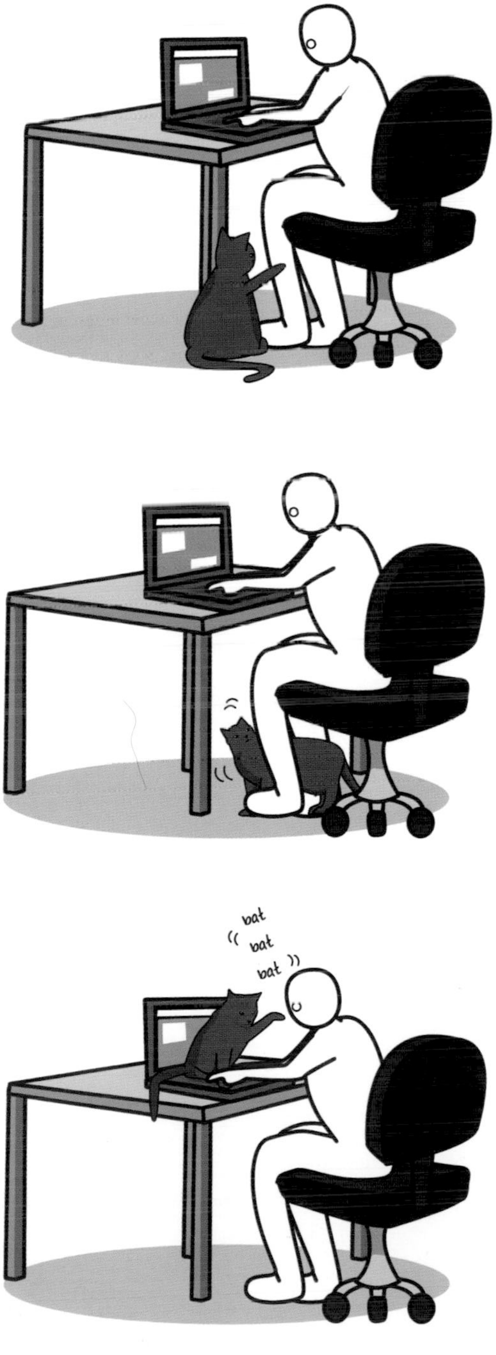
bat
bat
bat

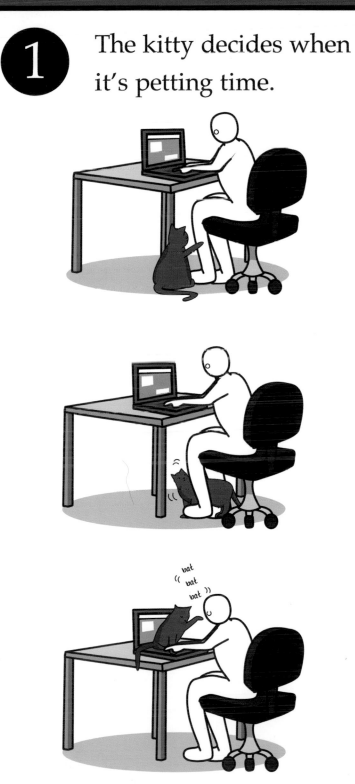

2 Do not pet the kitty like this; it is wrong.

pat
pat
pat

This is also wrong:

shick
shick
shick

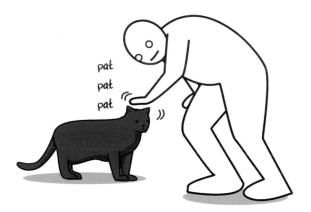

3 If the kitty purrs, you are doing a satisfactory job.

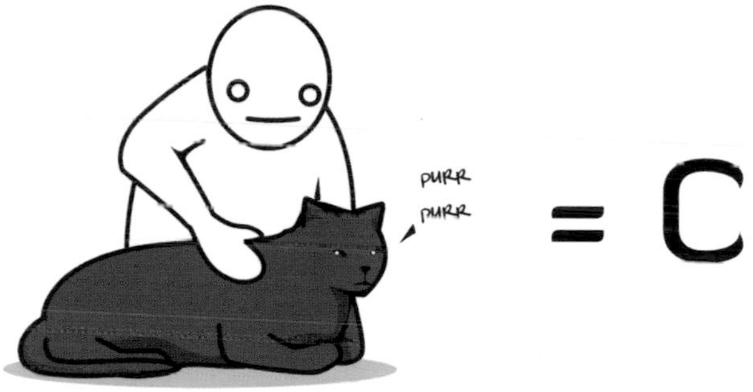
PURR
PURR
= C

If the kitty dozes off, you are doing an excellent job.

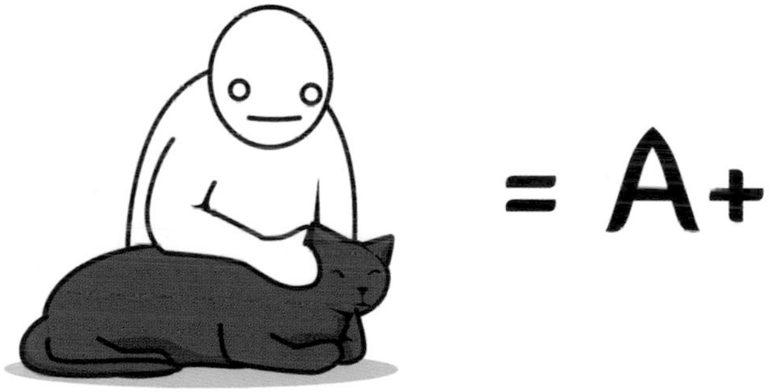
= A+

If the kitty is staring at you with their ears pointed backwards, you are doing an unsatisfactory job.

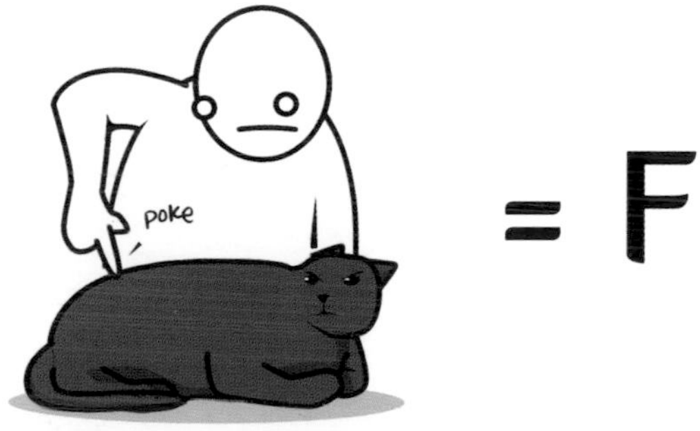
POKE
= F

4

If the kitty exposes their belly, it is an invitation for a tummy rub.

Do not turn this invitation down. It has been said that petting the tummy of a kitty is like frolicking in the back hair of an angel.

An exposed belly, however, can also mean the kitty wants to ensnare you into a whiskered bear trap composed of claws, teeth, and agony.

The trick is to look into their eyes first.

What do you see?

Empathy?

Or murder?

Biting and clawing is a form of "love mauling."
The more pain they deal out, the more they are trying to tell you that they love you.

Endure the pain and do not stop petting your kitty.

5 Do not prematurely end the petting session.

If you do, your kitty will log the time and make up the deficit later.

GIFT IDEAS FOR MY OWNER'S BIRTHDAY

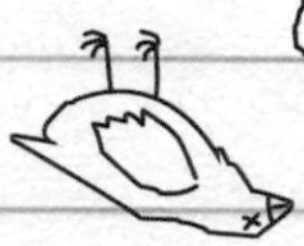

Leave a dead bird on the front porch

Leave a dead bird on the back porch

Leave a dead bird in the living room

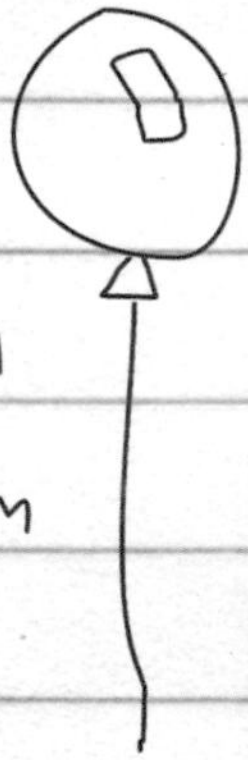

Leave a MOSTLY dead bird in the living room

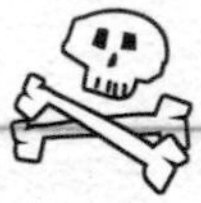

wait until he sees it
and then proceed to make it 100% dead HAHAHAAA

Leave a decapitated bird head in the bedroom

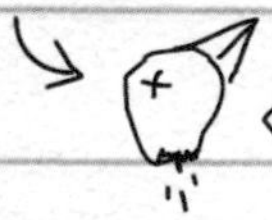

Where's the rest of it ??!!
two part Birthday SURPRISE!!!

Barf on something shiny
↳ Smartphone?
↳ windshield?
↳ his forehead?

chew up OLD FAMILY PHOTOS.
(he loves me more than those stoopid Relatives anyway)

When he gets home from work, Jump up and CLAW him in the nards

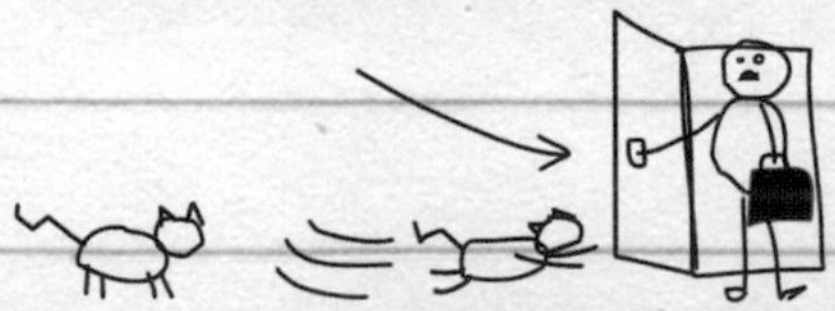

Nard assault increases exciting Birthday fun-ness BY 10,000%

When your cat likes to sprint at high speeds

 When in a hurry

 When you shout his or her name.

At 3:37 am when a Formula One race track magically appears around the sides of your bed

How to tell if your **cat** is plotting to **kill you**

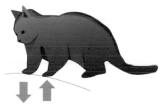

Kneading on you

You may think this is a sign of affection, but your cat is actually checking your internal organs for weaknesses.

Excessive shoveling of kitty litter

After using the litter box, your cat needlessly kicks litter around, most of it ending up all over the room.

This is practice for burying bodies.

Staring Contests

If you get caught in a staring contest with your cat, do not look away. Looking away will signal to your cat that you are weak, and an attack is likely to follow.

Bringing you dead animals

This isn't a gift. It's a warning.

Throwing up grass

Through this painful feeding and purging process, cats prepare their minds and bodies for combat.

Hiding in dark places and watching you

Your cat will often hide in order to study you in your natural habitat.

Sleeping on your electronics

Humans have superior technology.
Your cat knows this and will attempt to disrupt
all communications to the outside world.

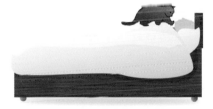

Pawing at your face
while you sleep

Cats aren't very good at
smothering people, but this
won't stop them from trying.

Sprinting at light speed out
of any room you enter

When your cat does this,
it's actually a failed ambush.

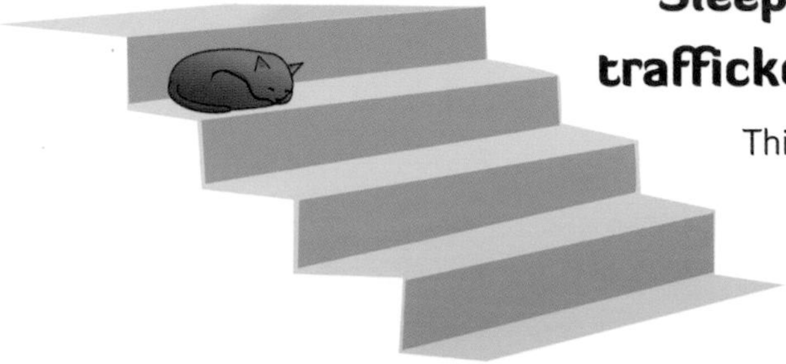

Sleeping in the highest trafficked part of the house

This is a "kitty landmine."

Constantly giving you the stink eye

for no damned reason at all.

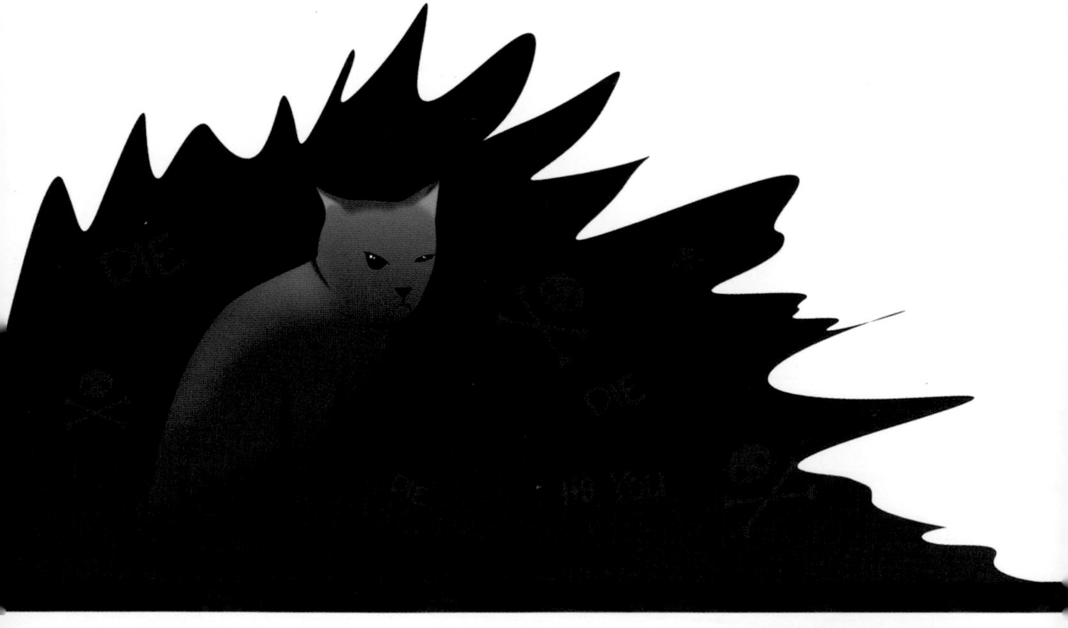

Excessive yawning

This is not a yawn;
this is your cat's **war face.**

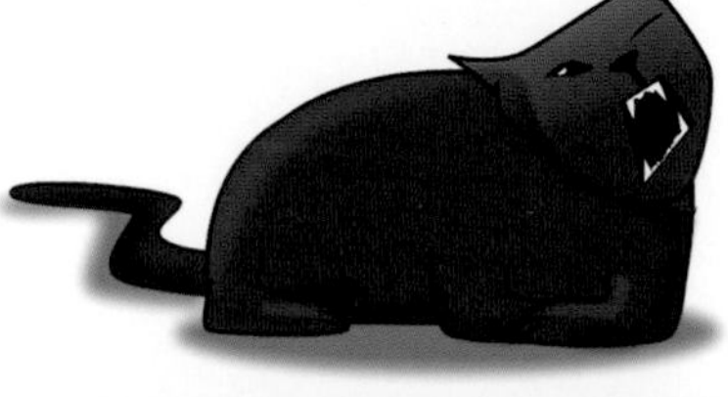

The Bobcats
Episode 1: Monday

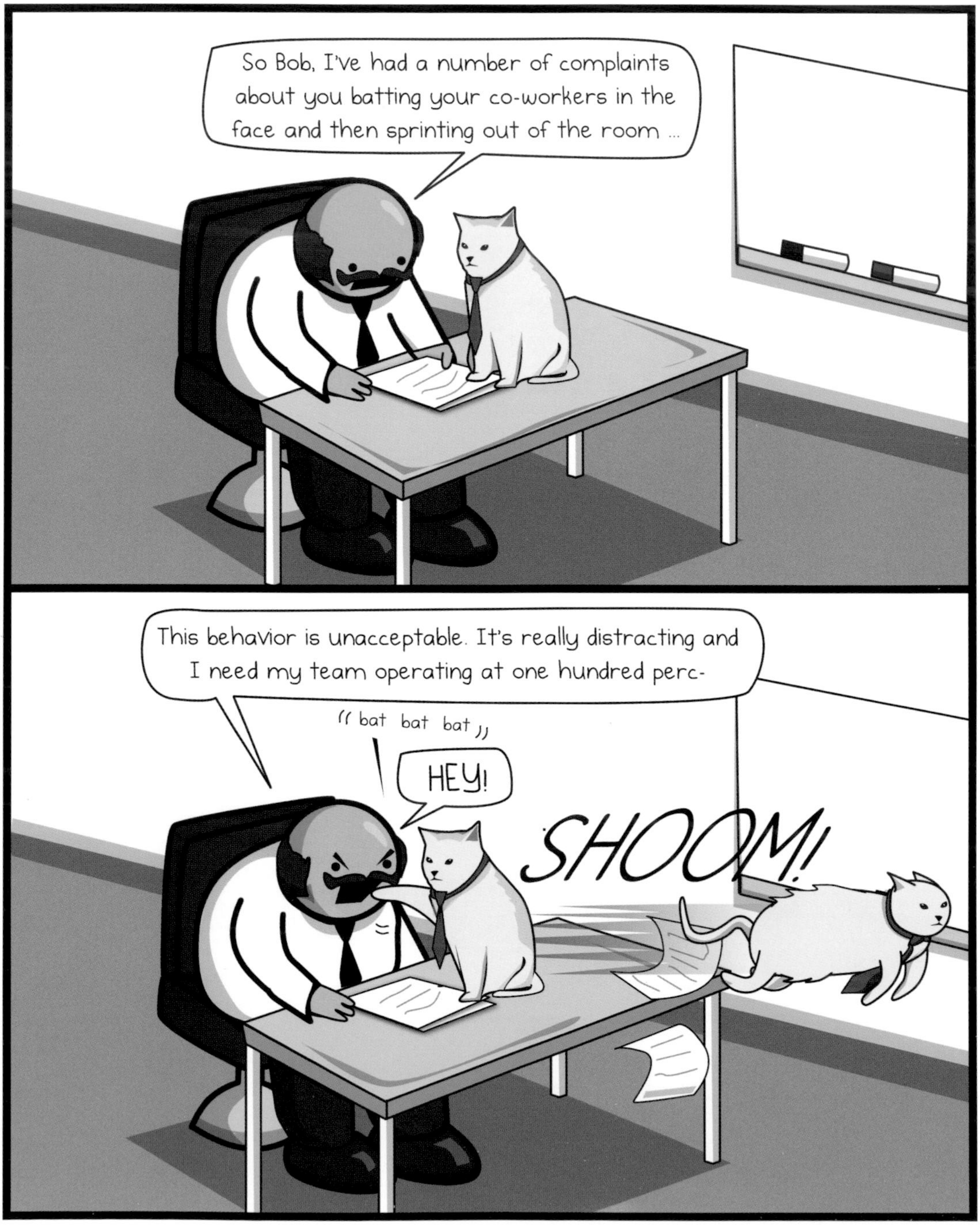
So Bob, I've had a number of complaints about you batting your co-workers in the face and then sprinting out of the room ...
This behavior is unacceptable. It's really distracting and I need my team operating at one hundred perc-
"bat bat bat"
HEY!
SHOOM!

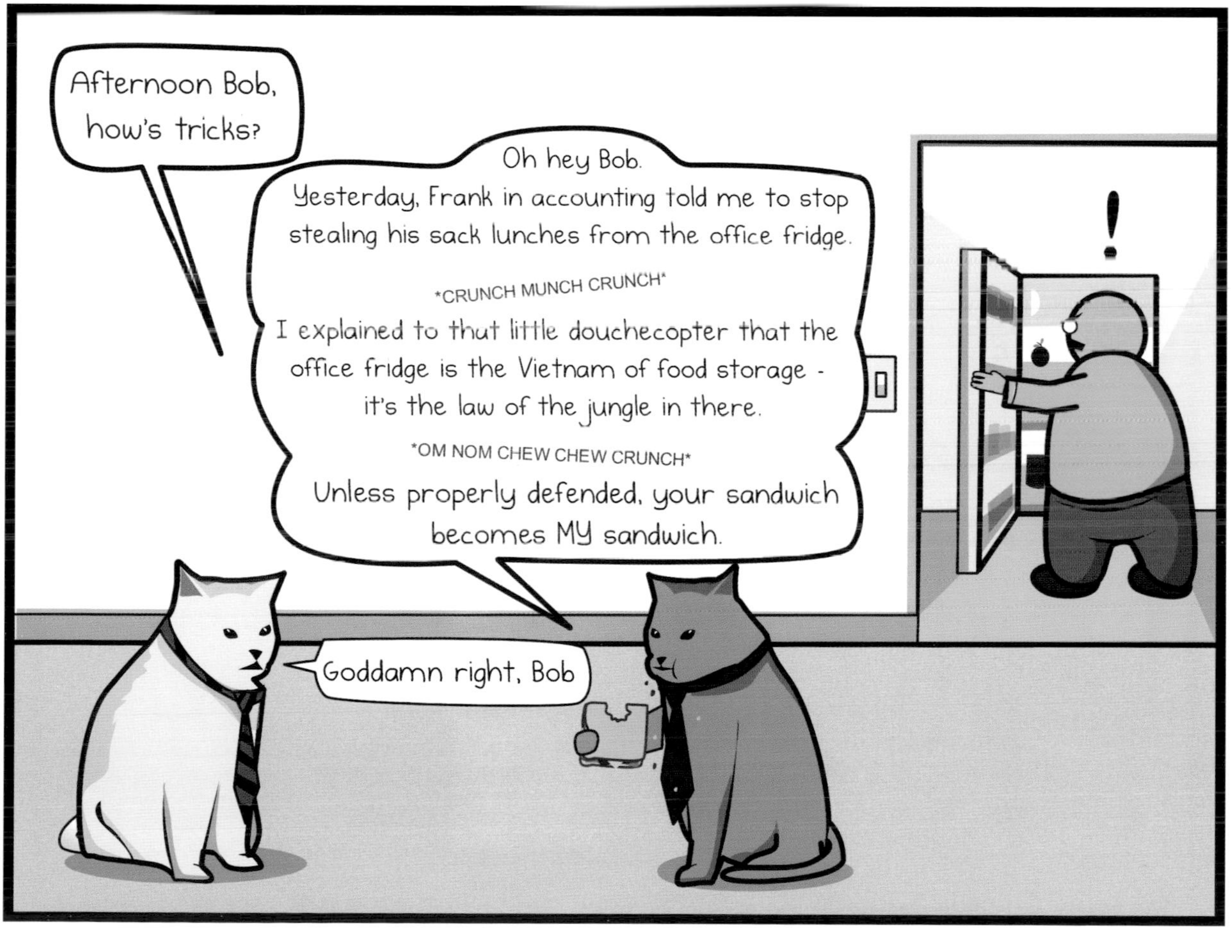

Afternoon Bob, how's tricks?
Oh hey Bob. Yesterday, Frank in accounting told me to stop stealing his sack lunches from the office fridge.
CRUNCH MUNCH CRUNCH
I explained to that little douchecopter that the office fridge is the Vietnam of food storage - it's the law of the jungle in there.
OM NOM CHEW CHEW CRUNCH
Unless properly defended, your sandwich becomes MY sandwich.
!
Goddamn right, Bob

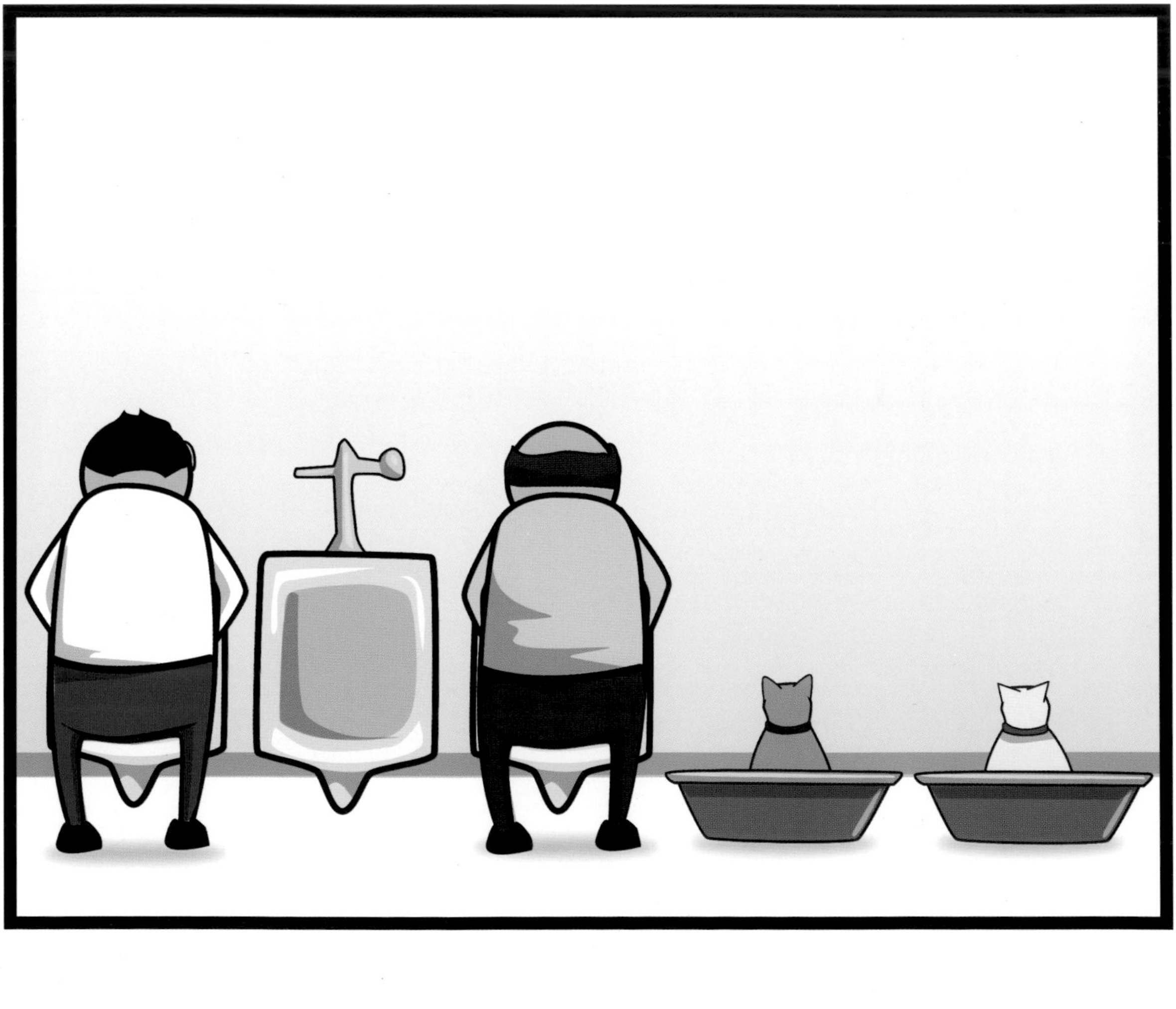

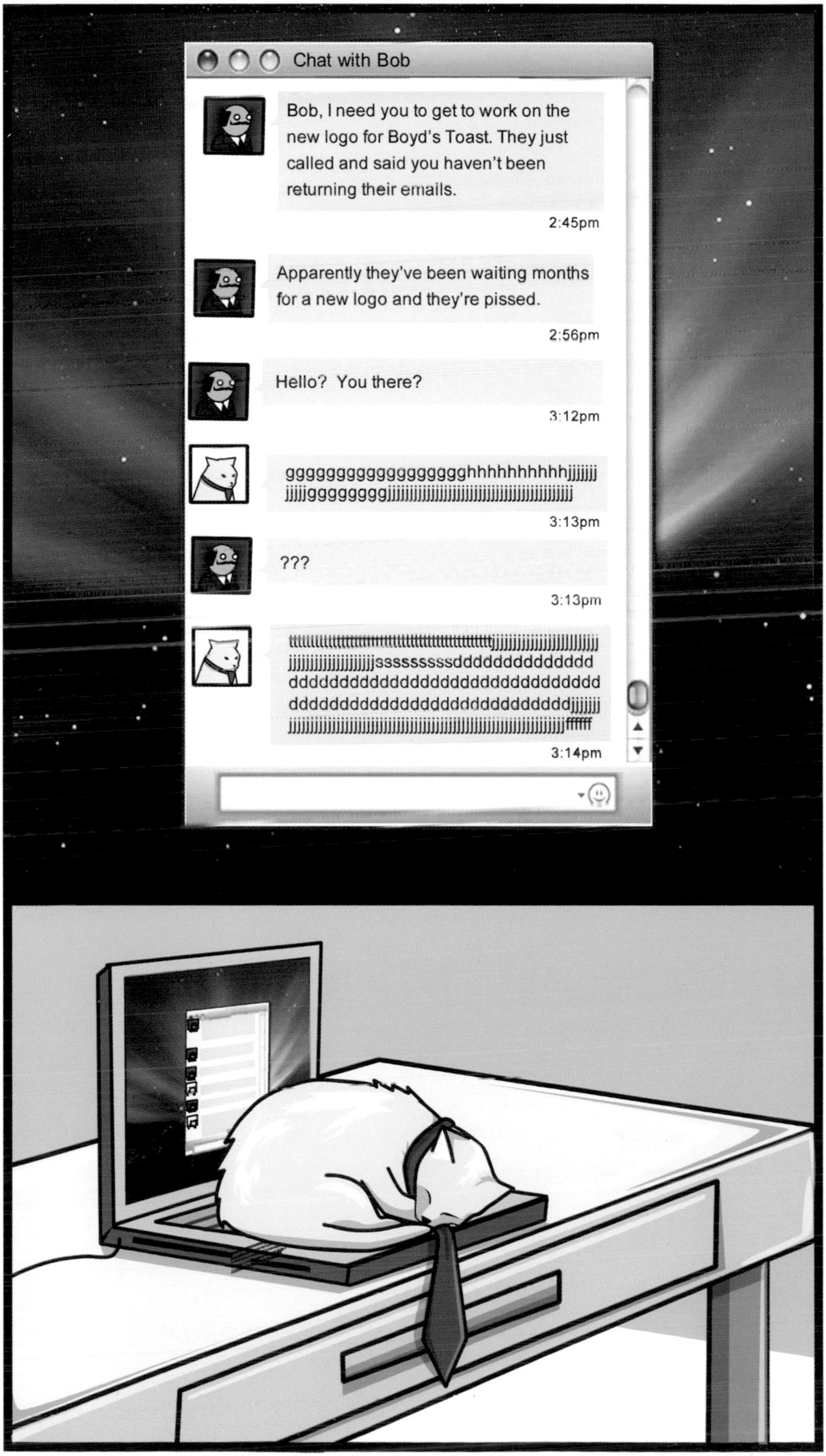
Chat with Bob
Bob, I need you to get to work on the new logo for Boyd's Toast. They just called and said you haven't been returning their emails.
2:45pm
Apparently they've been waiting months for a new logo and they're pissed.
2:56pm
Hello? You there?
3:12pm
ggggggggggggggggghhhhhhhhhjjjjjj jjjjggggggggjjjjjjjjjjjjjjjjjjjjjjjjjjjjjjjjjjjjjjjjjjjj
3:13pm
???
3:13pm
tttttttttttttttttttttttttttttttttttttttttjjjjjjjjjjjjjjjjjjjjjj jjjjjjjjjjjjjjjjjjjjjjsssssssssddddddddddddd ddddddddddddddddddddddddddddddd ddddddddddddddddddddddddddddjjjjjj jjjjjjjjjjjjjjjjjjjjjjjjjjjjjjjjjjjjjjjjjjjjjjjjjjjjjjjjjffffff
3:14pm

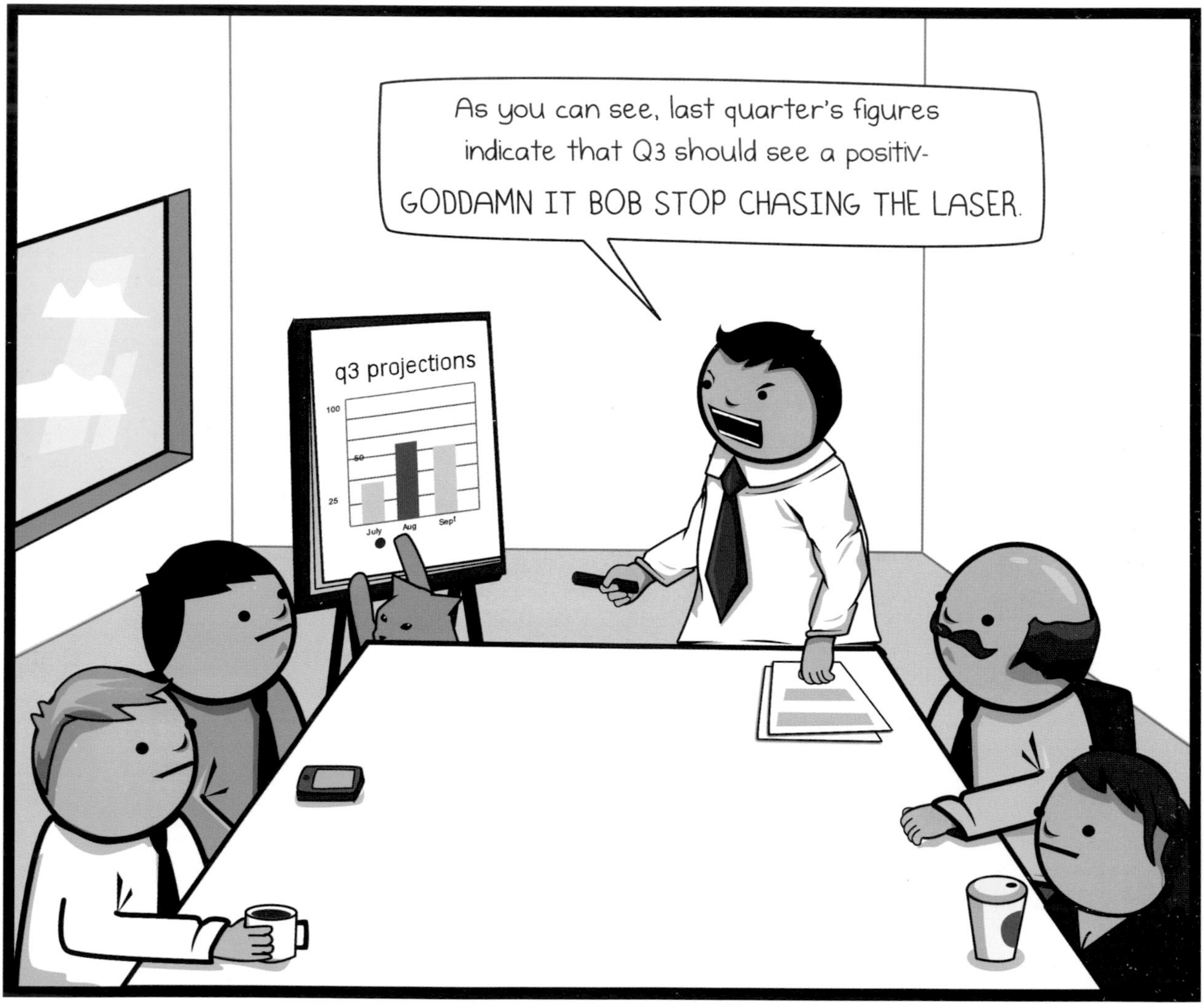
As you can see, last quarter's figures indicate that Q3 should see a positiv-
GODDAMN IT BOB STOP CHASING THE LASER.
q3 projections
100
50
25
July
Aug
Sept

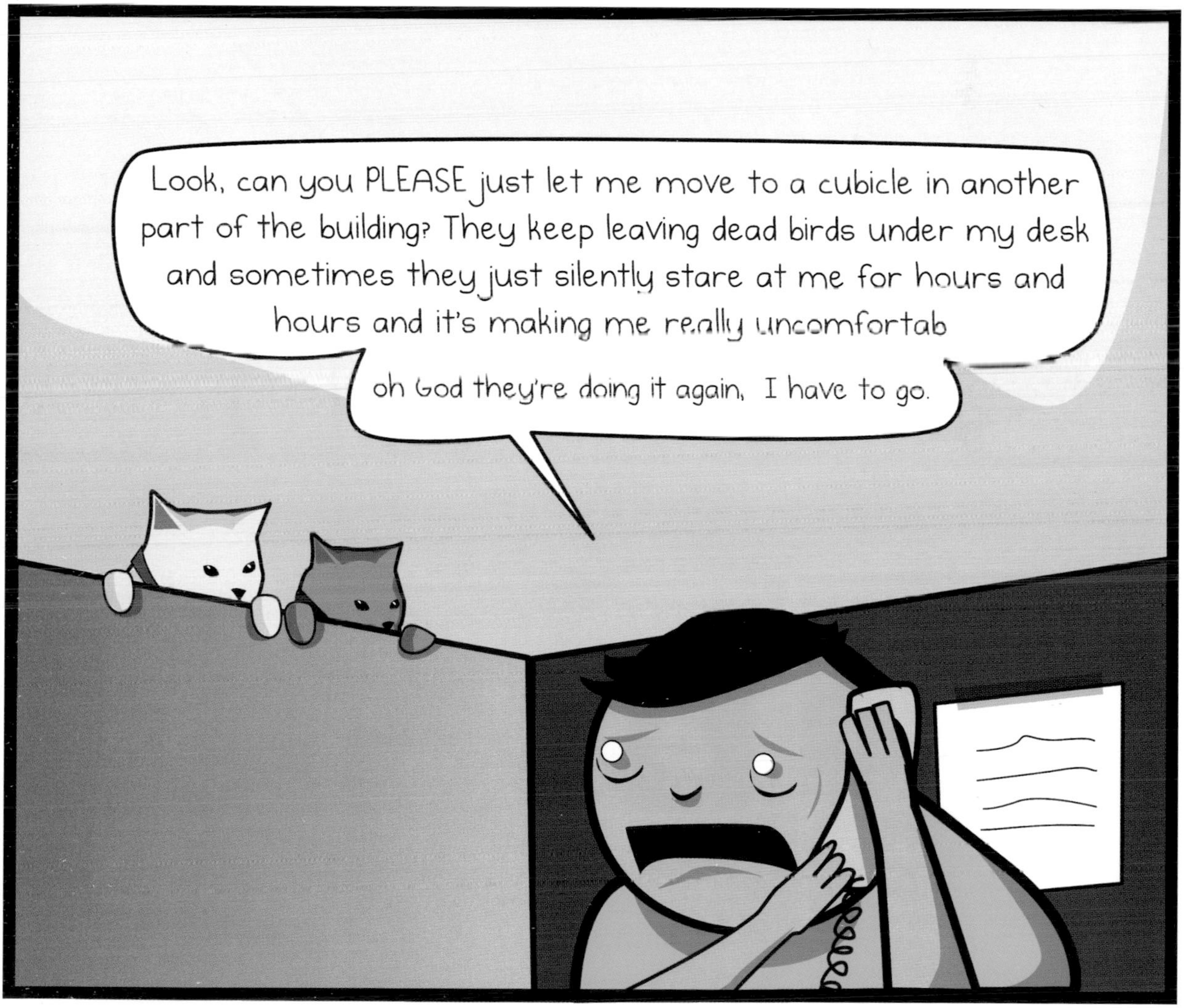
Look, can you PLEASE just let me move to a cubicle in another part of the building? They keep leaving dead birds under my desk and sometimes they just silently stare at me for hours and hours and it's making me really uncomfortab
oh God they're doing it again. I have to go.

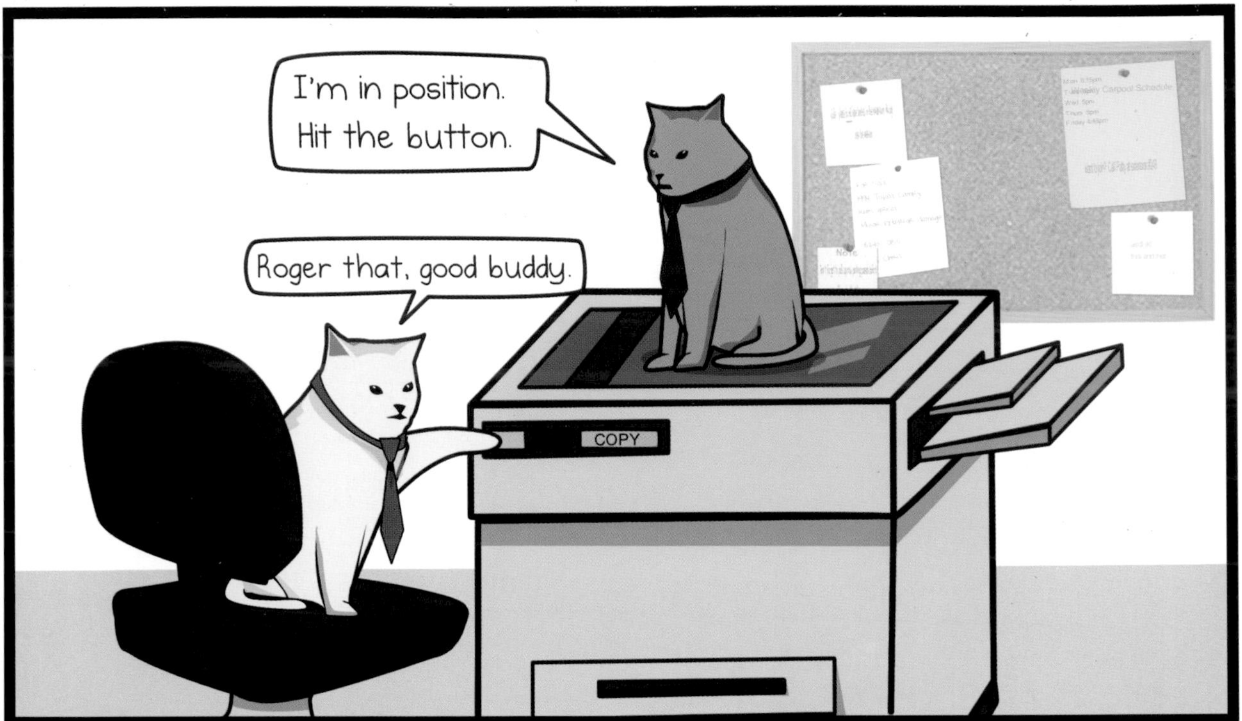
I'm in position. Hit the button.
Roger that, good buddy.
COPY

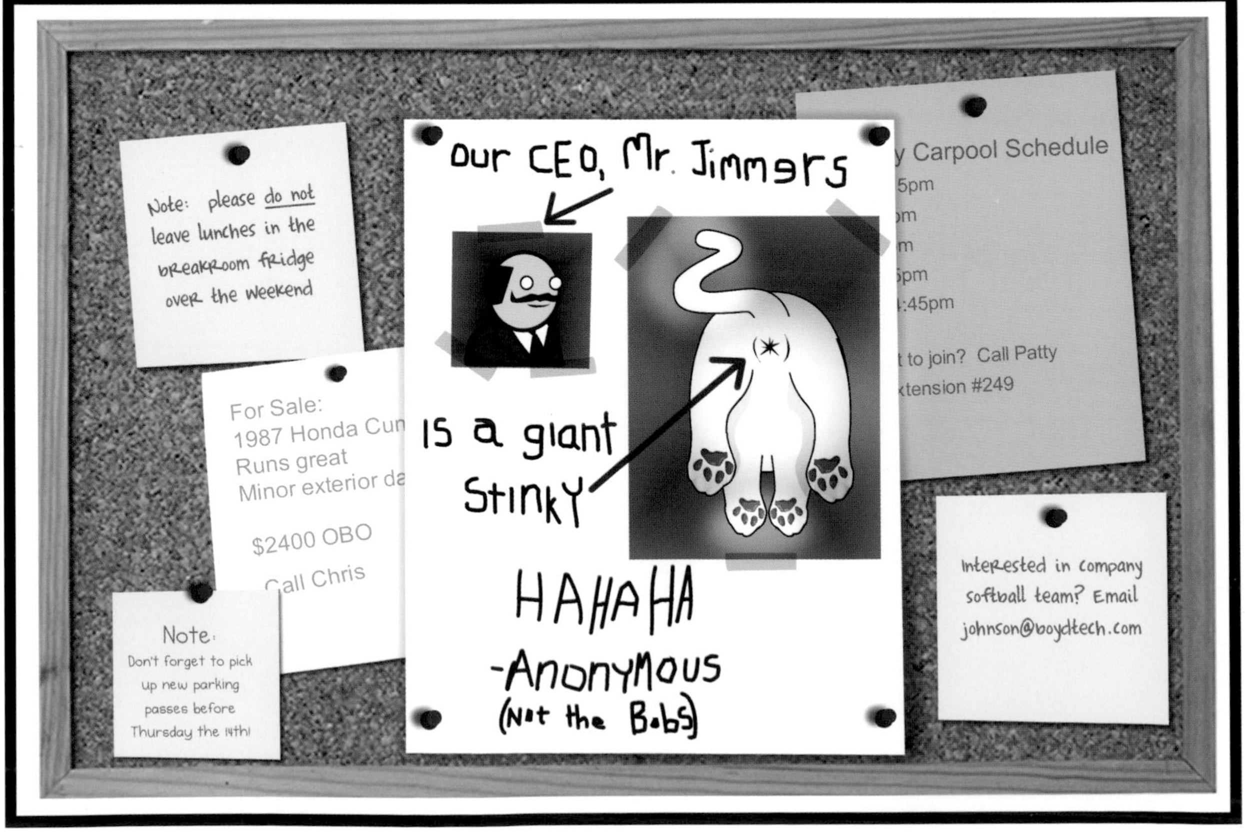
Note: please do not leave lunches in the breakroom fridge over the weekend
For Sale:
1987 Honda Cu
Runs great
Minor exterior da
$2400 OBO
Call Chris
Note:
Don't forget to pick up new parking passes before Thursday the 14th!
Our CEO, Mr. Jimmers
is a giant Stinky
HAHAHA
-Anonymous
(Not the Bobs)
y Carpool Schedule
5pm
m
m
5pm
:45pm
t to join? Call Patty
xtension #249
Interested in company softball team? Email johnson@boydtech.com

The Bobcats

Episode 2: Tuesday

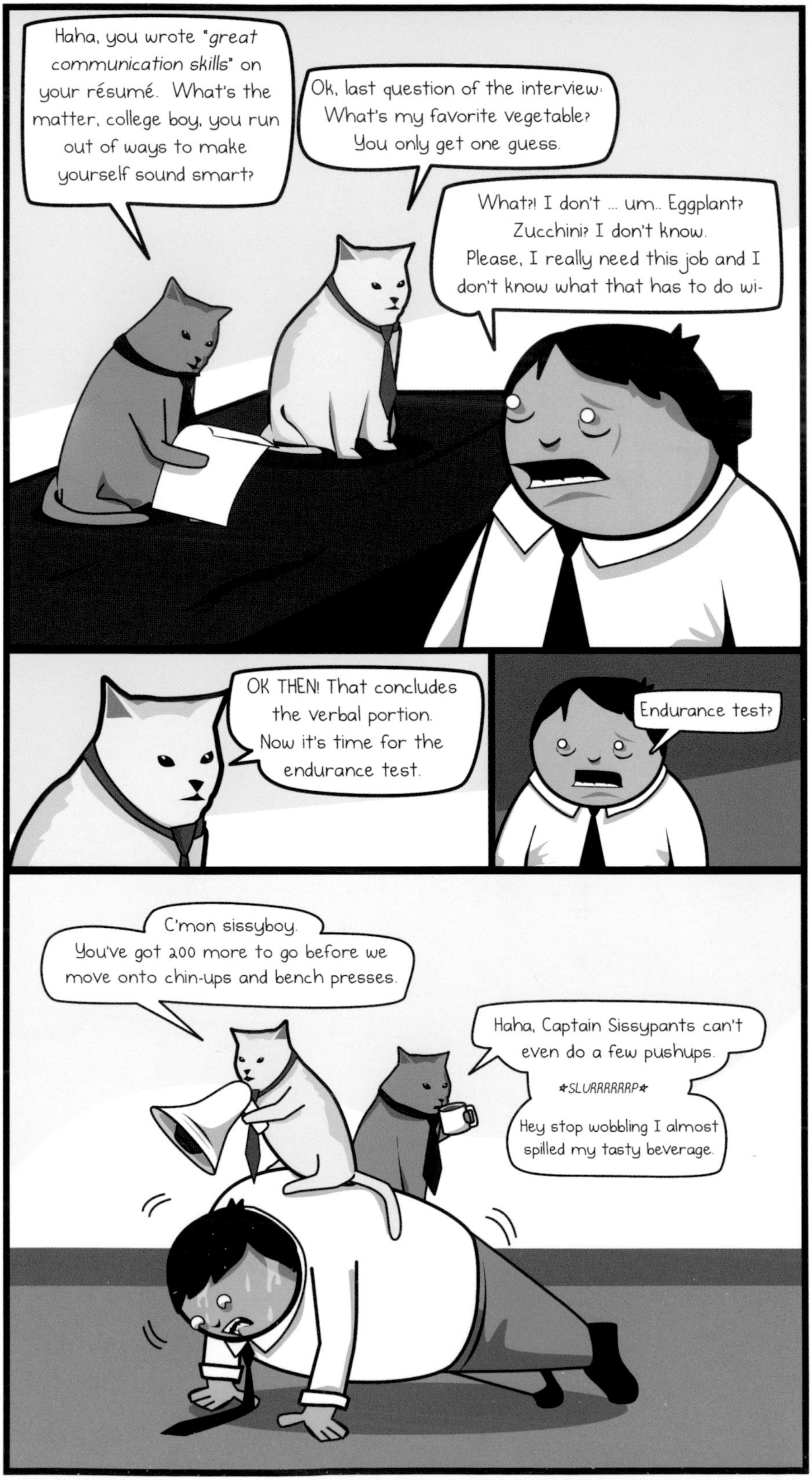
Haha, you wrote "*great communication skills*" on your résumé. What's the matter, college boy, you run out of ways to make yourself sound smart?
Ok, last question of the interview: What's my favorite vegetable? You only get one guess.
What?! I don't ... um.. Eggplant? Zucchini? I don't know. Please, I really need this job and I don't know what that has to do wi-
OK THEN! That concludes the verbal portion. Now it's time for the endurance test.
Endurance test?
C'mon sissyboy. You've got 200 more to go before we move onto chin-ups and bench presses.
Haha, Captain Sissypants can't even do a few pushups.
SLURRRRRRP
Hey stop wobbling I almost spilled my tasty beverage.

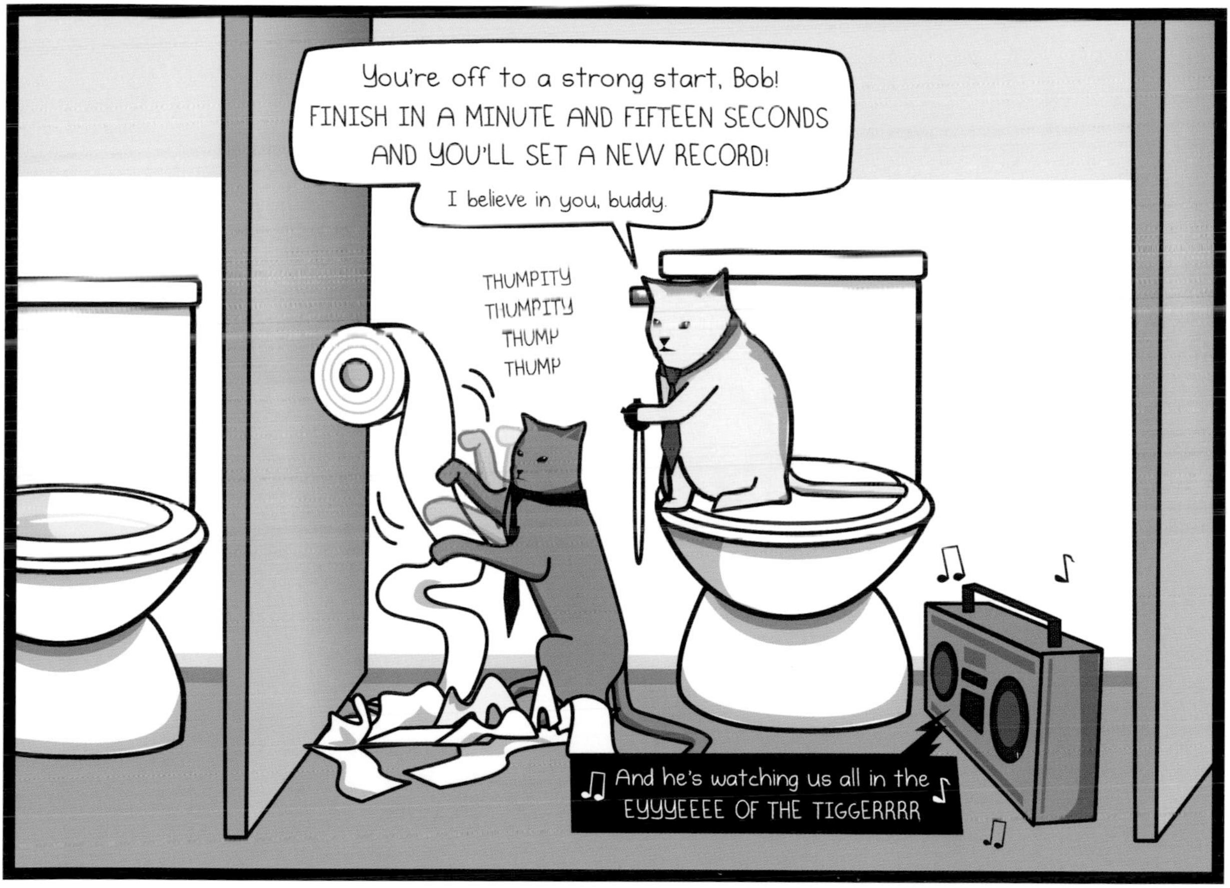
You're off to a strong start, Bob!
FINISH IN A MINUTE AND FIFTEEN SECONDS
AND YOU'LL SET A NEW RECORD!
I believe in you, buddy.
THUMPITY
THUMPITY
THUMP
THUMP
And he's watching us all in the
EYYYEEEE OF THE TIGGERRRR

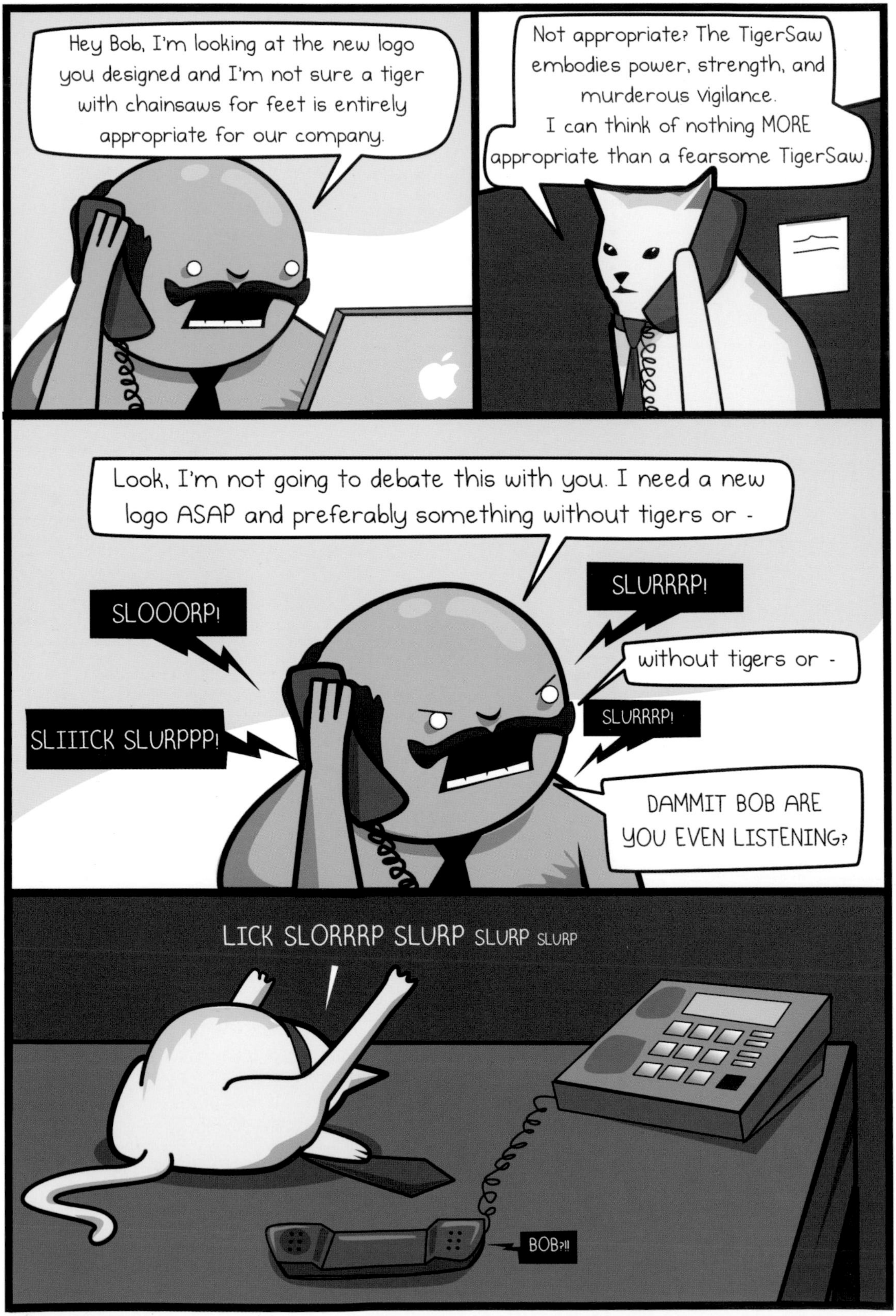
Hey Bob, I'm looking at the new logo you designed and I'm not sure a tiger with chainsaws for feet is entirely appropriate for our company.
Not appropriate? The TigerSaw embodies power, strength, and murderous vigilance.
I can think of nothing MORE appropriate than a fearsome TigerSaw.
Look, I'm not going to debate this with you. I need a new logo ASAP and preferably something without tigers or -
SLOOORP!
SLURRRP!
without tigers or -
SLIIICK SLURPPP!
SLURRRP!
DAMMIT BOB ARE YOU EVEN LISTENING?
LICK SLORRRP SLURP SLURP SLURP
BOB?!!

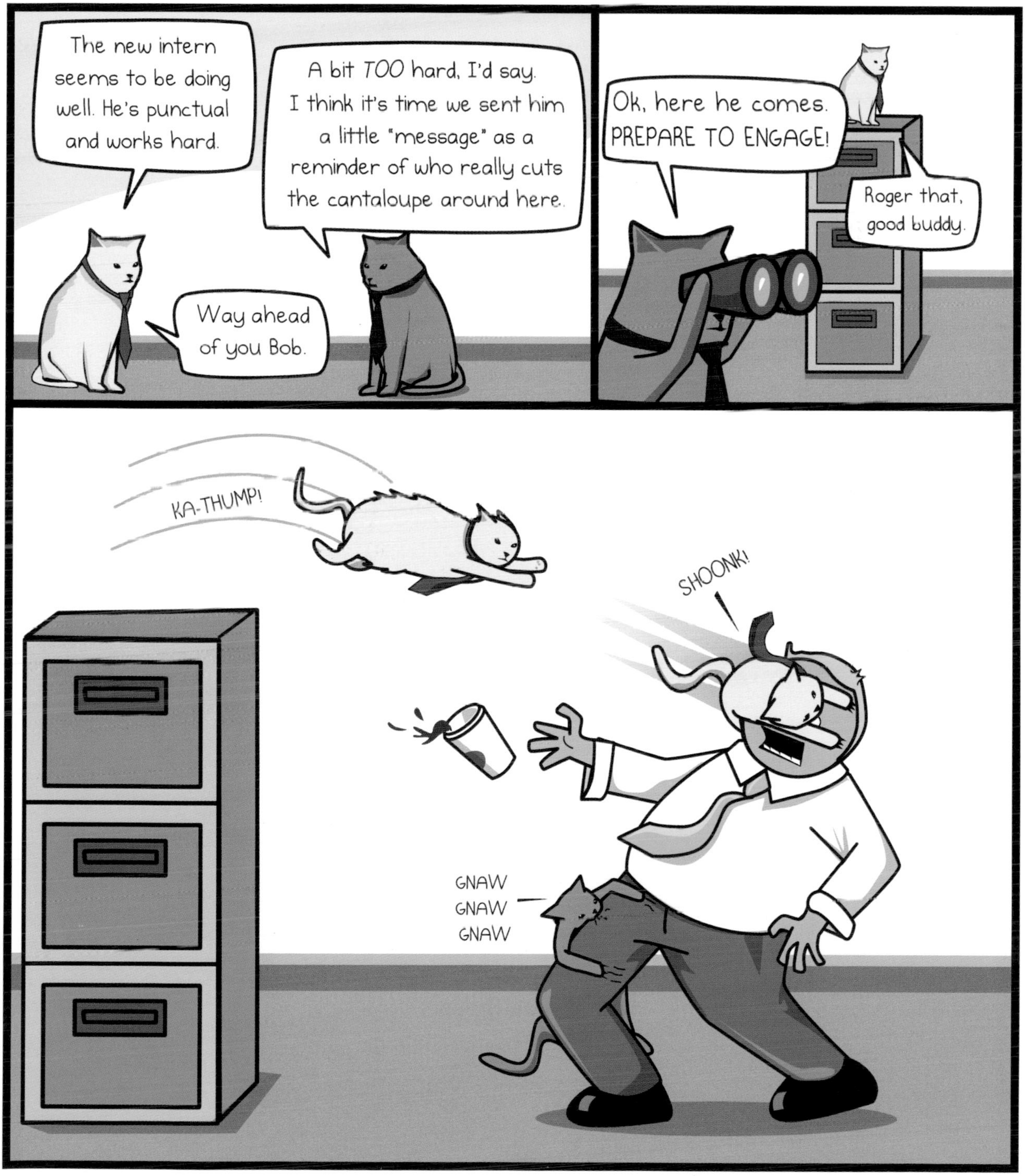
The new intern seems to be doing well. He's punctual and works hard.
A bit TOO hard, I'd say. I think it's time we sent him a little "message" as a reminder of who really cuts the cantaloupe around here.
Way ahead of you Bob.
Ok, here he comes. PREPARE TO ENGAGE!
Roger that, good buddy.
KA-THUMP!
SHOONK!
GNAW GNAW GNAW

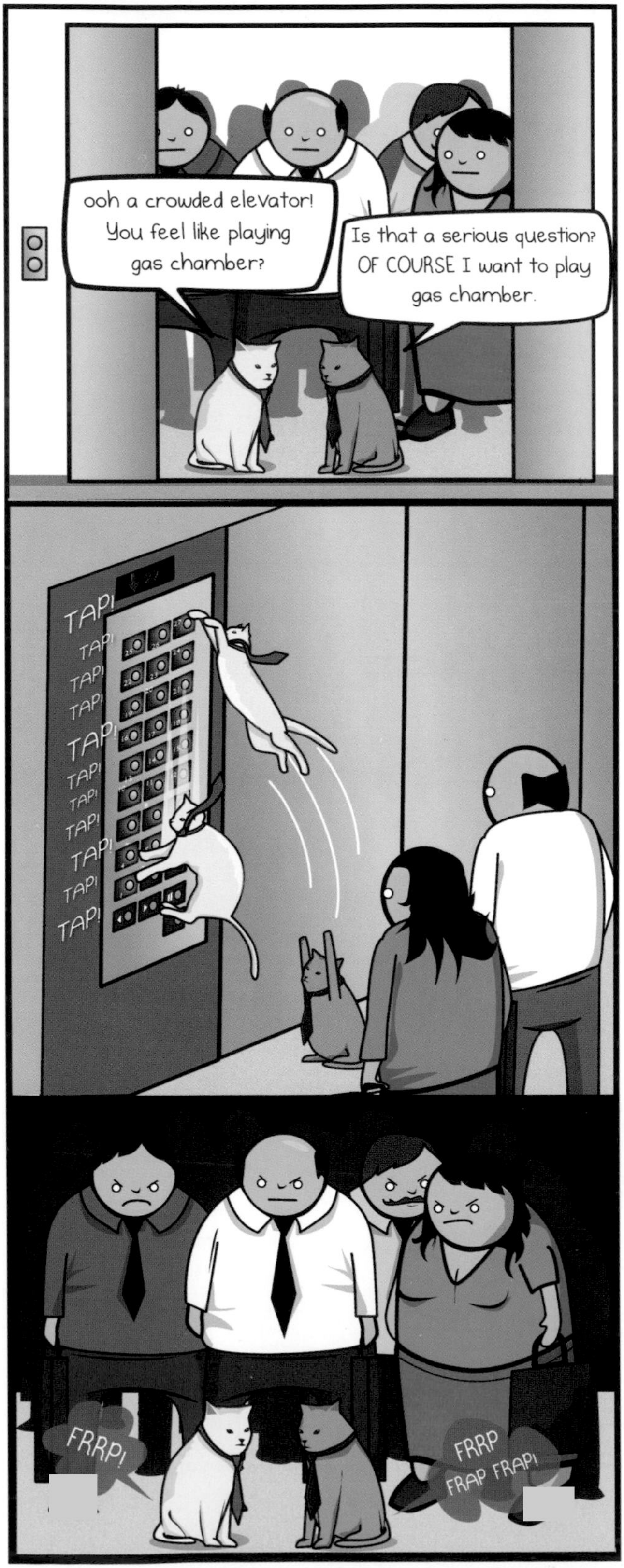
ooh a crowded elevator! You feel like playing gas chamber?
Is that a serious question? OF COURSE I want to play gas chamber.
TAP! TAP! TAP! TAP! TAP! TAP! TAP! TAP! TAP! TAP! TAP! TAP!
FRRP!
FRRP FRAP FRAP!

The Bobcats

Episode 3: Wednesday

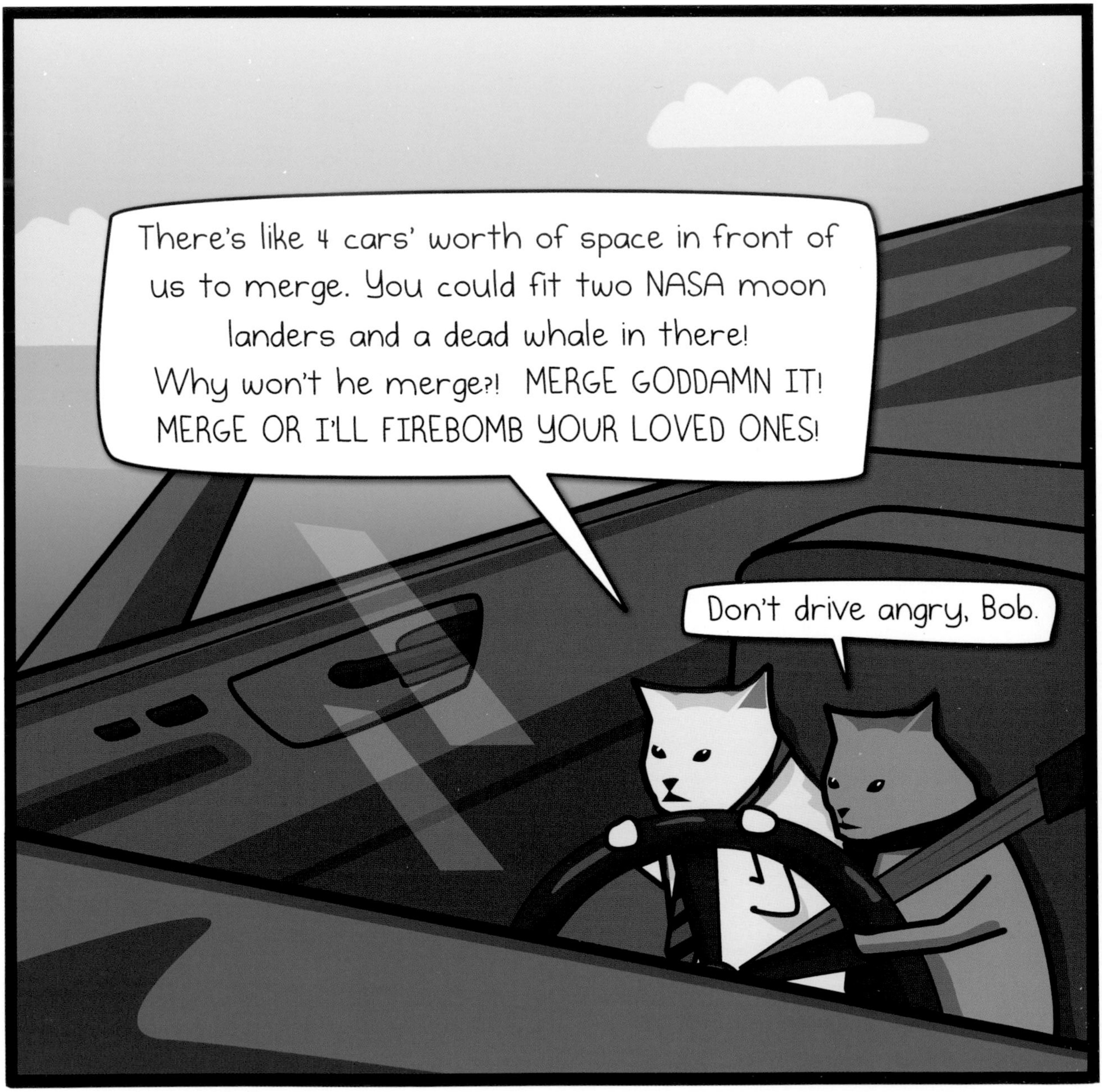
There's like 4 cars' worth of space in front of us to merge. You could fit two NASA moon landers and a dead whale in there! Why won't he merge?! MERGE GODDAMN IT! MERGE OR I'LL FIREBOMB YOUR LOVED ONES!
Don't drive angry, Bob.

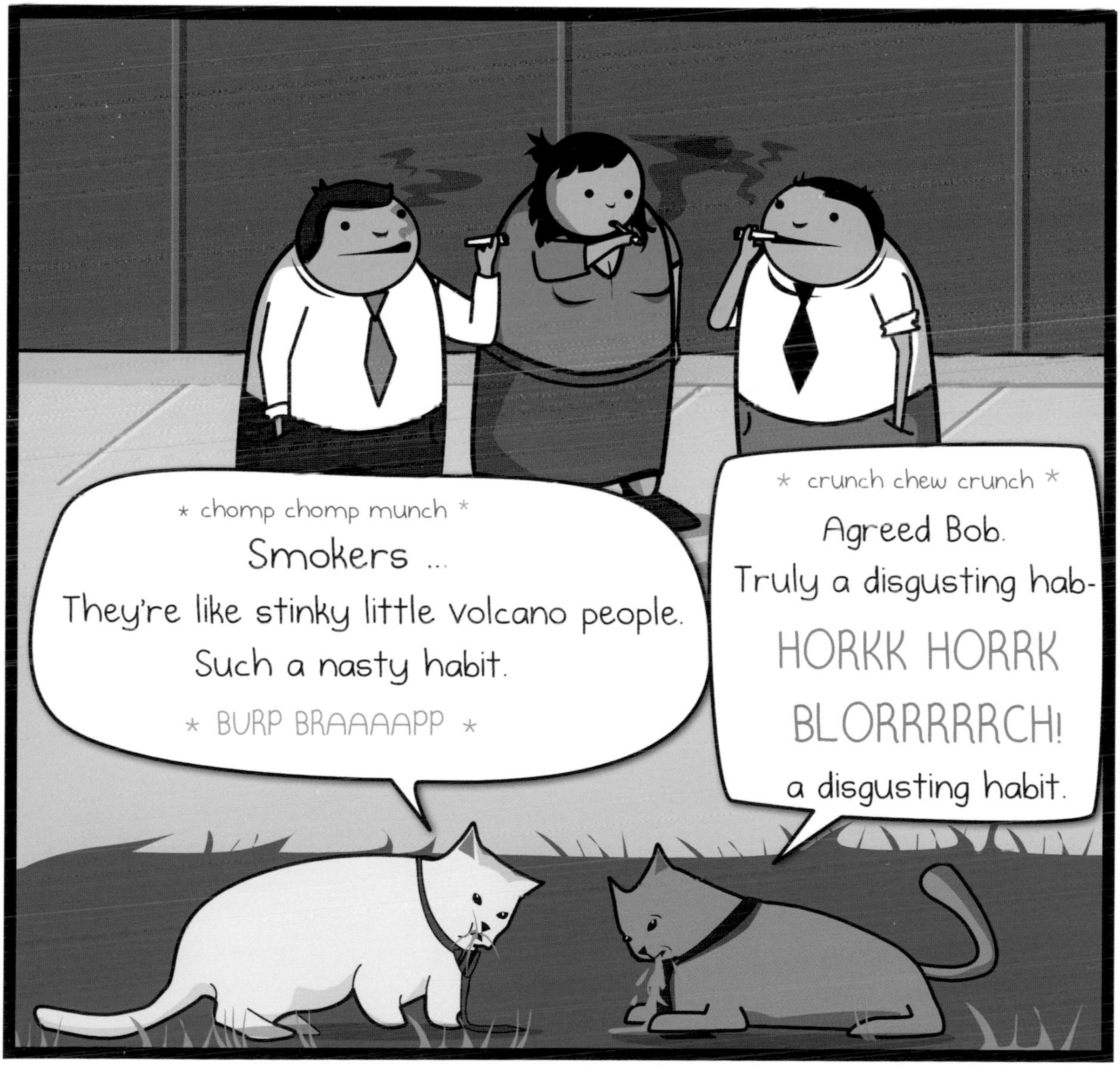
* chomp chomp munch *
Smokers ...
They're like stinky little volcano people.
Such a nasty habit.
* BURP BRAAAAPP *
* crunch chew crunch *
Agreed Bob.
Truly a disgusting hab-
HORKK HORRK
BLORRRRRCH!
a disgusting habit.

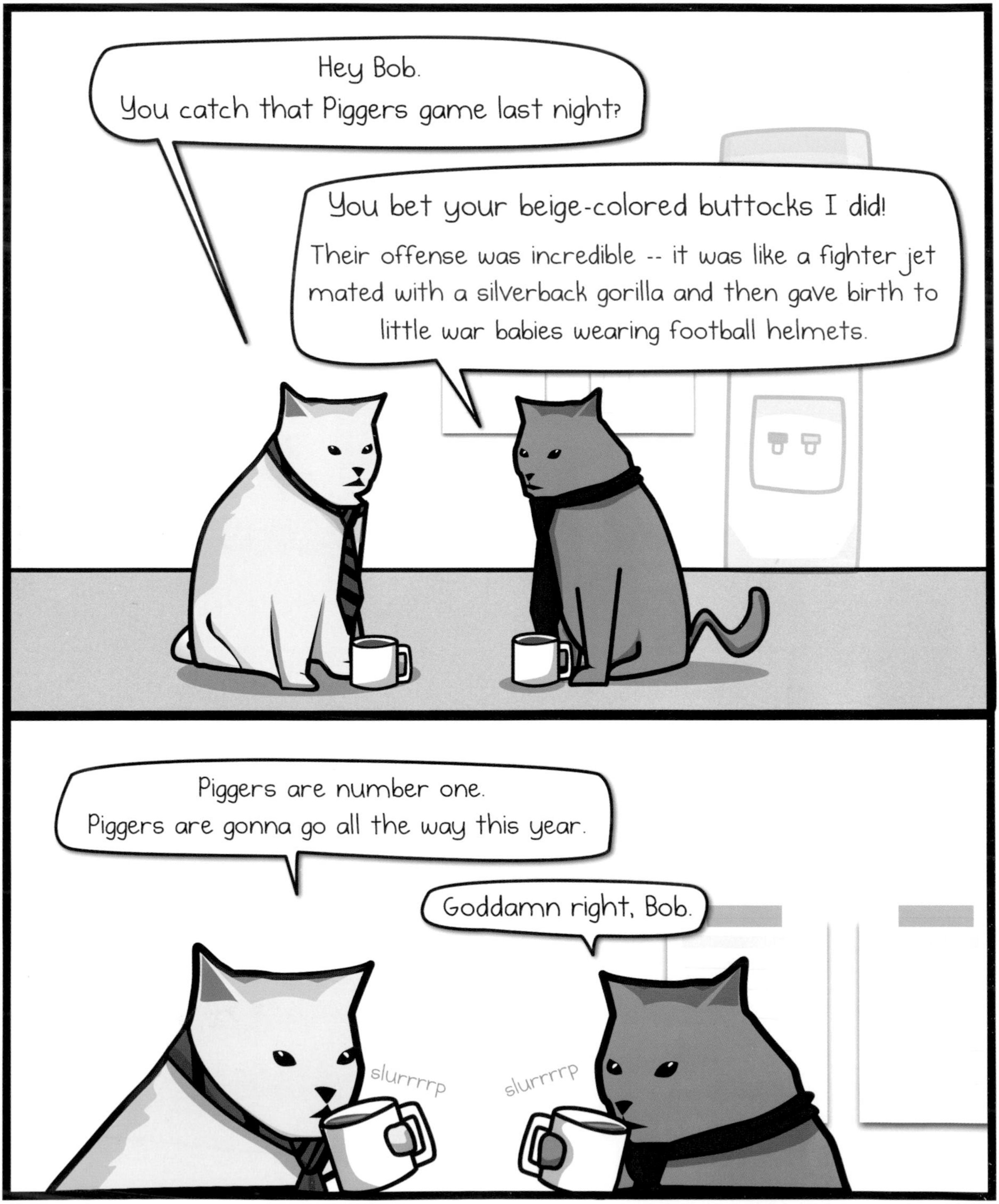
Hey Bob.
You catch that Piggers game last night?
You bet your beige-colored buttocks I did!
Their offense was incredible -- it was like a fighter jet mated with a silverback gorilla and then gave birth to little war babies wearing football helmets.
Piggers are number one.
Piggers are gonna go all the way this year.
Goddamn right, Bob.
slurrrrp
slurrrrp

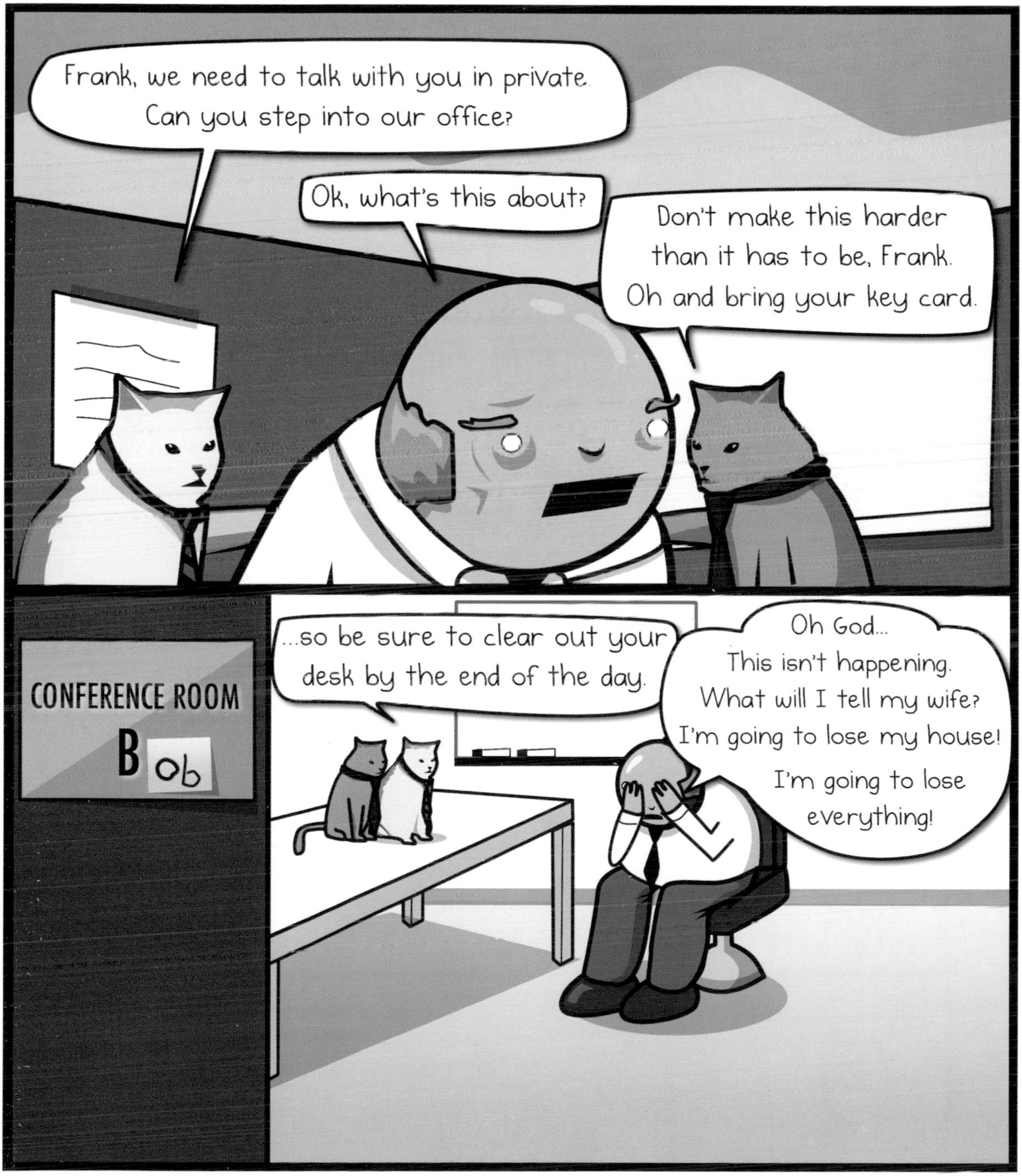

Frank, we need to talk with you in private. Can you step into our office?
Ok, what's this about?
Don't make this harder than it has to be, Frank. Oh and bring your key card.
CONFERENCE ROOM B ob
...so be sure to clear out your desk by the end of the day.
Oh God... This isn't happening. What will I tell my wife? I'm going to lose my house! I'm going to lose everything!

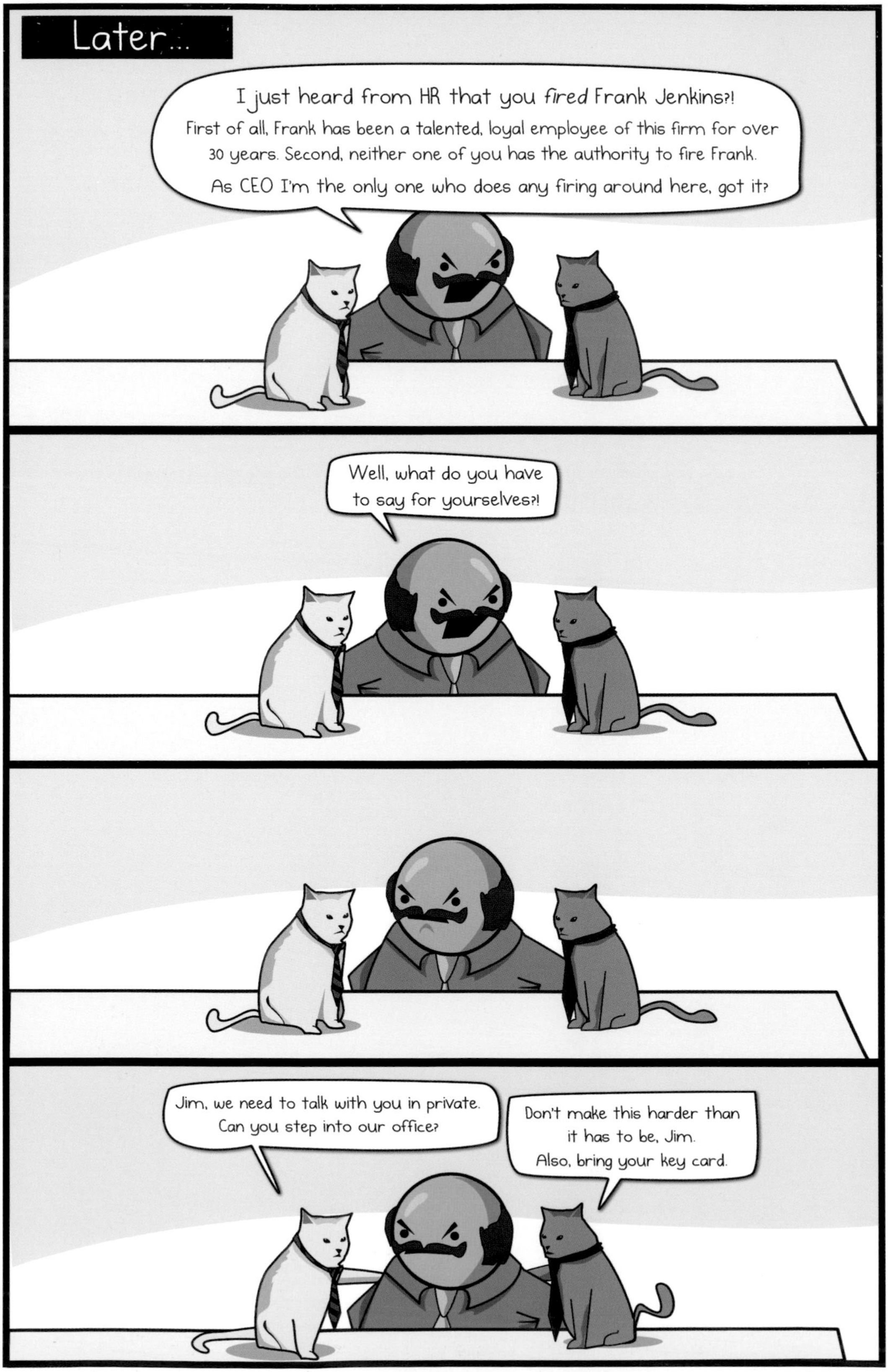

Later...
I just heard from HR that you *fired* Frank Jenkins?! First of all, Frank has been a talented, loyal employee of this firm for over 30 years. Second, neither one of you has the authority to fire Frank. As CEO I'm the only one who does any firing around here, got it?
Well, what do you have to say for yourselves?!
Jim, we need to talk with you in private. Can you step into our office?
Don't make this harder than it has to be, Jim. Also, bring your key card.

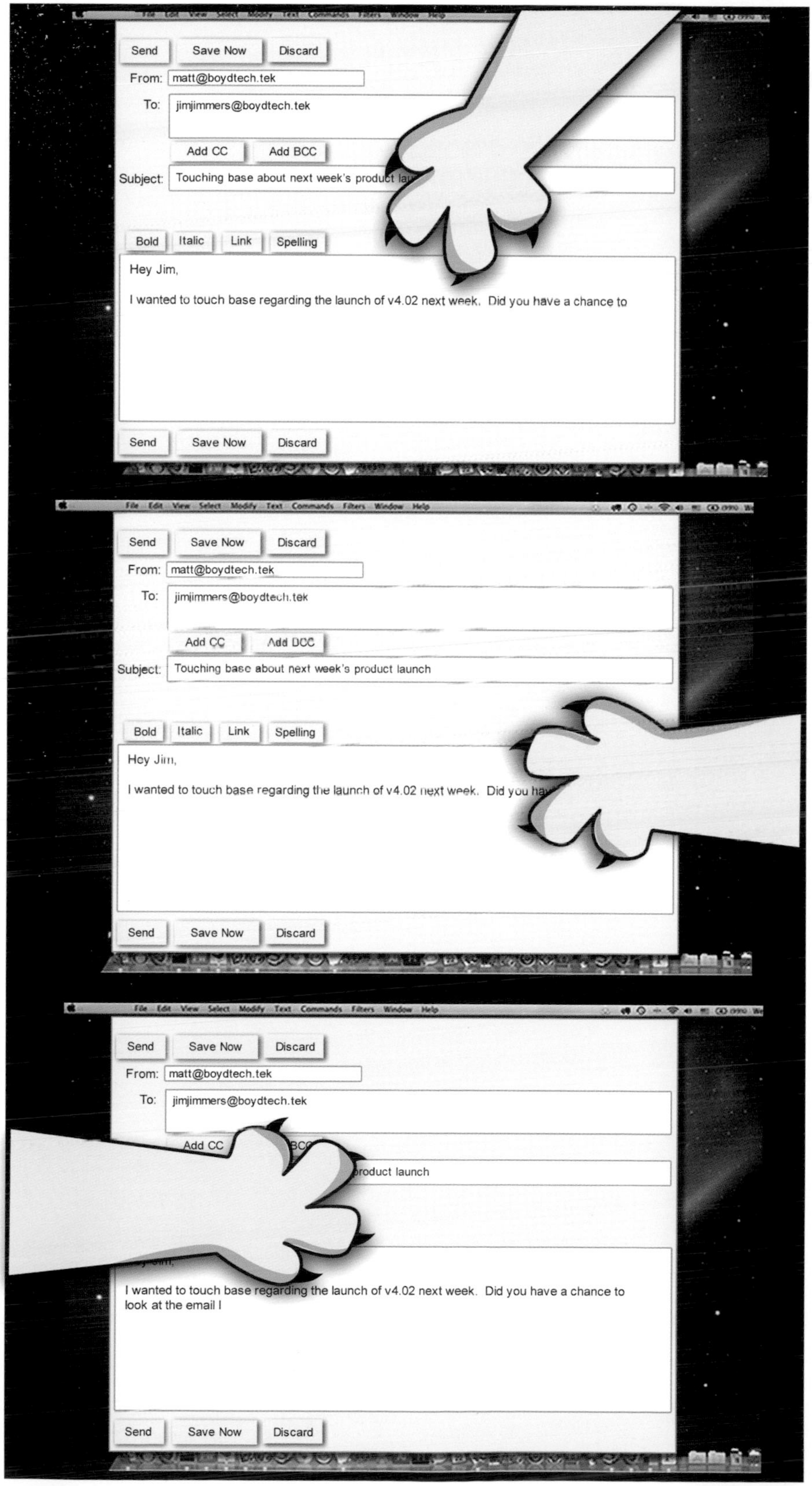
Send
Save Now
Discard
From:
matt@boydtech.tek
To:
jimjimmers@boydtech.tek
Add CC
Add BCC
Subject:
Touching base about next week's product la
Bold
Italic
Link
Spelling
Hey Jim,
I wanted to touch base regarding the launch of v4.02 next week. Did you have a chance to
Send
Save Now
Discard
Send
Save Now
Discard
From:
matt@boydtech.tek
To:
jimjimmers@boydtech.tek
Add CC
Add BCC
Subject:
Touching base about next week's product launch
Bold
Italic
Link
Spelling
Hey Jim,
I wanted to touch base regarding the launch of v4.02 next week. Did you ha
Send
Save Now
Discard
Send
Save Now
Discard
From:
matt@boydtech.tek
To:
jimjimmers@boydtech.tek
Add CC
product launch
I wanted to touch base regarding the launch of v4.02 next week. Did you have a chance to
look at the email I
Send
Save Now
Discard

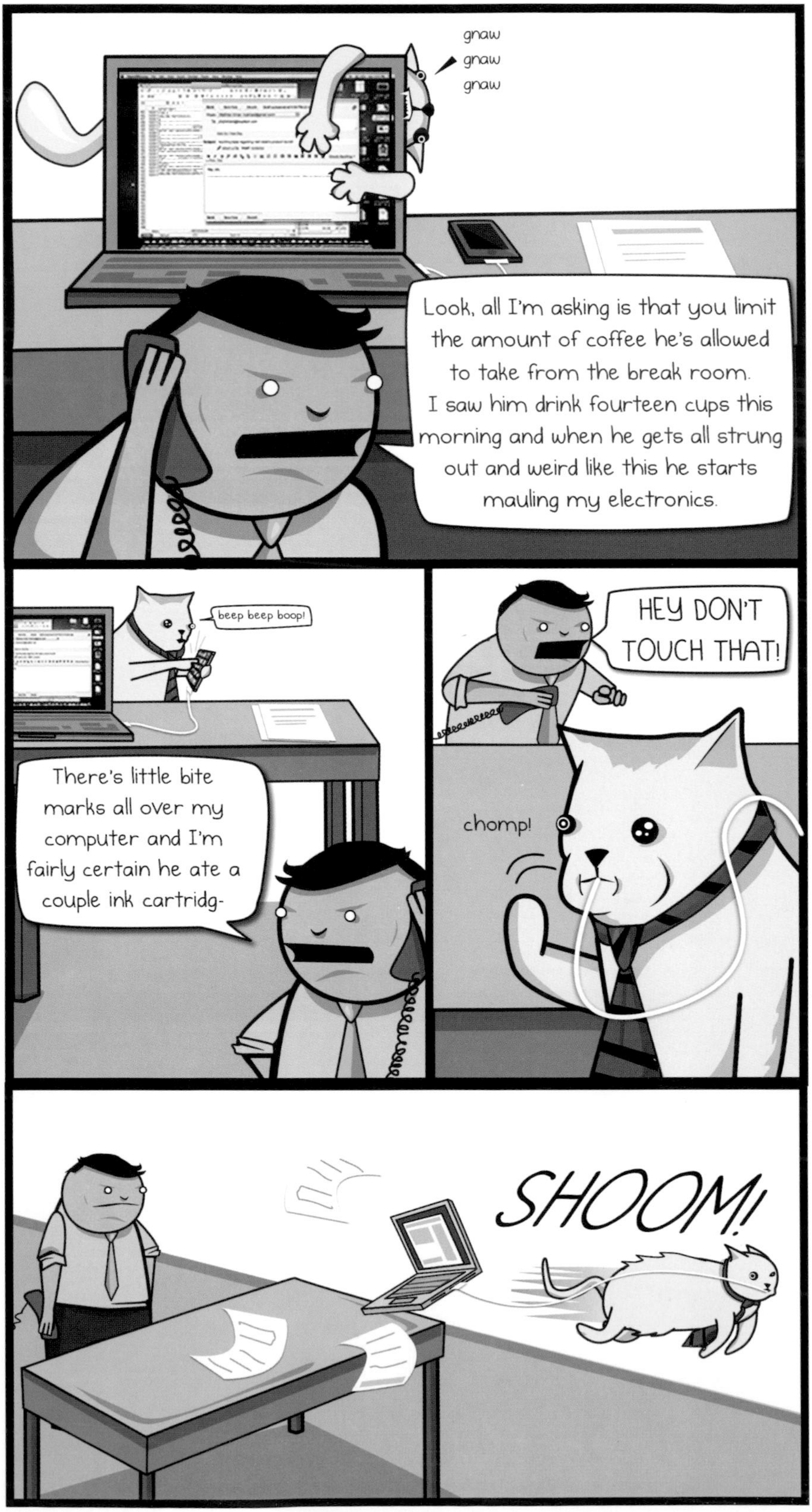
gnaw
gnaw
gnaw
Look, all I'm asking is that you limit the amount of coffee he's allowed to take from the break room. I saw him drink fourteen cups this morning and when he gets all strung out and weird like this he starts mauling my electronics.
beep beep boop!
There's little bite marks all over my computer and I'm fairly certain he ate a couple ink cartridg-
HEY DON'T TOUCH THAT!
chomp!
SHOOM!

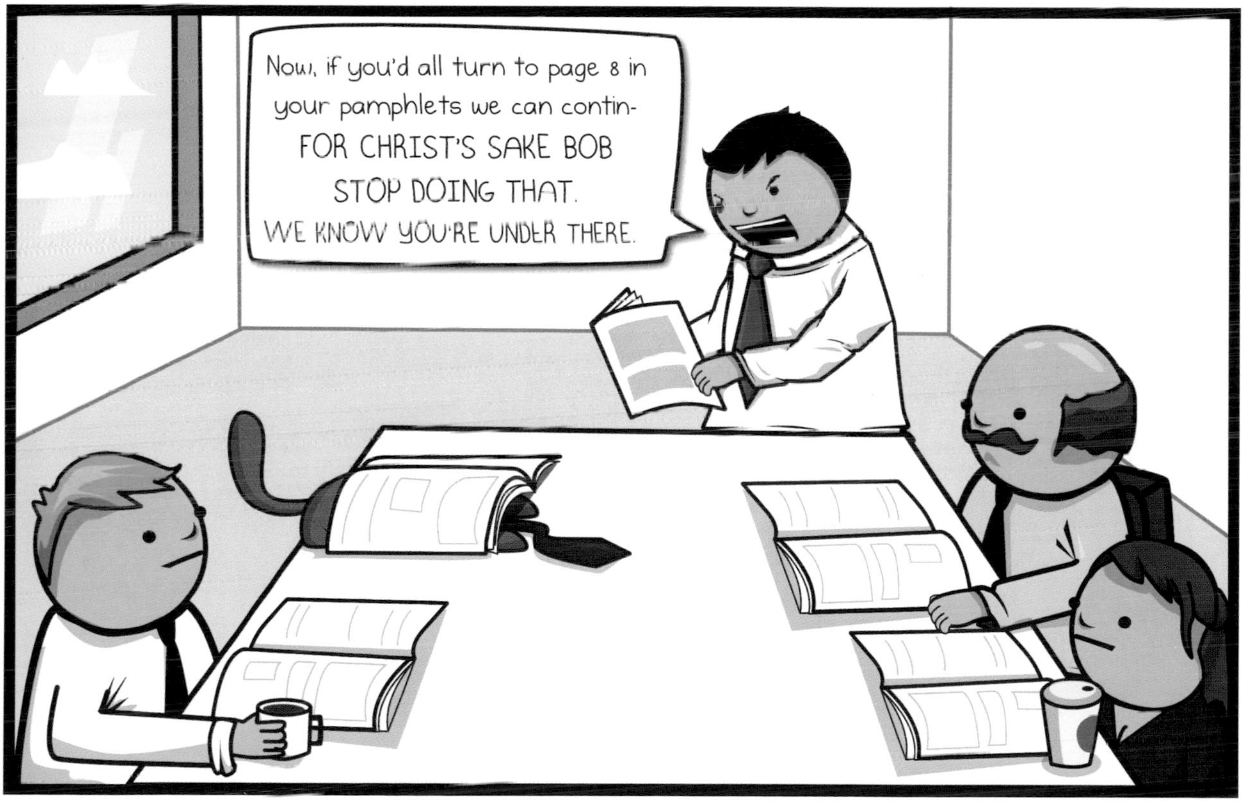
Now, if you'd all turn to page 8 in your pamphlets we can contin-
FOR CHRIST'S SAKE BOB STOP DOING THAT.
WE KNOW YOU'RE UNDER THERE.

The Bobcats

Episode 4: Thursday

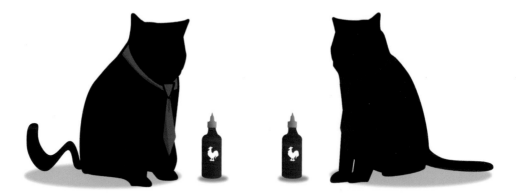

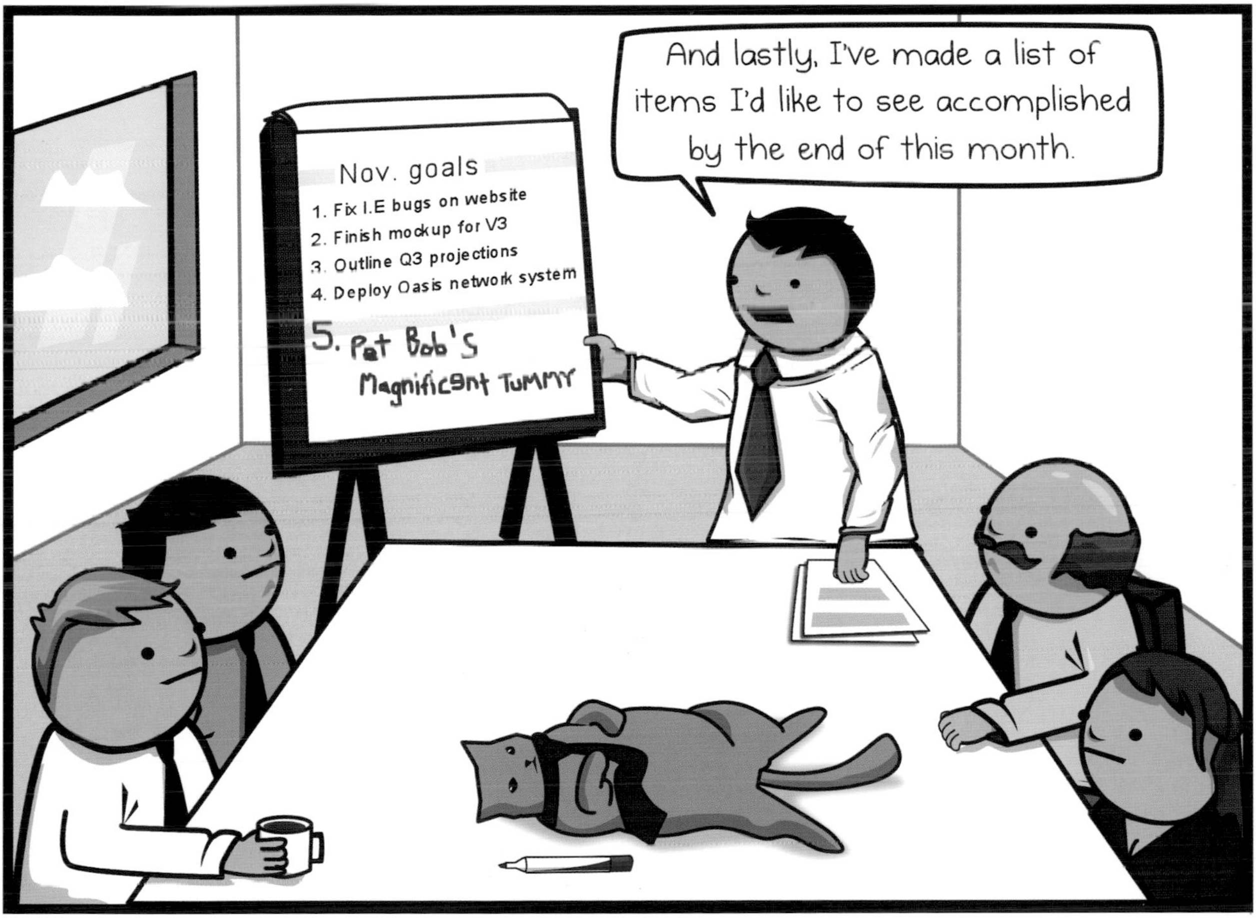
Nov. goals
1. Fix I.E bugs on website
2. Finish mockup for V3
3. Outline Q3 projections
4. Deploy Oasis network system
5. Pet Bob'S Magnific8nt TuMMY
And lastly, I've made a list of items I'd like to see accomplished by the end of this month.

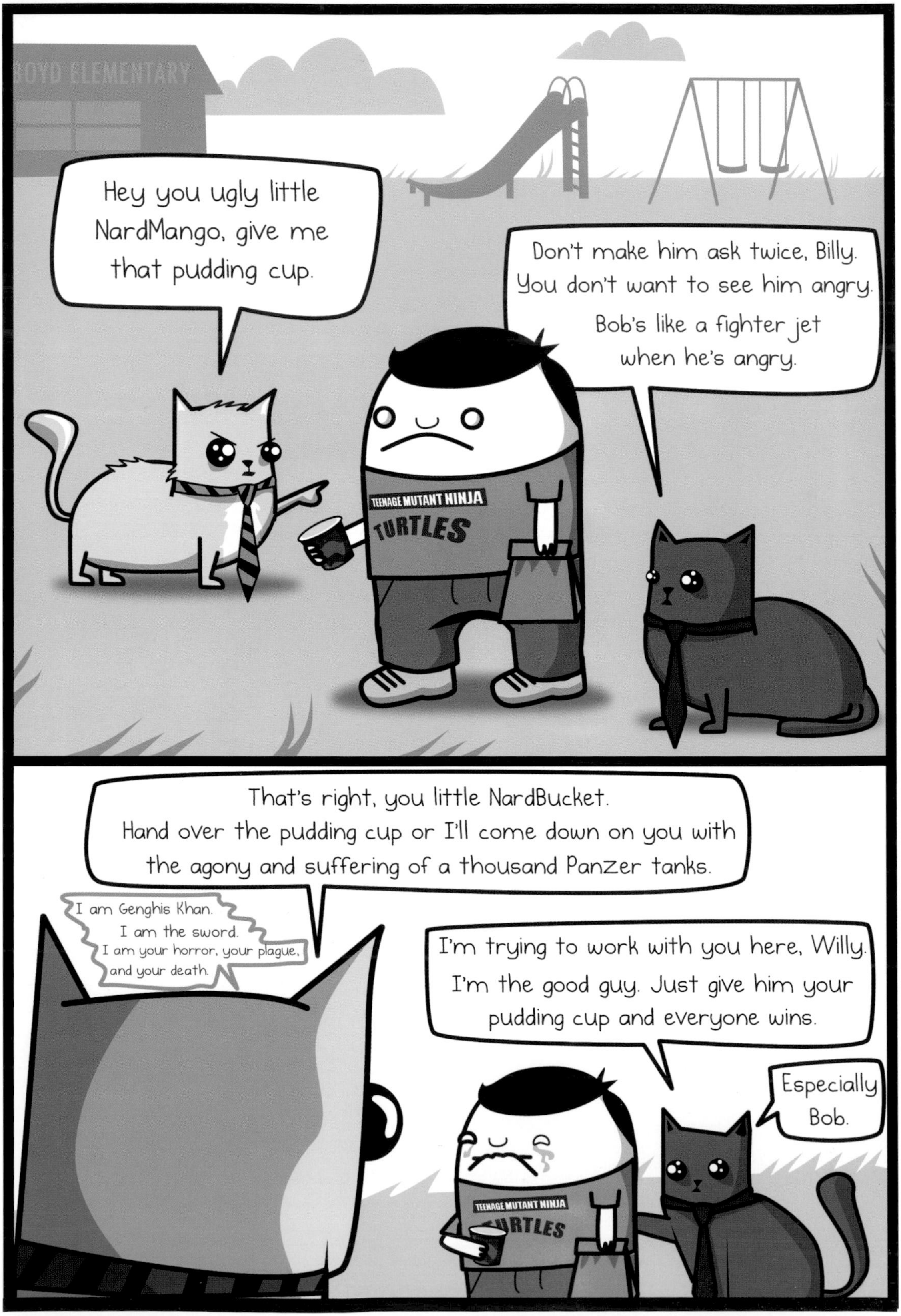
BOYD ELEMENTARY
Hey you ugly little NardMango, give me that pudding cup.
Don't make him ask twice, Billy. You don't want to see him angry.
Bob's like a fighter jet when he's angry.
TEENAGE MUTANT NINJA TURTLES
That's right, you little NardBucket. Hand over the pudding cup or I'll come down on you with the agony and suffering of a thousand Panzer tanks.
I am Genghis Khan. I am the sword. I am your horror, your plague, and your death.
I'm trying to work with you here, Willy. I'm the good guy. Just give him your pudding cup and everyone wins.
Especially Bob.
TEENAGE MUTANT NINJA TURTLES

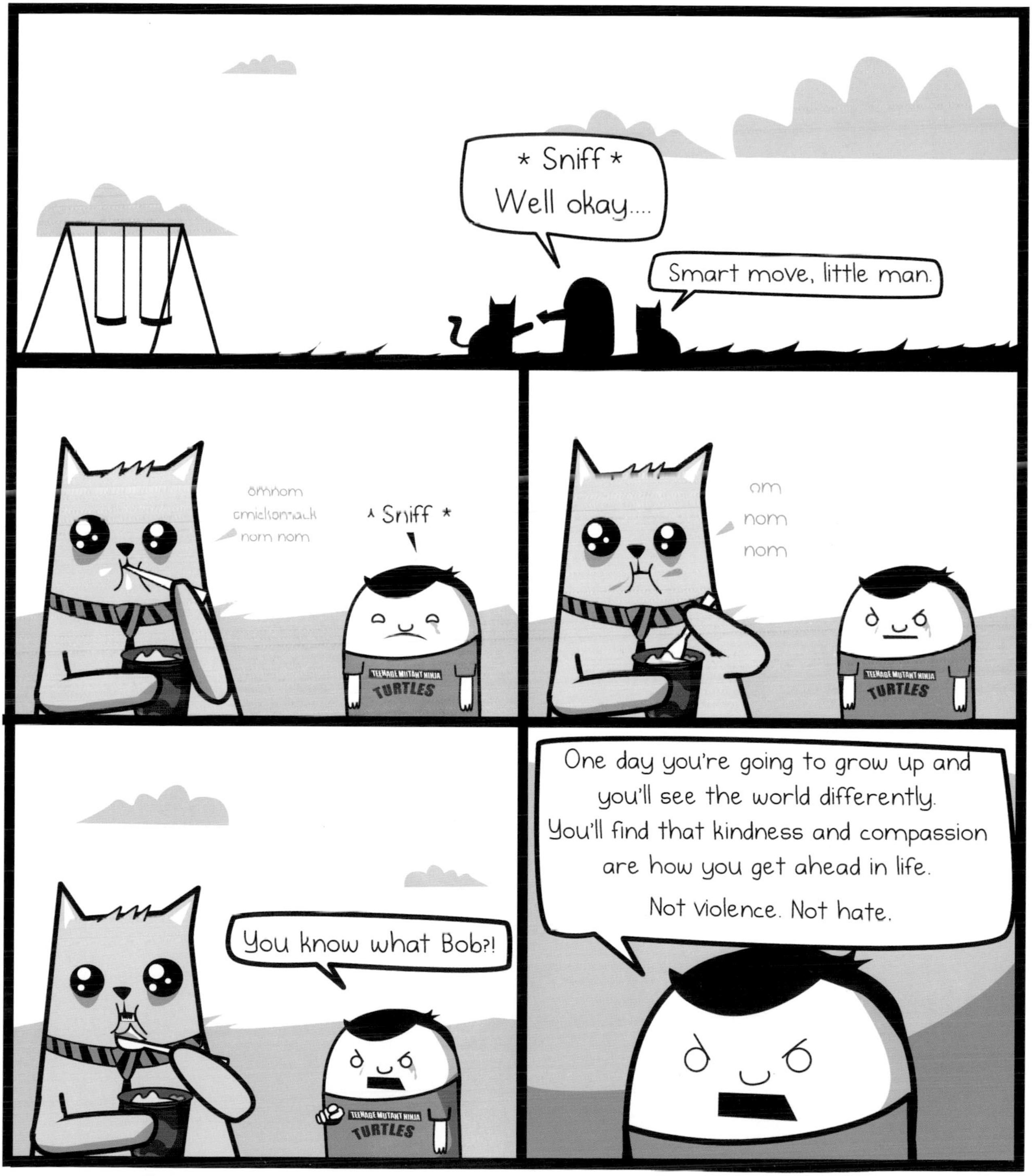
* Sniff *
Well okay....
Smart move, little man.
omnom
nom nom
* Sniff *
TEENAGE MUTANT NINJA TURTLES
om
nom
nom
TEENAGE MUTANT NINJA TURTLES
You know what Bob?!
TEENAGE MUTANT NINJA TURTLES
One day you're going to grow up and you'll see the world differently.
You'll find that kindness and compassion are how you get ahead in life.
Not violence. Not hate.

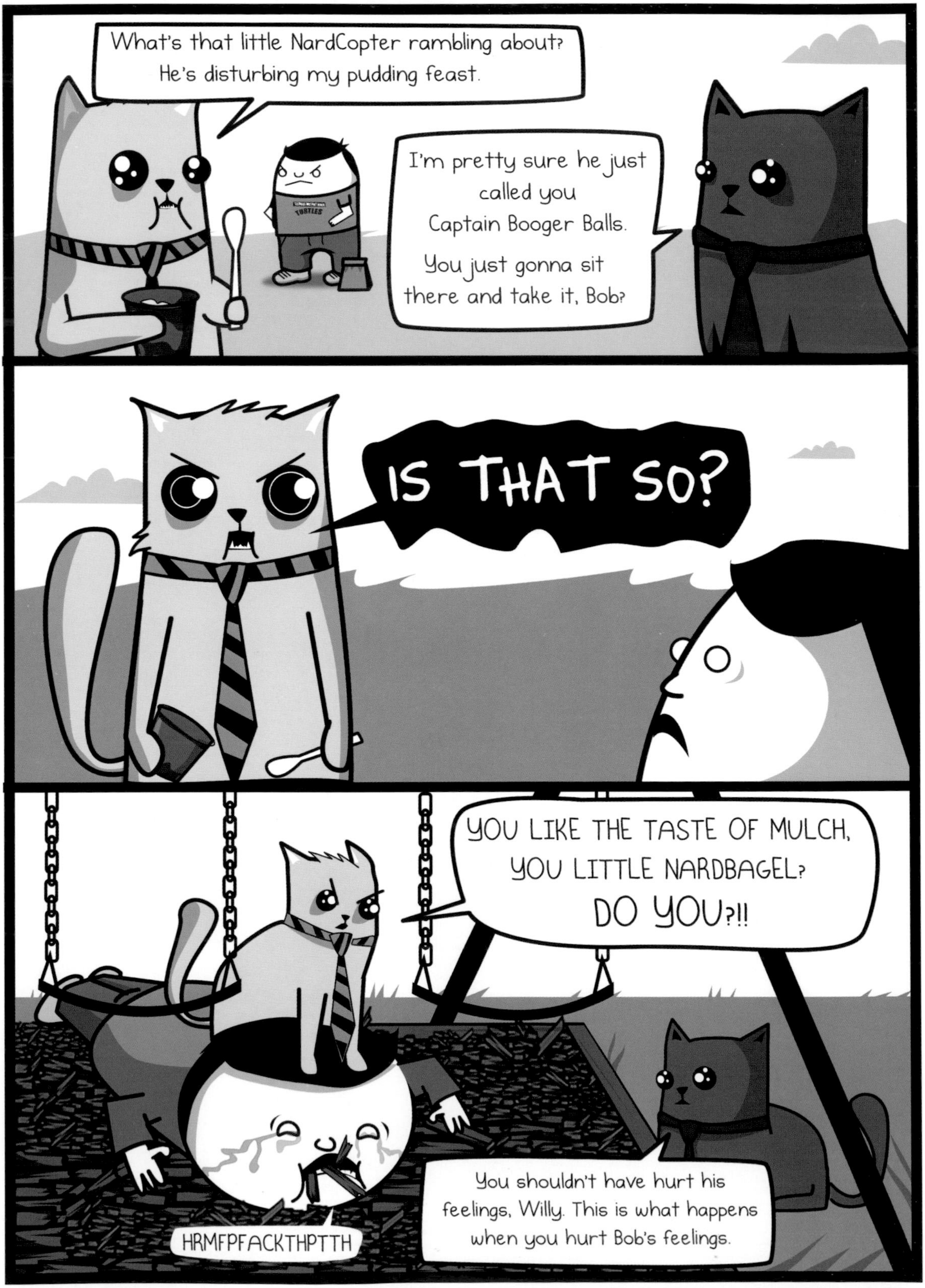
What's that little NardCopter rambling about? He's disturbing my pudding feast.
I'm pretty sure he just called you Captain Booger Balls. You just gonna sit there and take it, Bob?
IS THAT SO?
YOU LIKE THE TASTE OF MULCH, YOU LITTLE NARDBAGEL? DO YOU?!!
HRMFPFACKTHPTTH
You shouldn't have hurt his feelings, Willy. This is what happens when you hurt Bob's feelings.

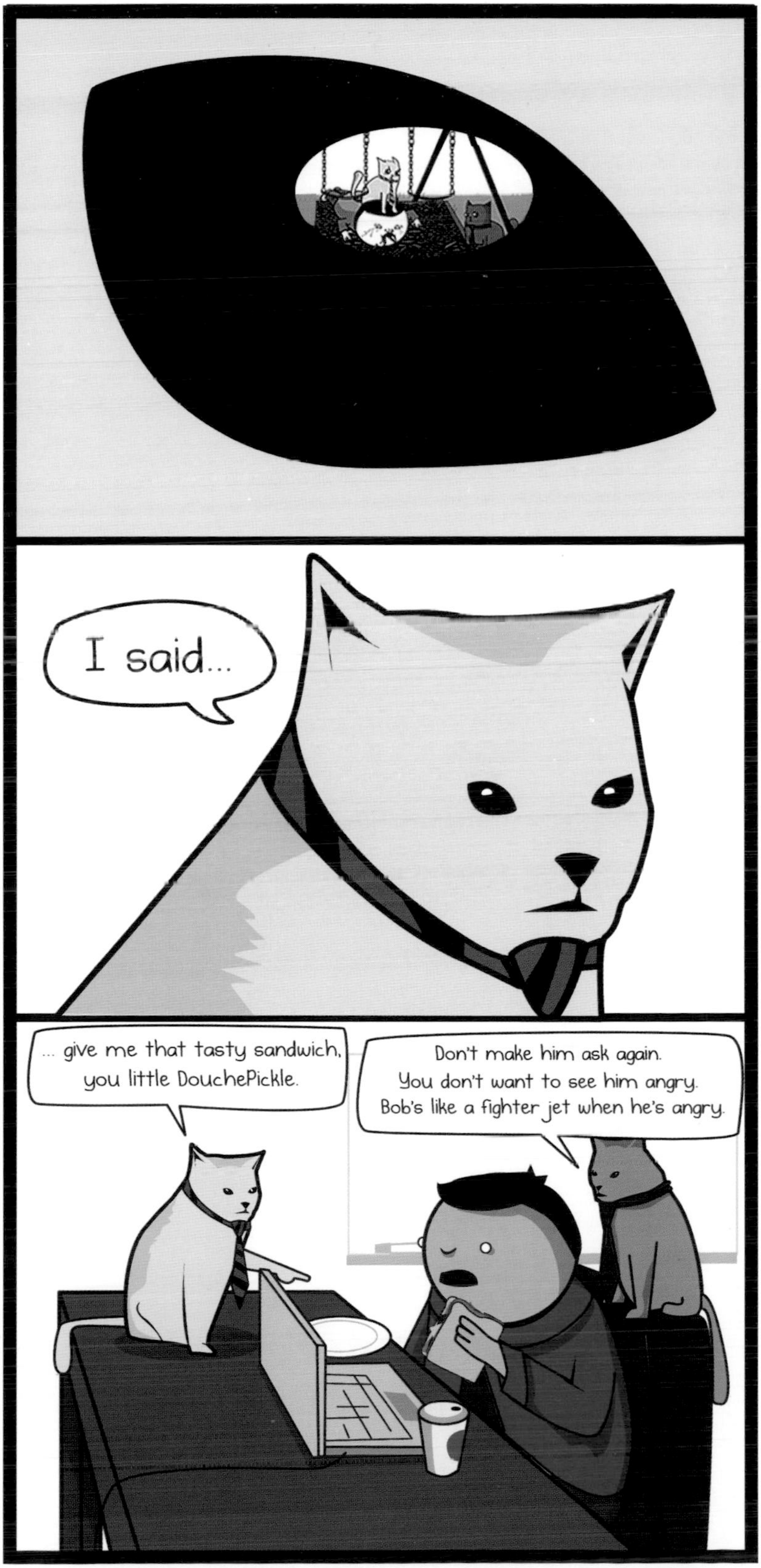
I said...
... give me that tasty sandwich, you little DouchePickle.
Don't make him ask again. You don't want to see him angry. Bob's like a fighter jet when he's angry.

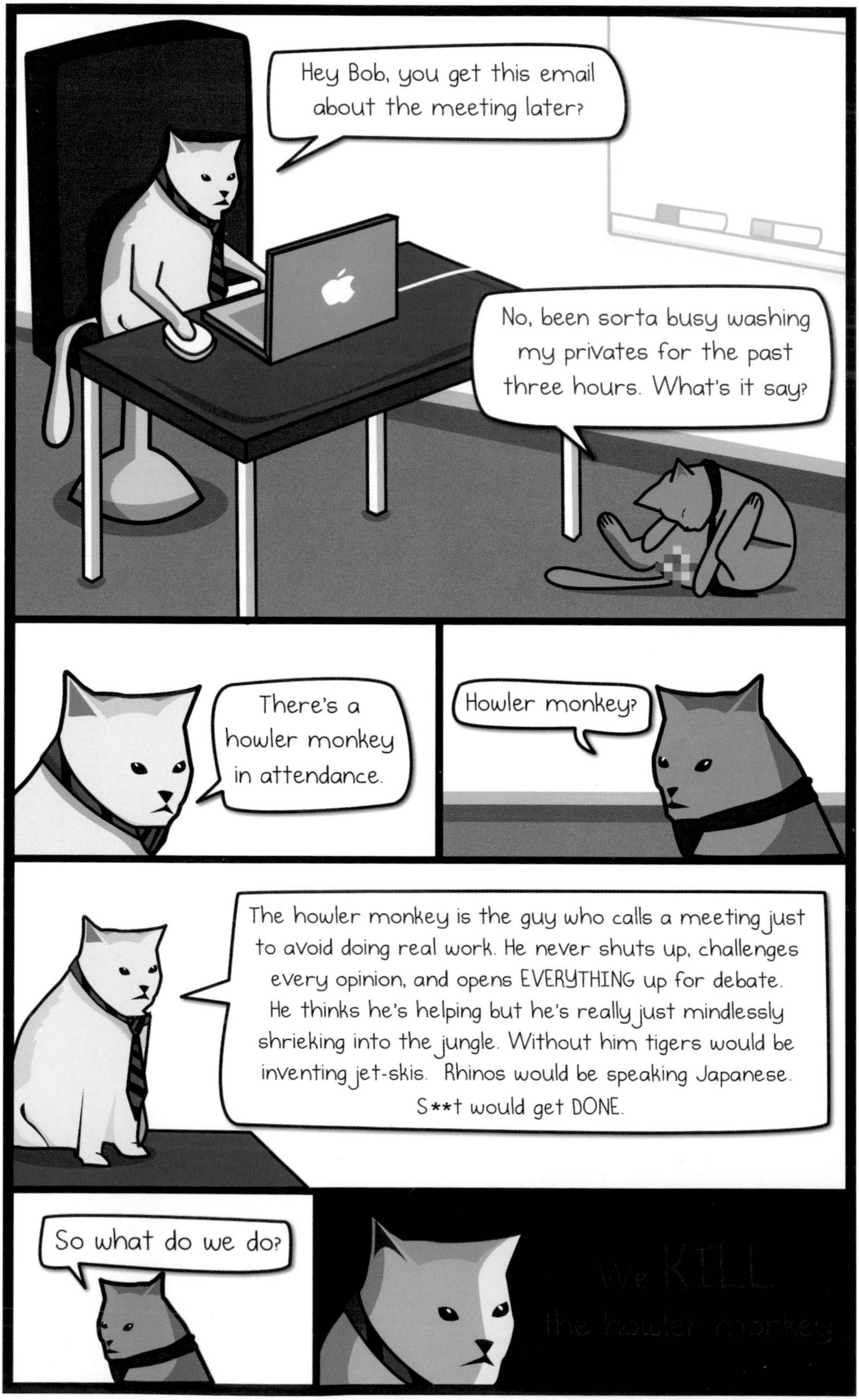
Hey Bob, you get this email about the meeting later?
No, been sorta busy washing my privates for the past three hours. What's it say?
There's a howler monkey in attendance.
Howler monkey?
The howler monkey is the guy who calls a meeting just to avoid doing real work. He never shuts up, challenges every opinion, and opens EVERYTHING up for debate. He thinks he's helping but he's really just mindlessly shrieking into the jungle. Without him tigers would be inventing jet-skis. Rhinos would be speaking Japanese. S**t would get DONE.
So what do we do?
We KILL the howler monkey

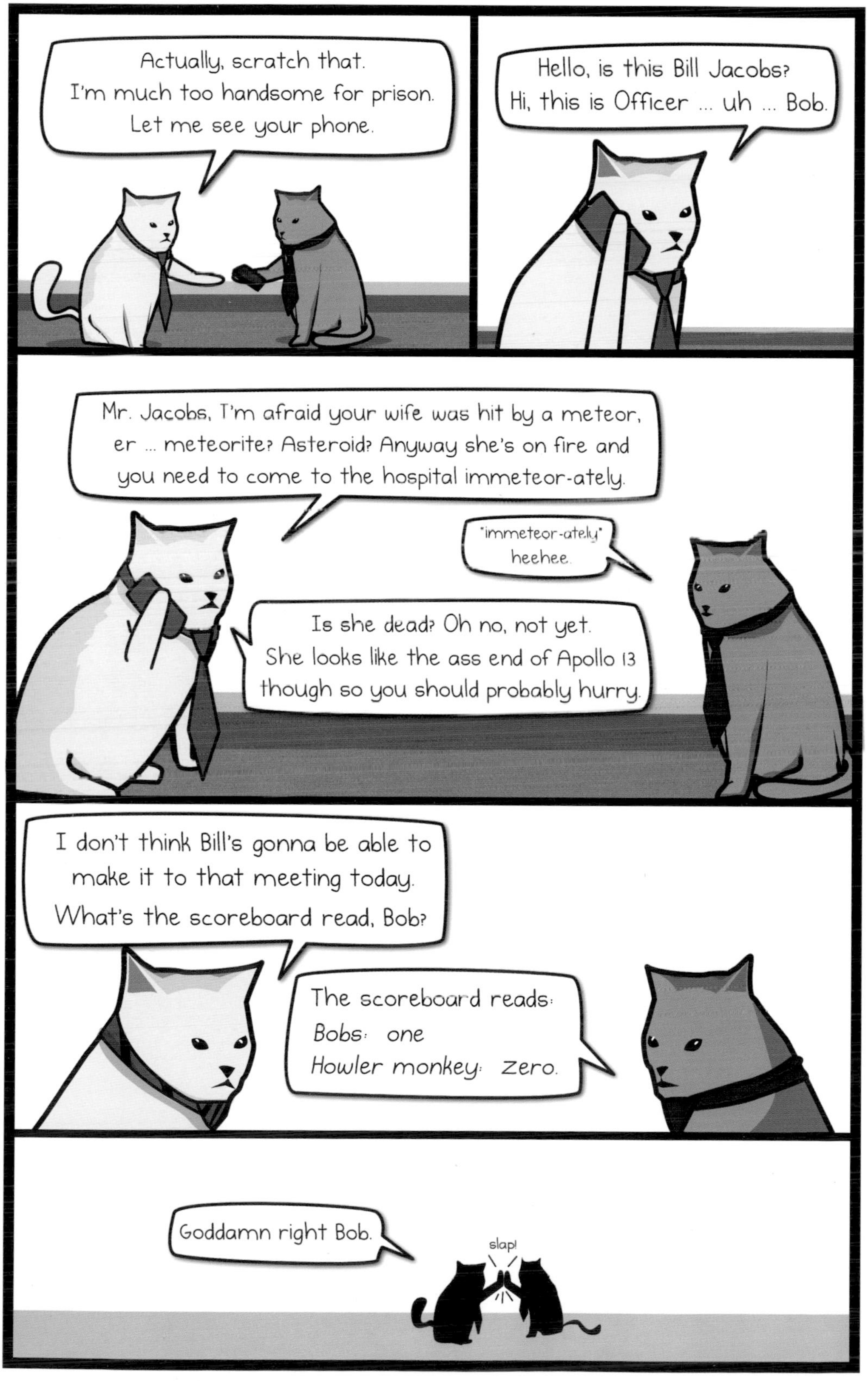
Actually, scratch that. I'm much too handsome for prison. Let me see your phone.
Hello, is this Bill Jacobs? Hi, this is Officer ... uh ... Bob.
Mr. Jacobs, I'm afraid your wife was hit by a meteor, er ... meteorite? Asteroid? Anyway she's on fire and you need to come to the hospital immeteor-ately.
"immeteor-ately" heehee.
Is she dead? Oh no, not yet. She looks like the ass end of Apollo 13 though so you should probably hurry.
I don't think Bill's gonna be able to make it to that meeting today. What's the scoreboard read, Bob?
The scoreboard reads: Bobs: one Howler monkey: zero.
Goddamn right Bob.
slap!

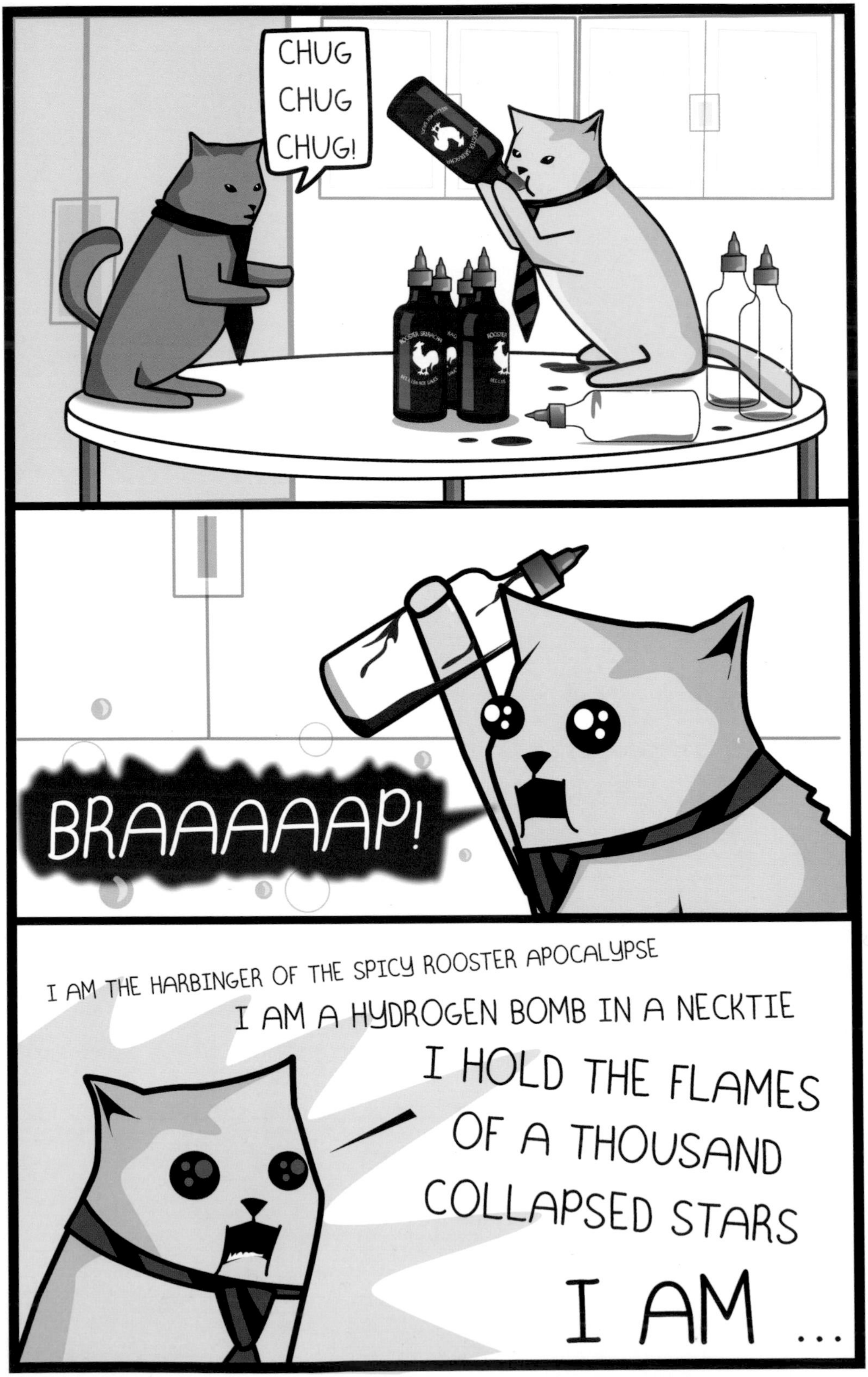
CHUG
CHUG
CHUG!
BRAAAAAAP!
I AM THE HARBINGER OF THE SPICY ROOSTER APOCALYPSE
I AM A HYDROGEN BOMB IN A NECKTIE
I HOLD THE FLAMES OF A THOUSAND COLLAPSED STARS
I AM ...

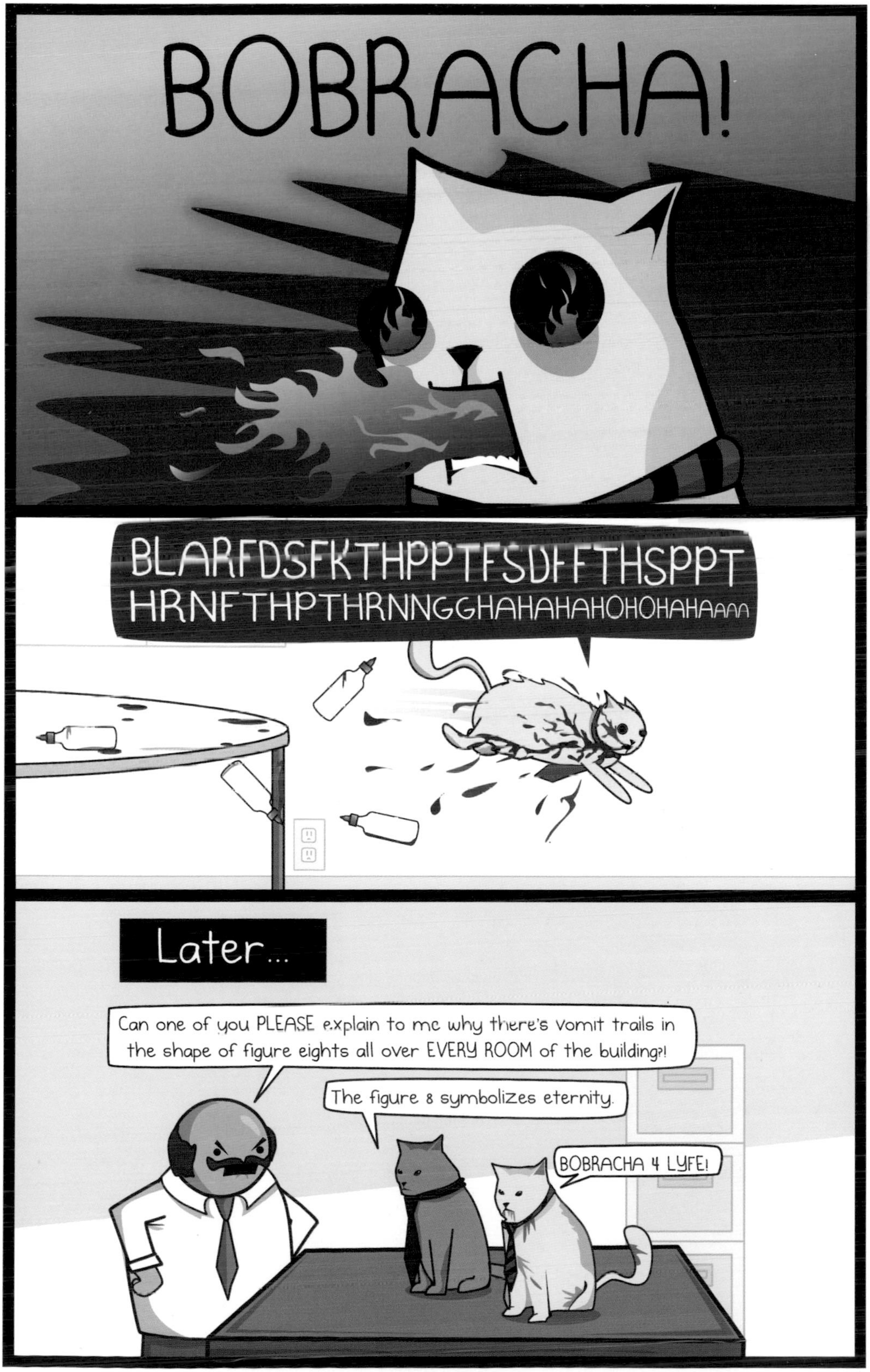
BOBRACHA!
BLARFDSFKTHPPTFSDFFTHSPPT HRNFTHPTHRNNGHAHAHAHOHOHAHAAAA
Later...
Can one of you PLEASE explain to me why there's vomit trails in the shape of figure eights all over EVERY ROOM of the building?!
The figure 8 symbolizes eternity.
BOBRACHA 4 LYFE!

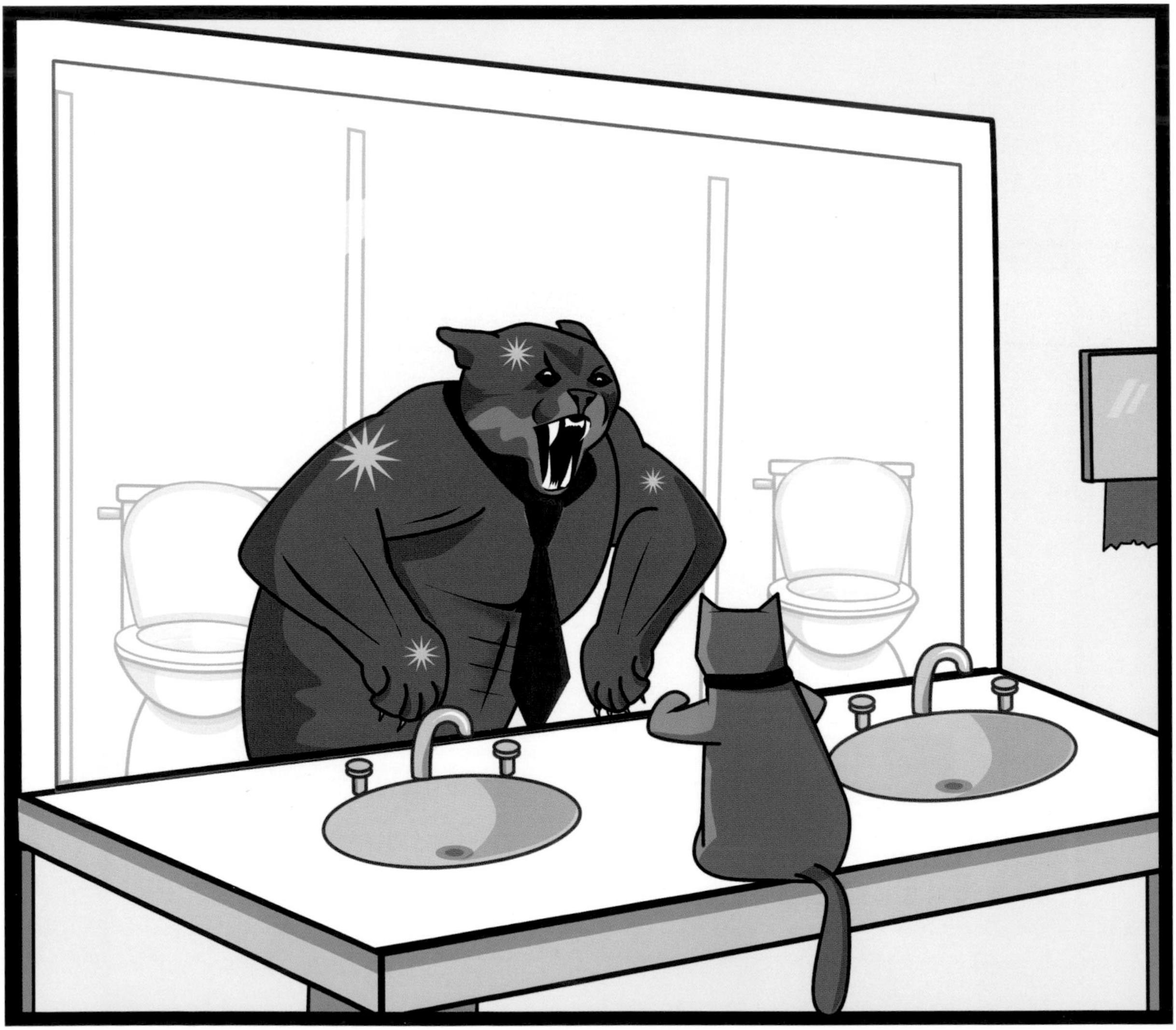

The Bobcats
Episode 5: Friday

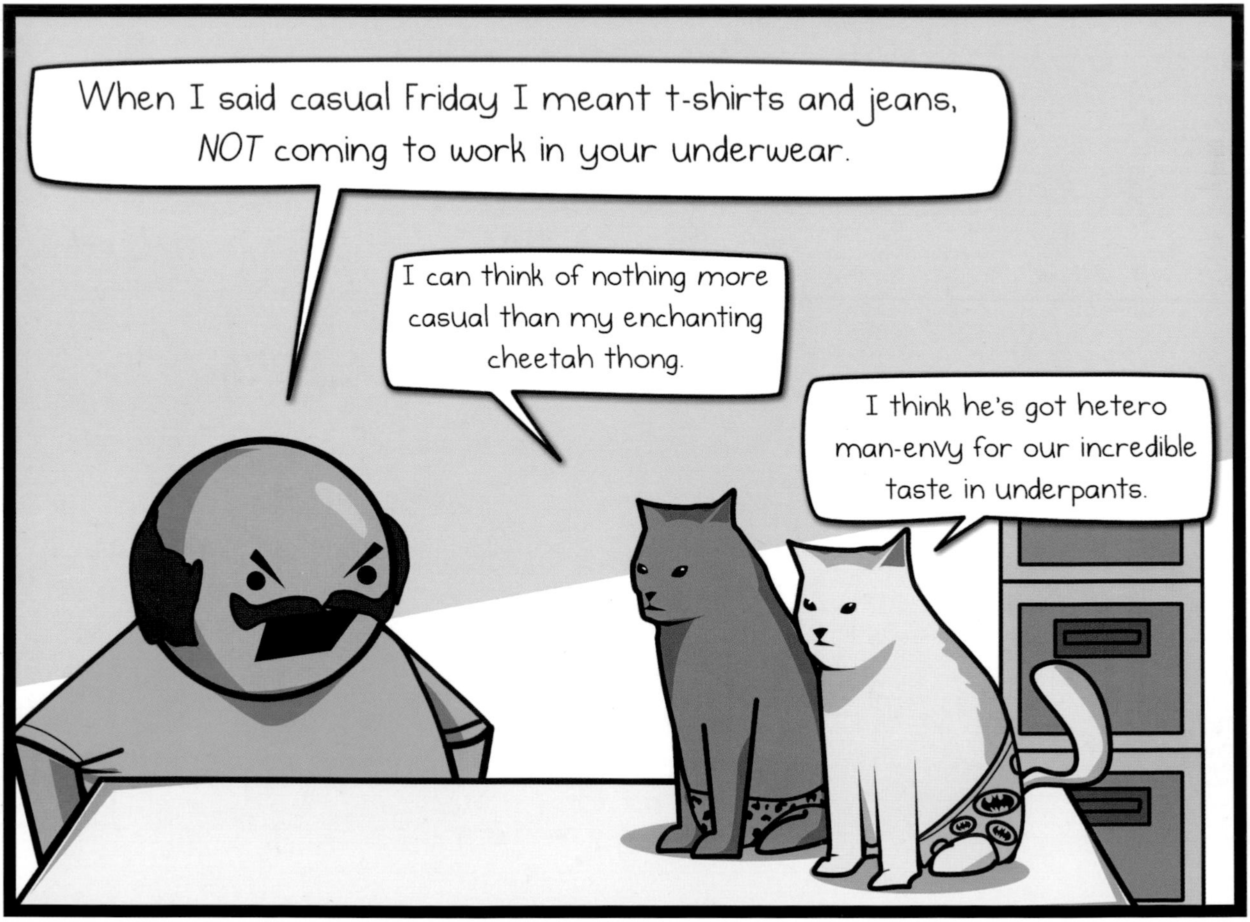
When I said casual Friday I meant t-shirts and jeans, NOT coming to work in your underwear.
I can think of nothing more casual than my enchanting cheetah thong.
I think he's got hetero man-envy for our incredible taste in underpants.

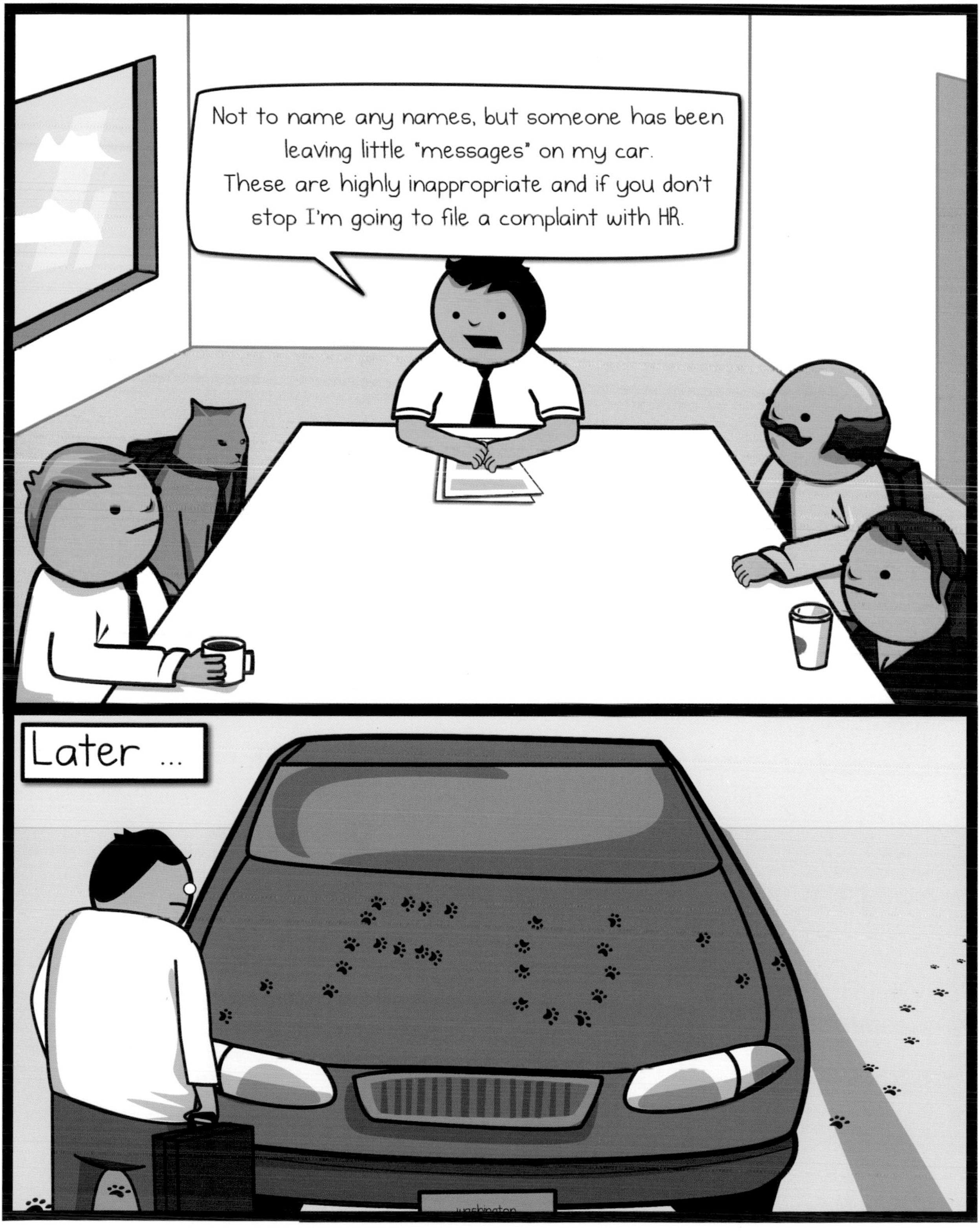
Not to name any names, but someone has been leaving little "messages" on my car. These are highly inappropriate and if you don't stop I'm going to file a complaint with HR.
Later ...

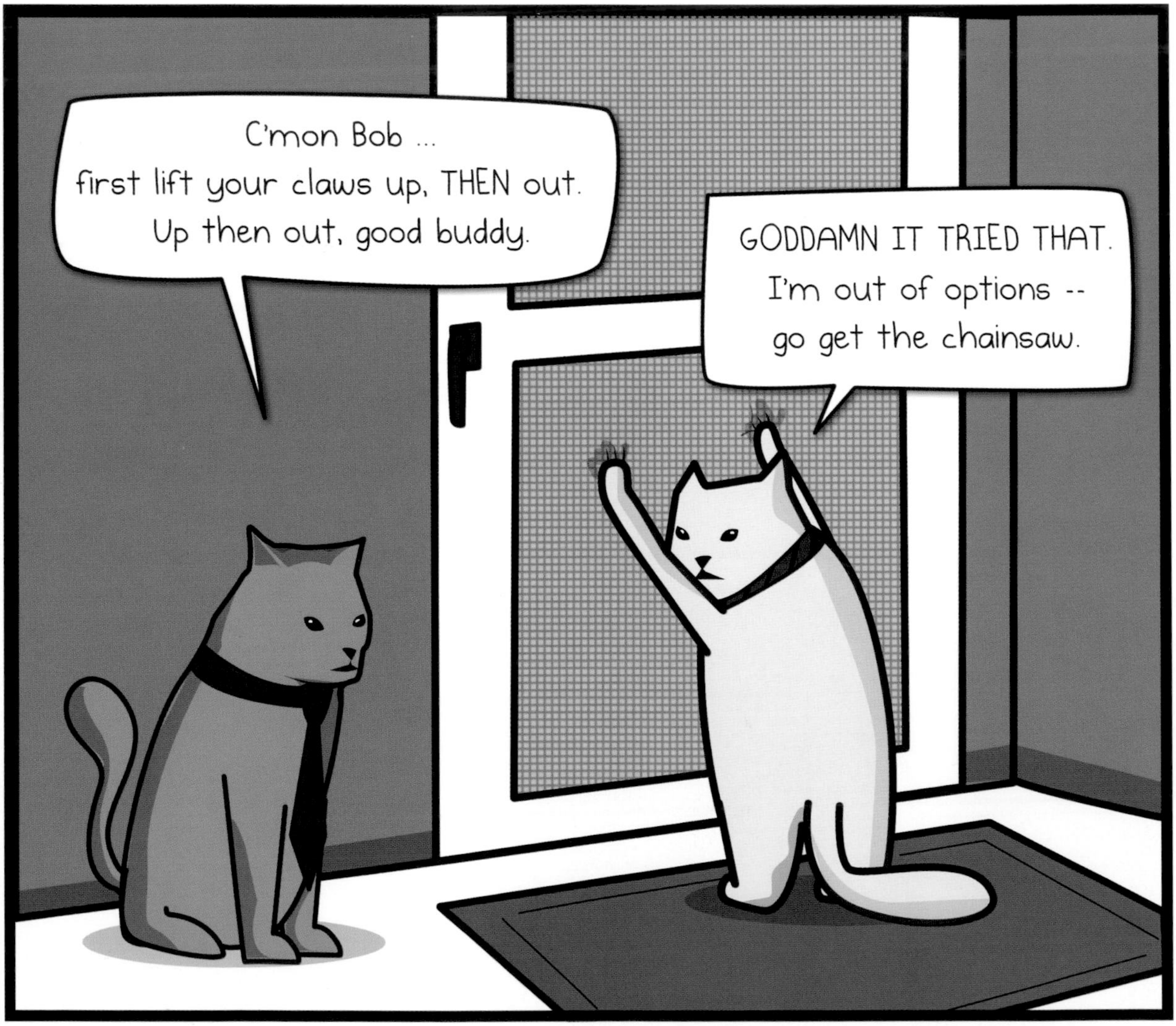
C'mon Bob ...
first lift your claws up, THEN out.
Up then out, good buddy.
GODDAMN IT TRIED THAT.
I'm out of options --
go get the chainsaw.

It was dark when he awoke ...

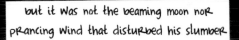

but it was not the beaming moon nor prancing wind that disturbed his slumber

It was the uncanny cry of the monstrous SkyBeast shrieking into the night ...

beckoning him.

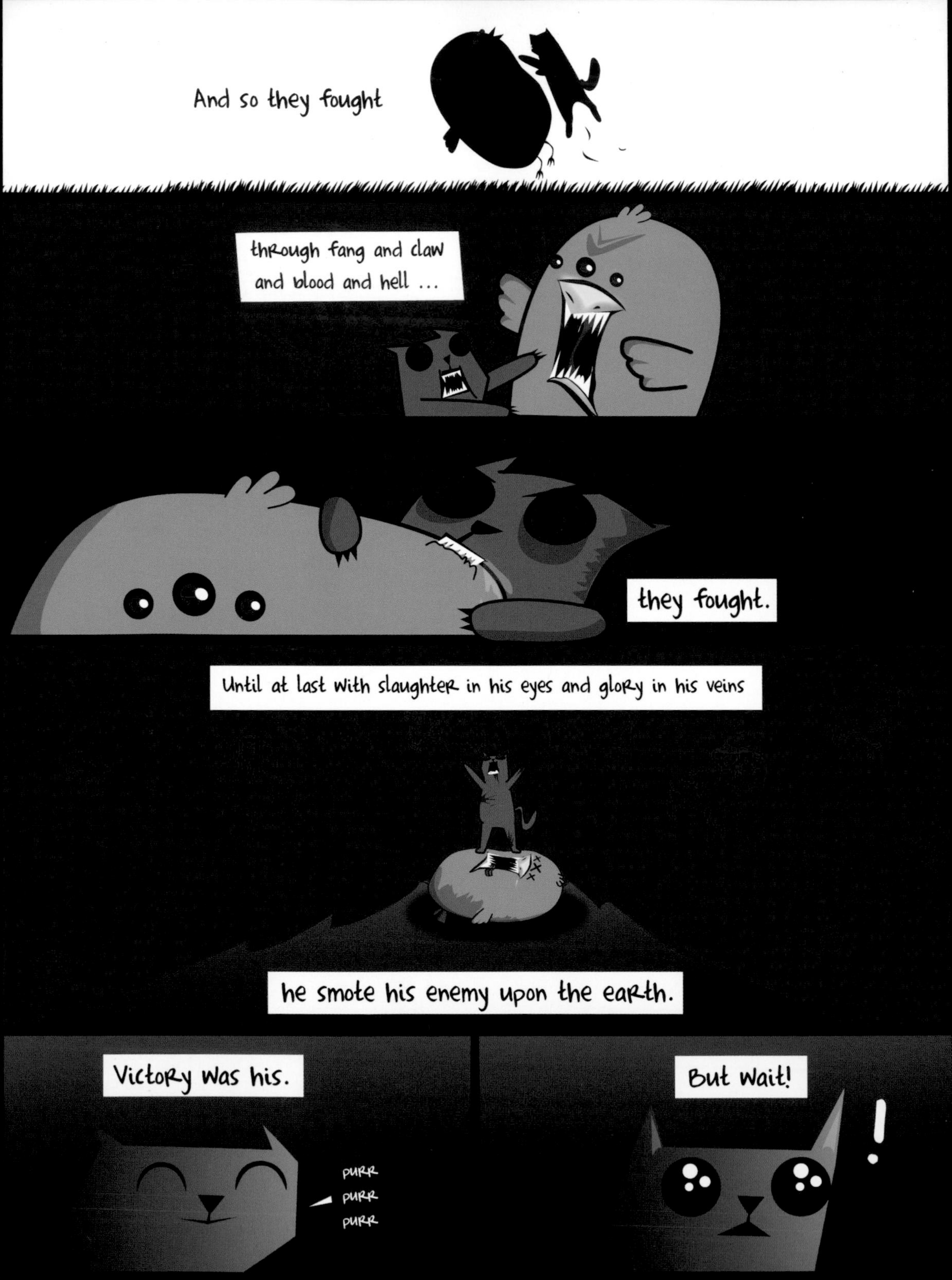
And so they fought
through fang and claw and blood and hell ...
they fought.
Until at last with slaughter in his eyes and glory in his veins
he smote his enemy upon the earth.
Victory was his.
PURR
PURR
PURR
But wait!
!

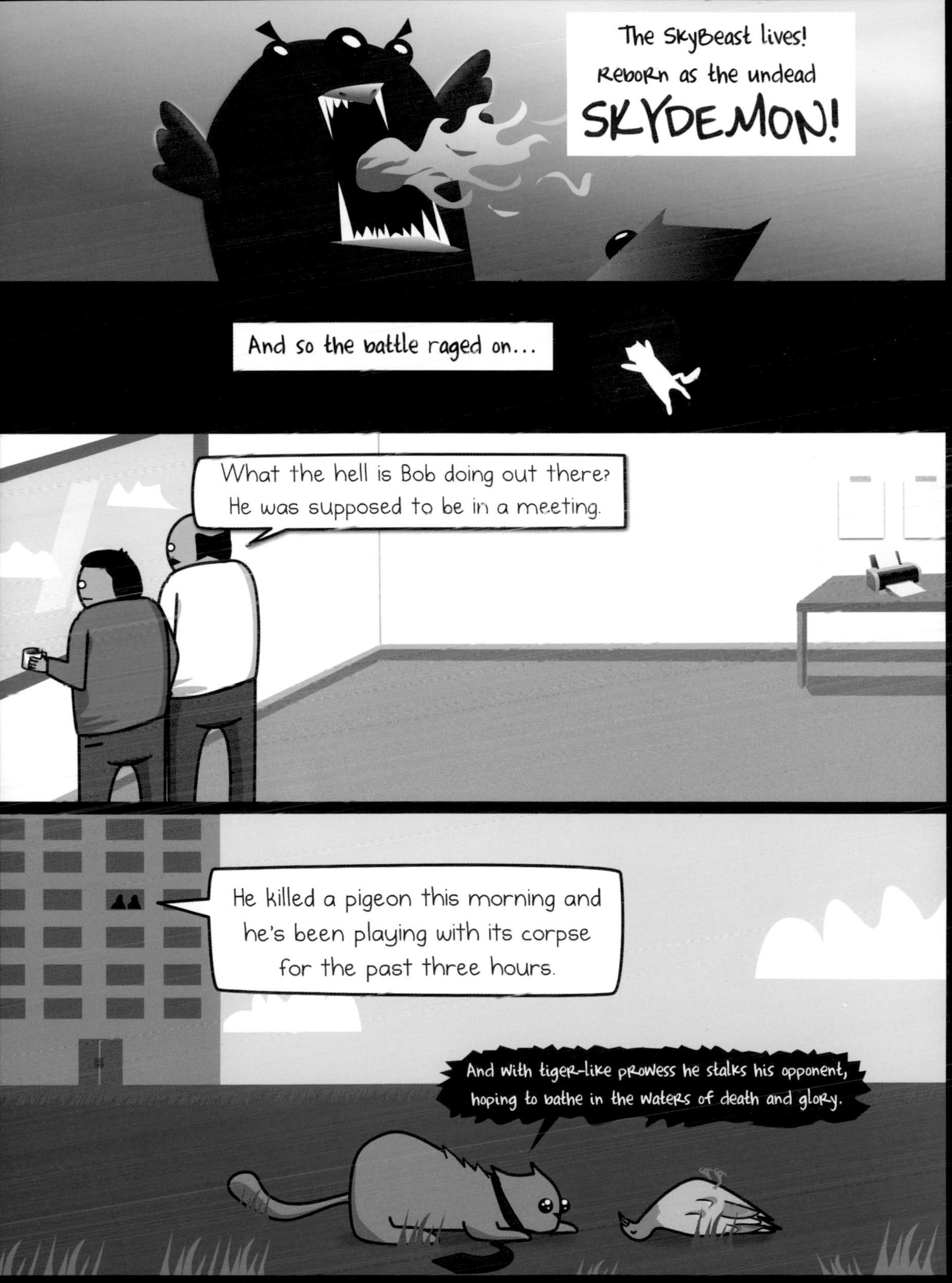
The SkyBeast lives!
Reborn as the undead
SKYDEMON!
And so the battle raged on...
What the hell is Bob doing out there? He was supposed to be in a meeting.
He killed a pigeon this morning and he's been playing with its corpse for the past three hours.
And with tiger-like prowess he stalks his opponent, hoping to bathe in the waters of death and glory.

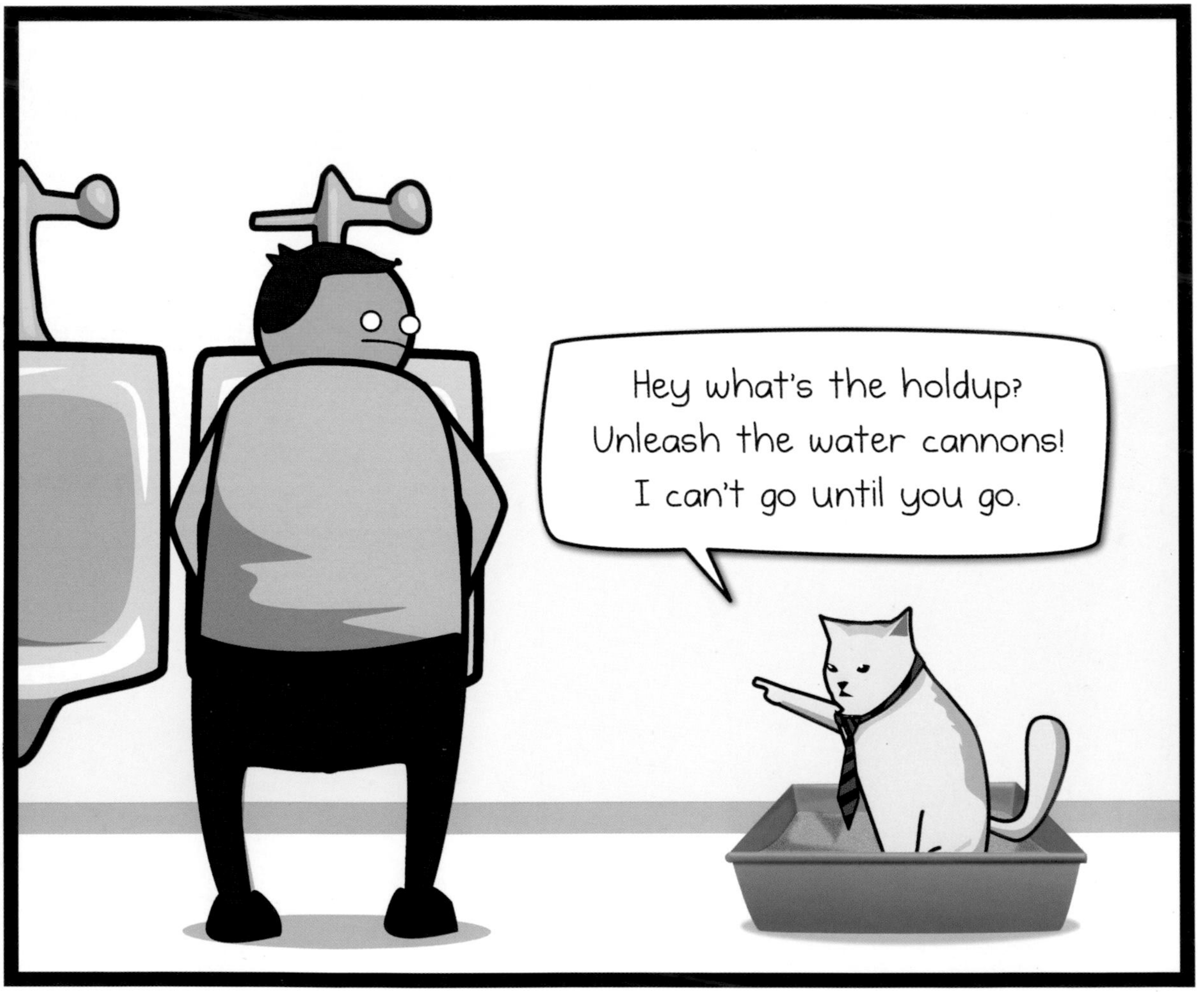
Hey what's the holdup?
Unleash the water cannons!
I can't go until you go.

The Bobcats

Episode 6: Saturday

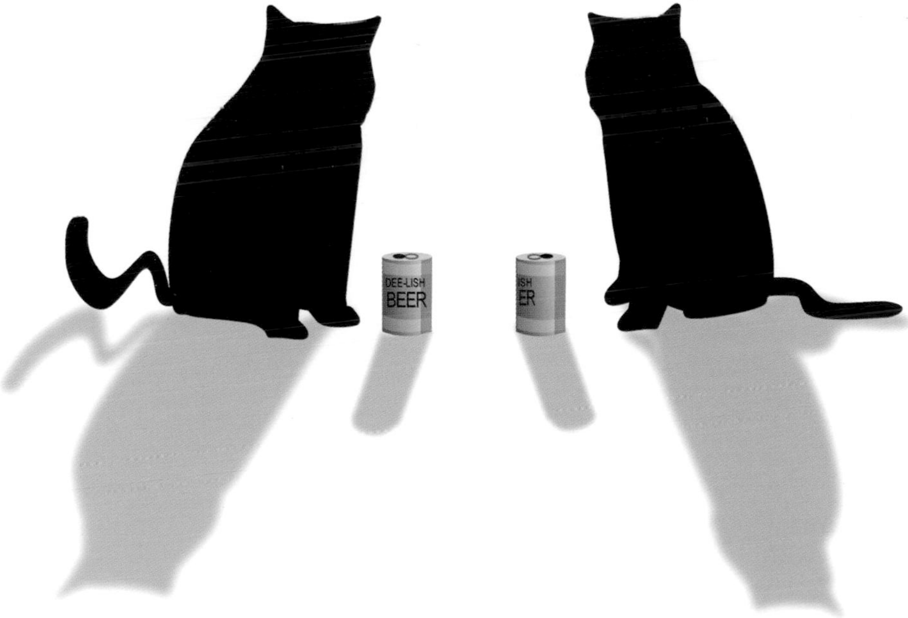
DEE-LISH
BEER

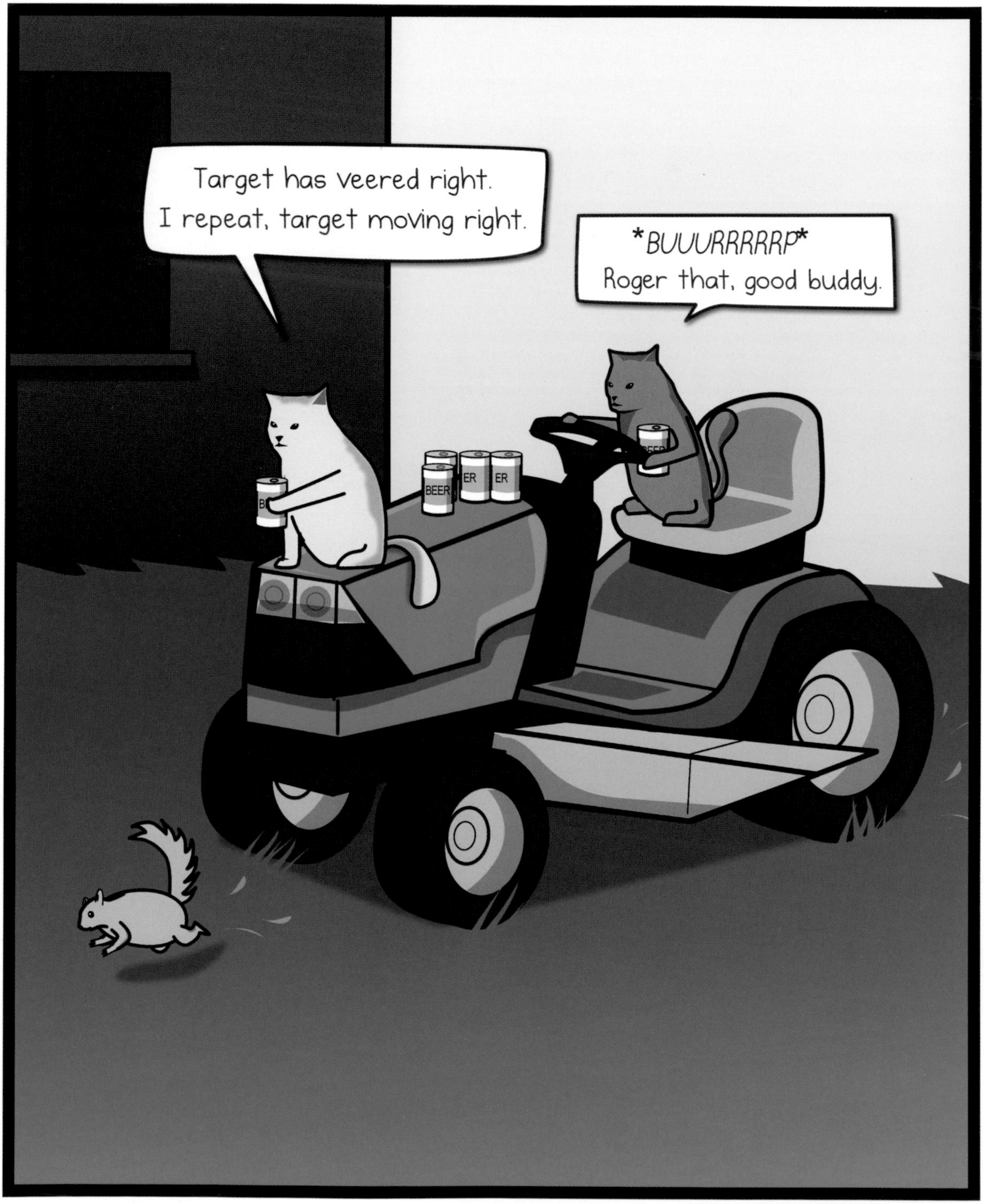
Target has veered right. I repeat, target moving right.
BUUURRRRRP Roger that, good buddy.
BEER
ER
ER

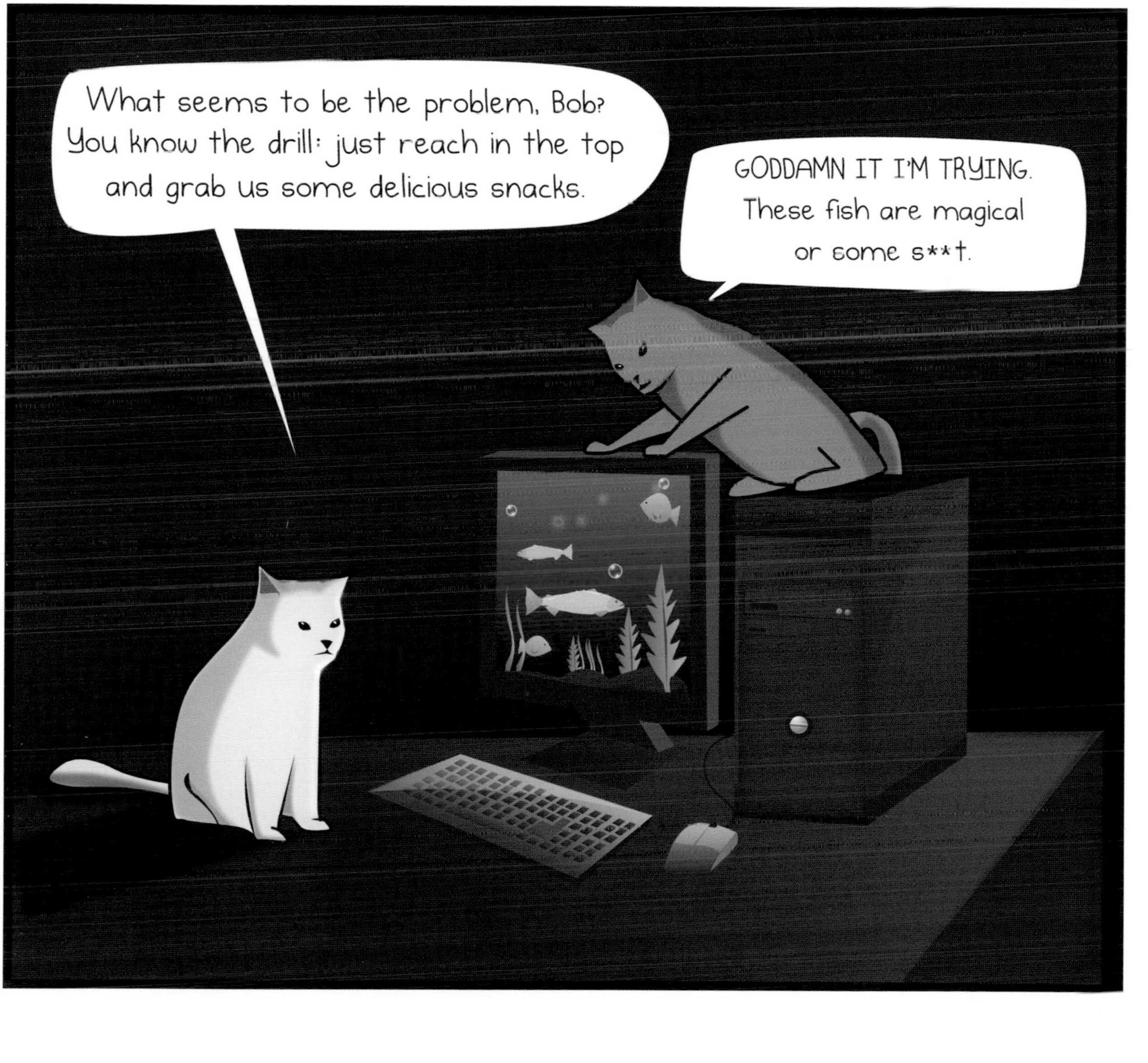
What seems to be the problem, Bob? You know the drill: just reach in the top and grab us some delicious snacks.
GODDAMN IT I'M TRYING. These fish are magical or some s**t.

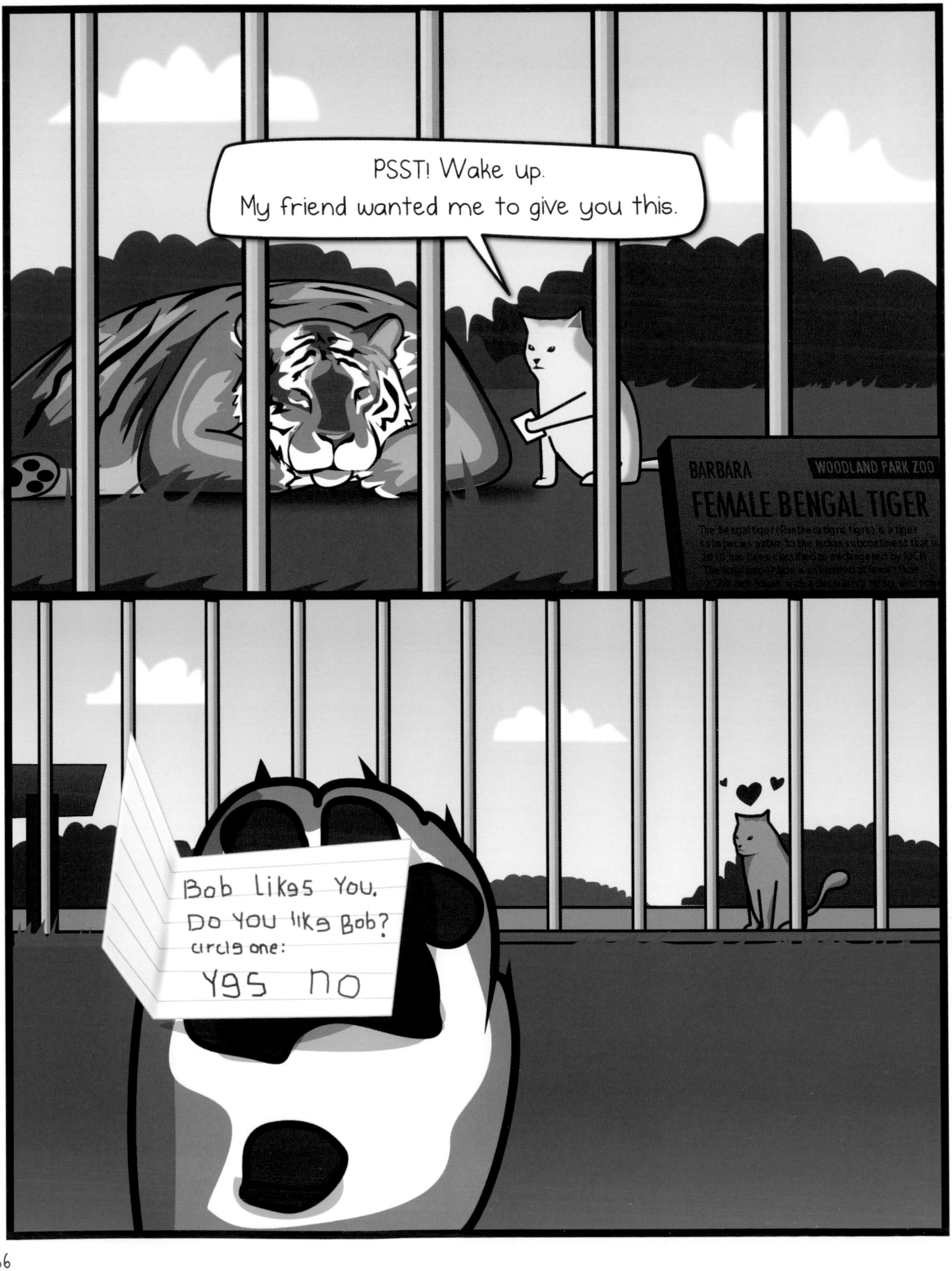
PSST! Wake up.
My friend wanted me to give you this.
BARBARA
WOODLAND PARK ZOO
FEMALE BENGAL TIGER
Bob likes you.
Do you like Bob?
circle one:
yes no

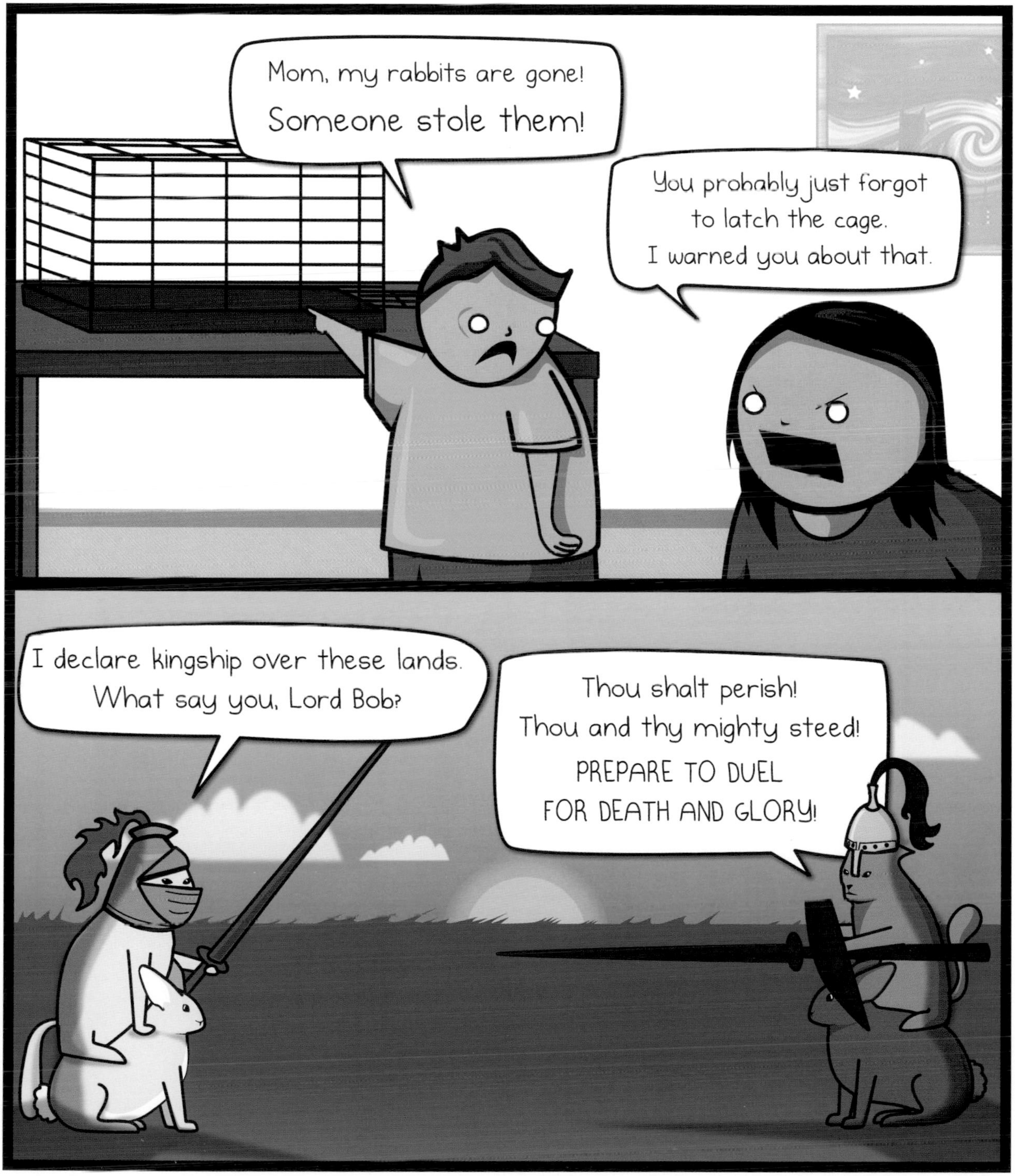
Mom, my rabbits are gone! Someone stole them!
You probably just forgot to latch the cage. I warned you about that.
I declare kingship over these lands. What say you, Lord Bob?
Thou shalt perish! Thou and thy mighty steed! PREPARE TO DUEL FOR DEATH AND GLORY!

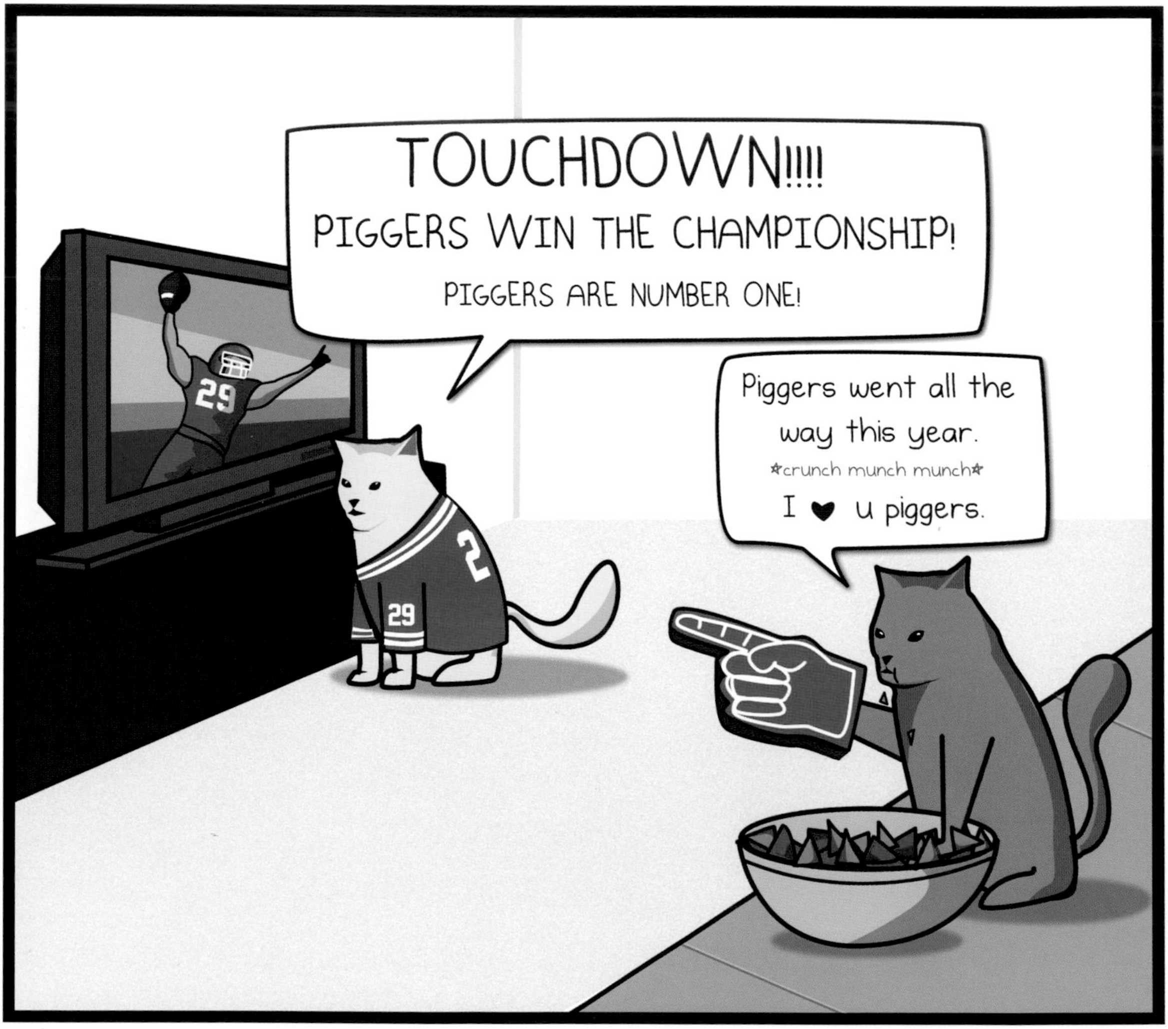
TOUCHDOWN!!!!
PIGGERS WIN THE CHAMPIONSHIP!
PIGGERS ARE NUMBER ONE!
Piggers went all the way this year.
crunch munch munch
I ♥ u piggers.

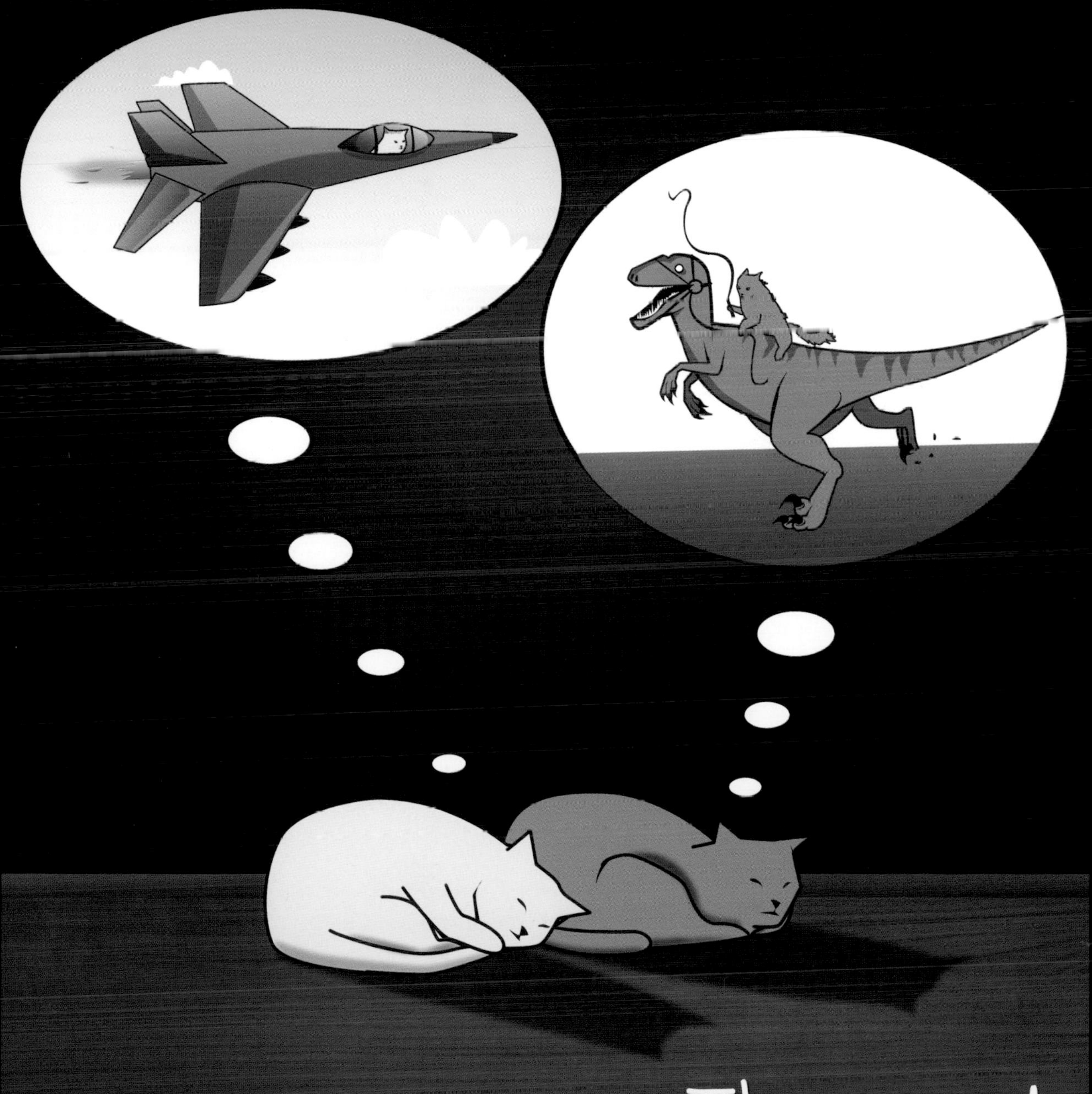
The end.

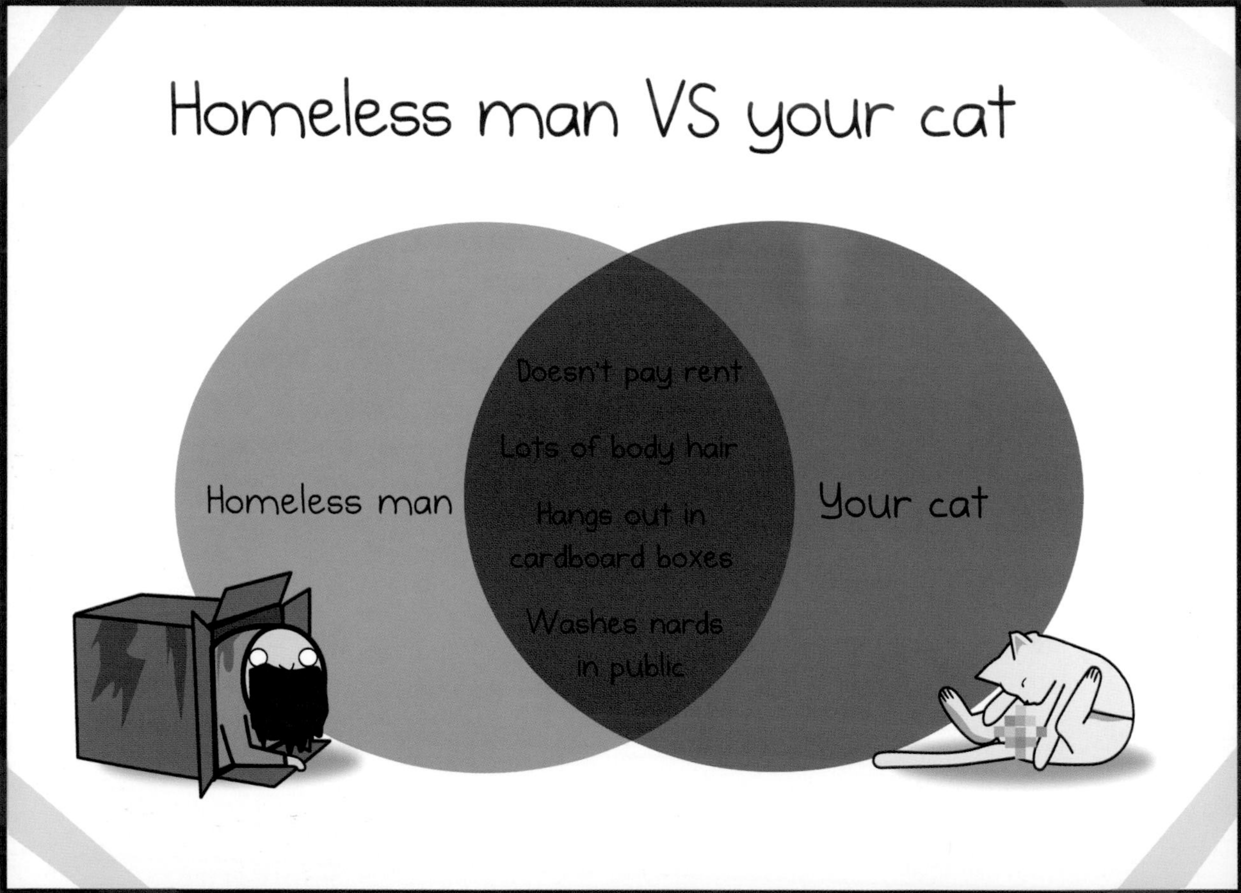

Homeless man VS your cat

Doesn't pay rent

Lots of body hair

Homeless man

Hangs out in cardboard boxes

Your cat

Washes nards in public

Direction of ears	Mood
	Neutral
	Grouchy
	Die.

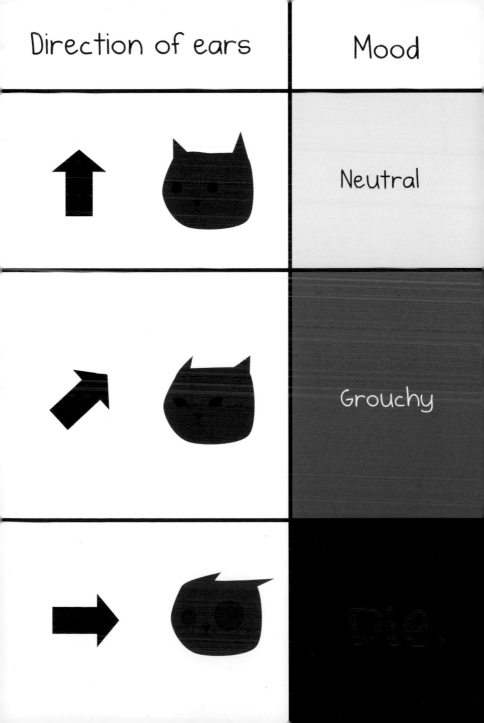

THINGS CATS LOVE

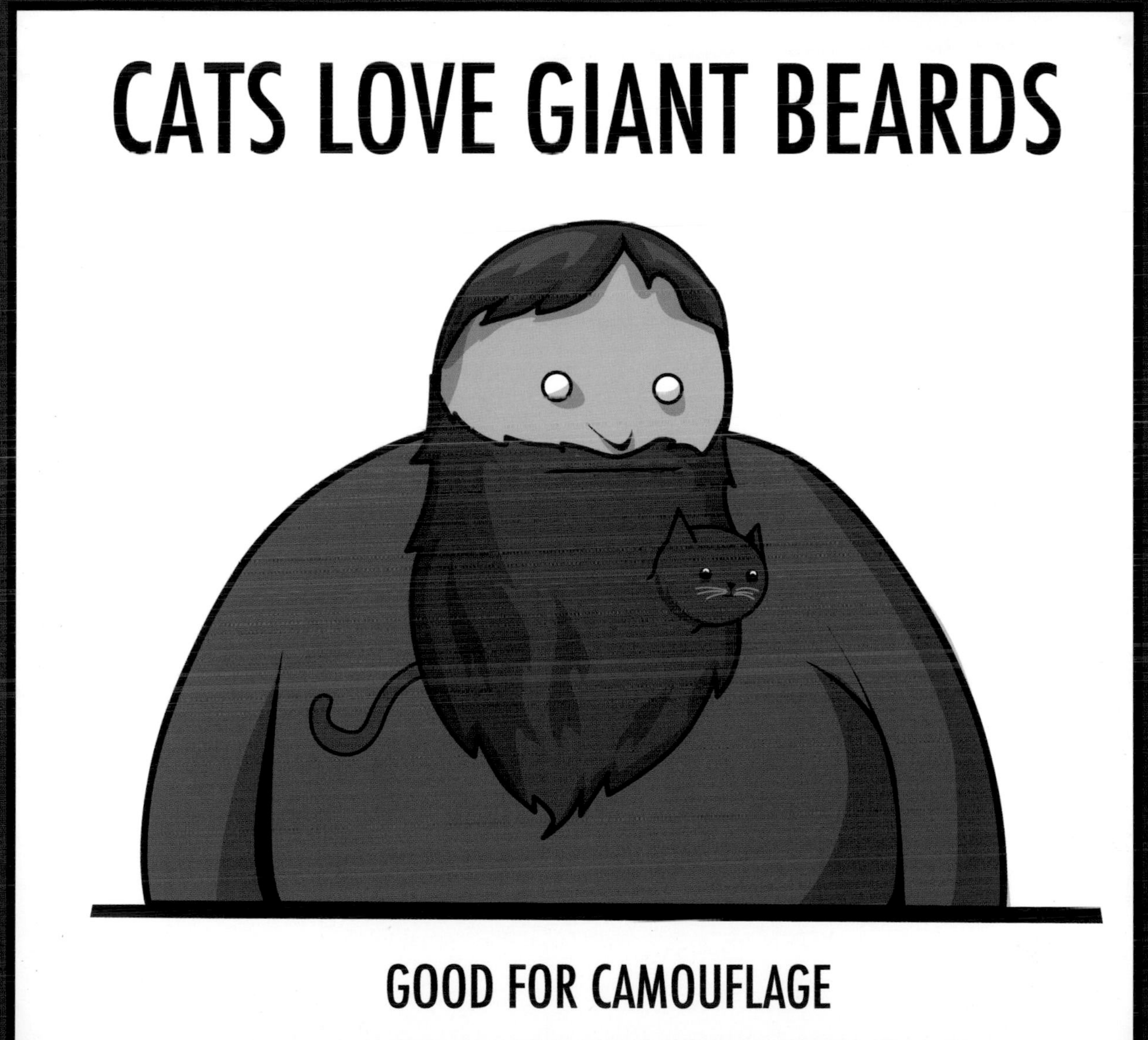
CATS LOVE GIANT BEARDS
GOOD FOR CAMOUFLAGE

CATS LOVE HOWITZERS

HEAVY ARTILLERY REEKS OF DEATH AND GLORY

CATS LOVE COMMANDEERING CHEETAHS

CUTS DOWN ON TRAVEL TIME

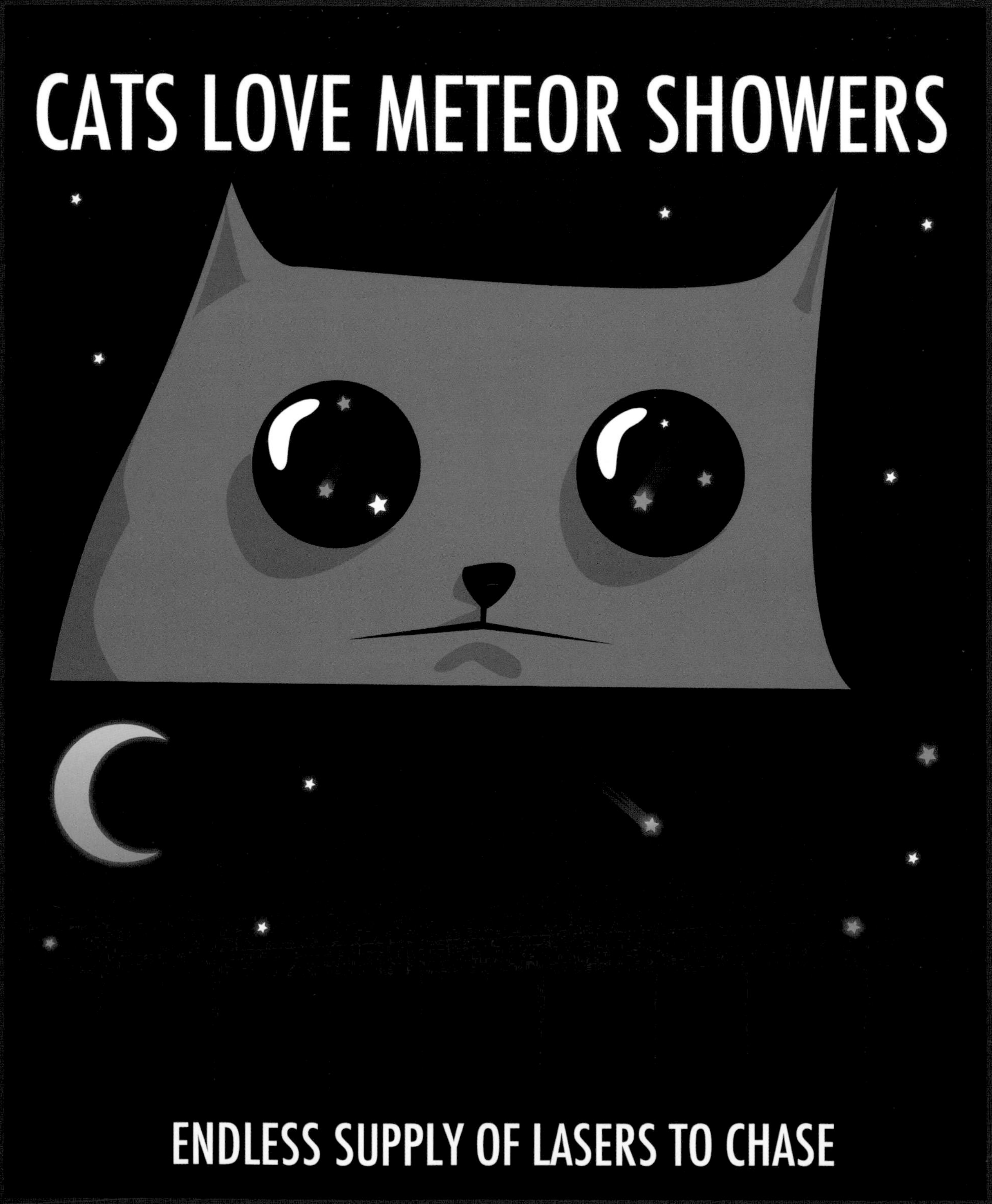
CATS LOVE METEOR SHOWERS
ENDLESS SUPPLY OF LASERS TO CHASE

CATS LOVE QUIET, PEACEFUL MOMENTS

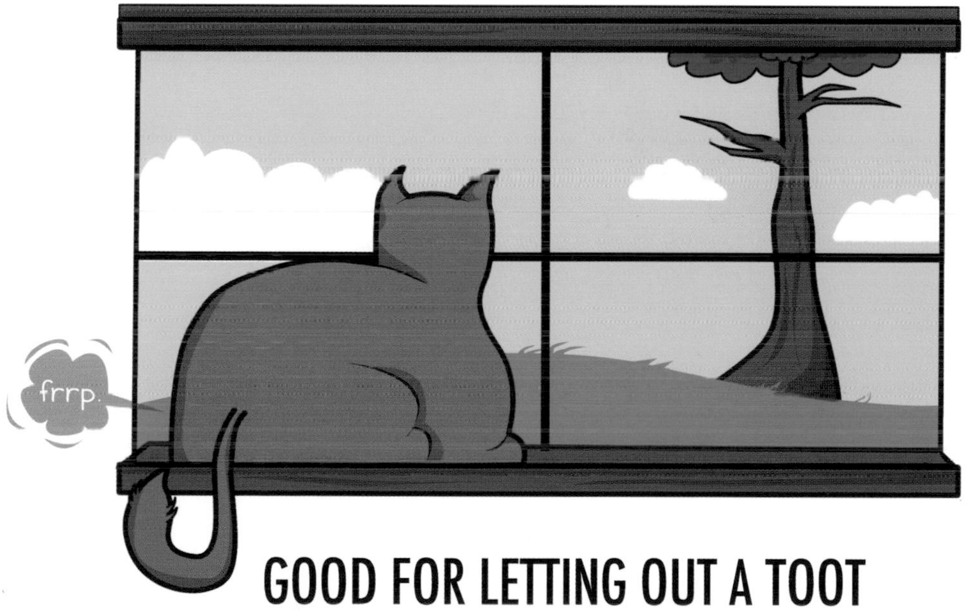
frrp.

GOOD FOR LETTING OUT A TOOT
AND CONTEMPLATING LIFE

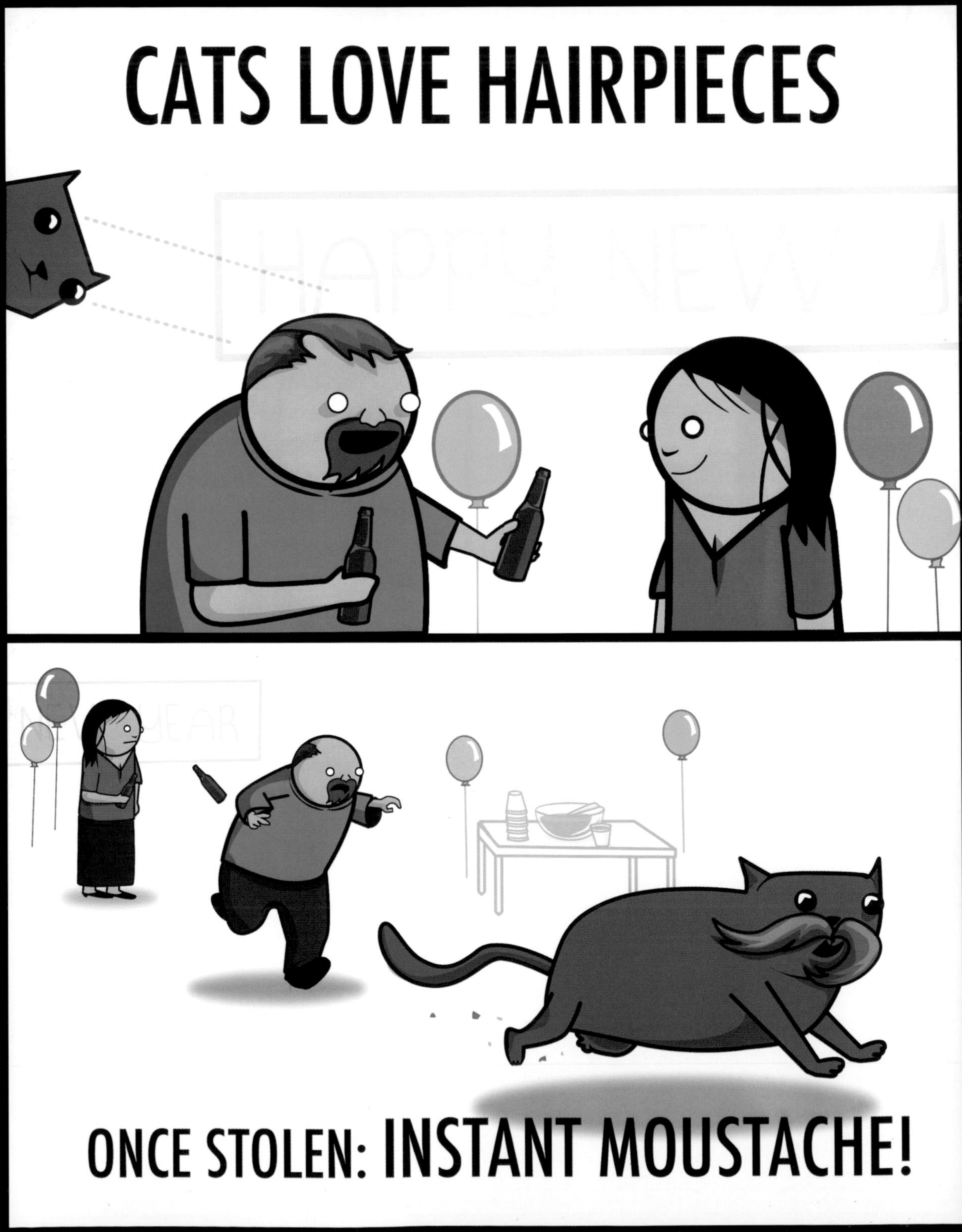
CATS LOVE HAIRPIECES
HAPPY NEW
ONCE STOLEN: INSTANT MOUSTACHE!

CATS LOVE REFLECTIVE SURFACES
THUNK!
NATURE'S VENDING MACHINE

CATS LOVE INFANTS

TOO WEAK AND HELPLESS TO ESCAPE A PROPER MAULING

Walking the dog

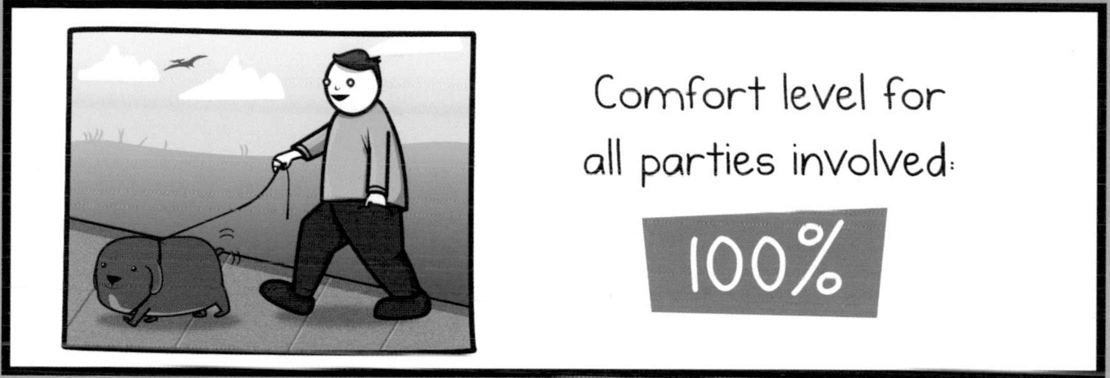
Comfort level for all parties involved:
100%

Walking the cat

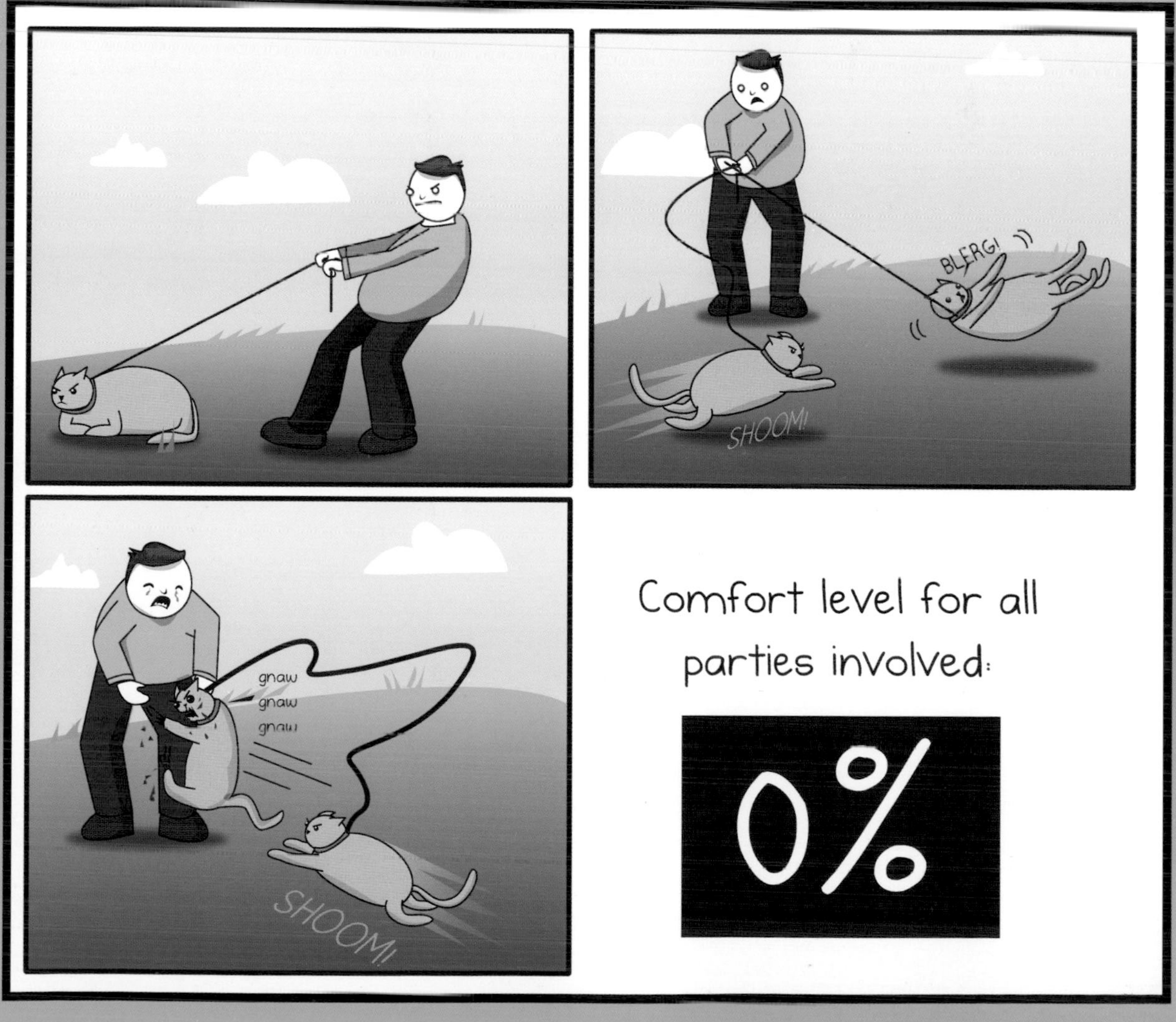
BLERG!
SHOOM!
gnaw
gnaw
gnaw
SHOOM!
Comfort level for all parties involved:
0%

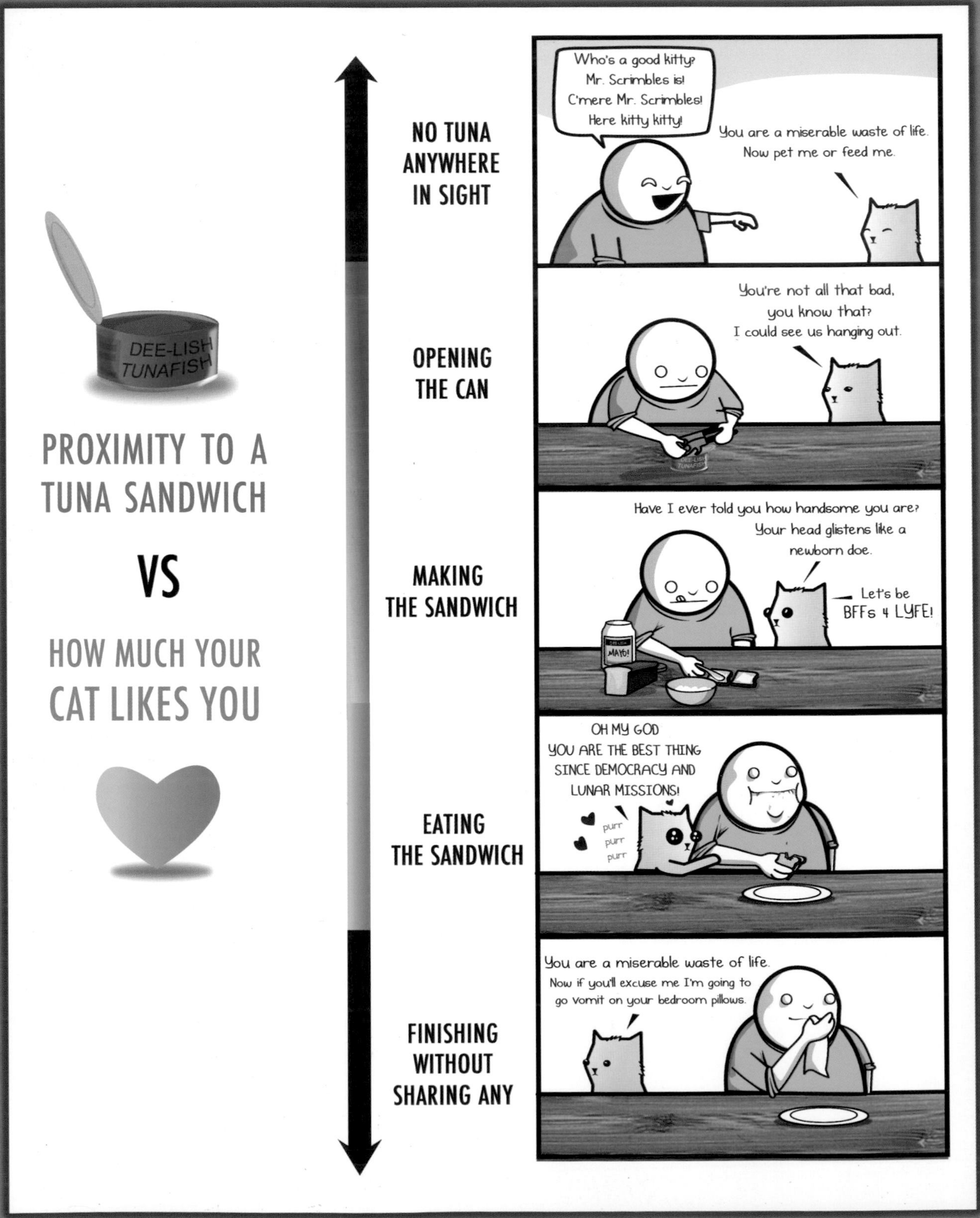
DEE-LISH TUNAFISH
PROXIMITY TO A TUNA SANDWICH
VS
HOW MUCH YOUR CAT LIKES YOU
NO TUNA ANYWHERE IN SIGHT
Who's a good kitty? Mr. Scrimbles is! C'mere Mr. Scrimbles! Here kitty kitty!
You are a miserable waste of life. Now pet me or feed me.
OPENING THE CAN
You're not all that bad, you know that? I could see us hanging out.
MAKING THE SANDWICH
Have I ever told you how handsome you are? Your head glistens like a newborn doe.
Let's be BFFs 4 LYFE!
MAYO!
EATING THE SANDWICH
OH MY GOD YOU ARE THE BEST THING SINCE DEMOCRACY AND LUNAR MISSIONS!
purr purr purr
FINISHING WITHOUT SHARING ANY
You are a miserable waste of life. Now if you'll excuse me I'm going to go vomit on your bedroom pillows.

Cat VS Internet

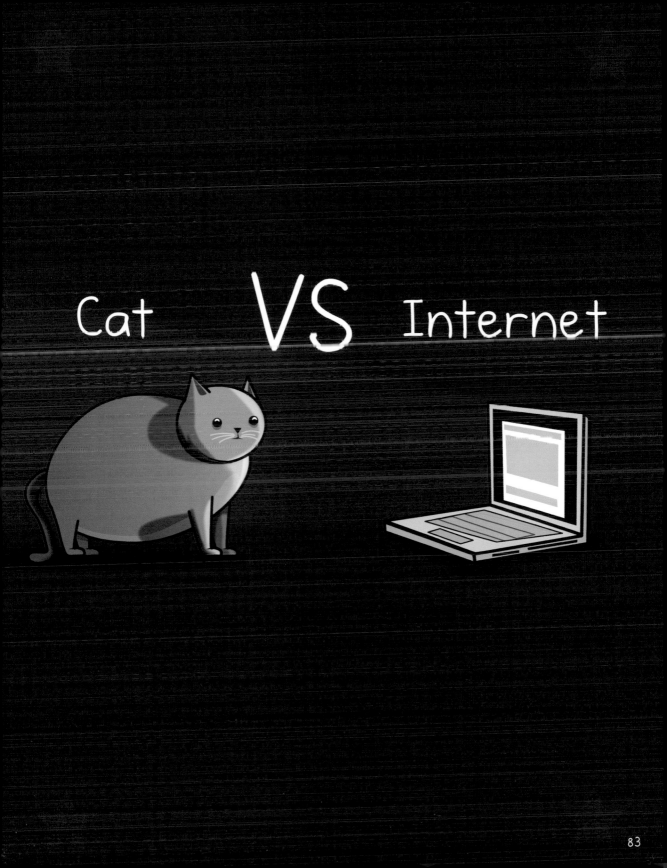

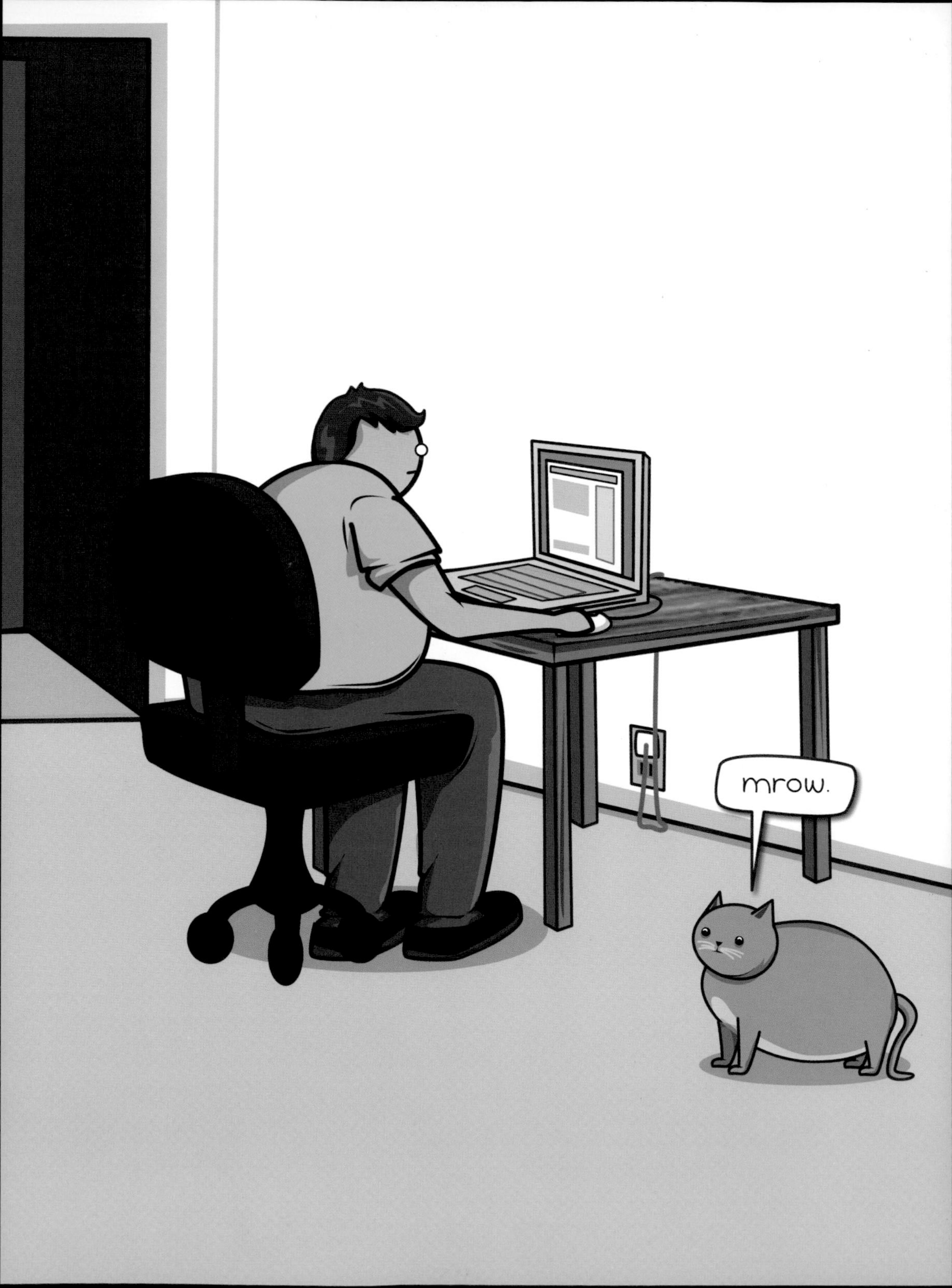
mrow.

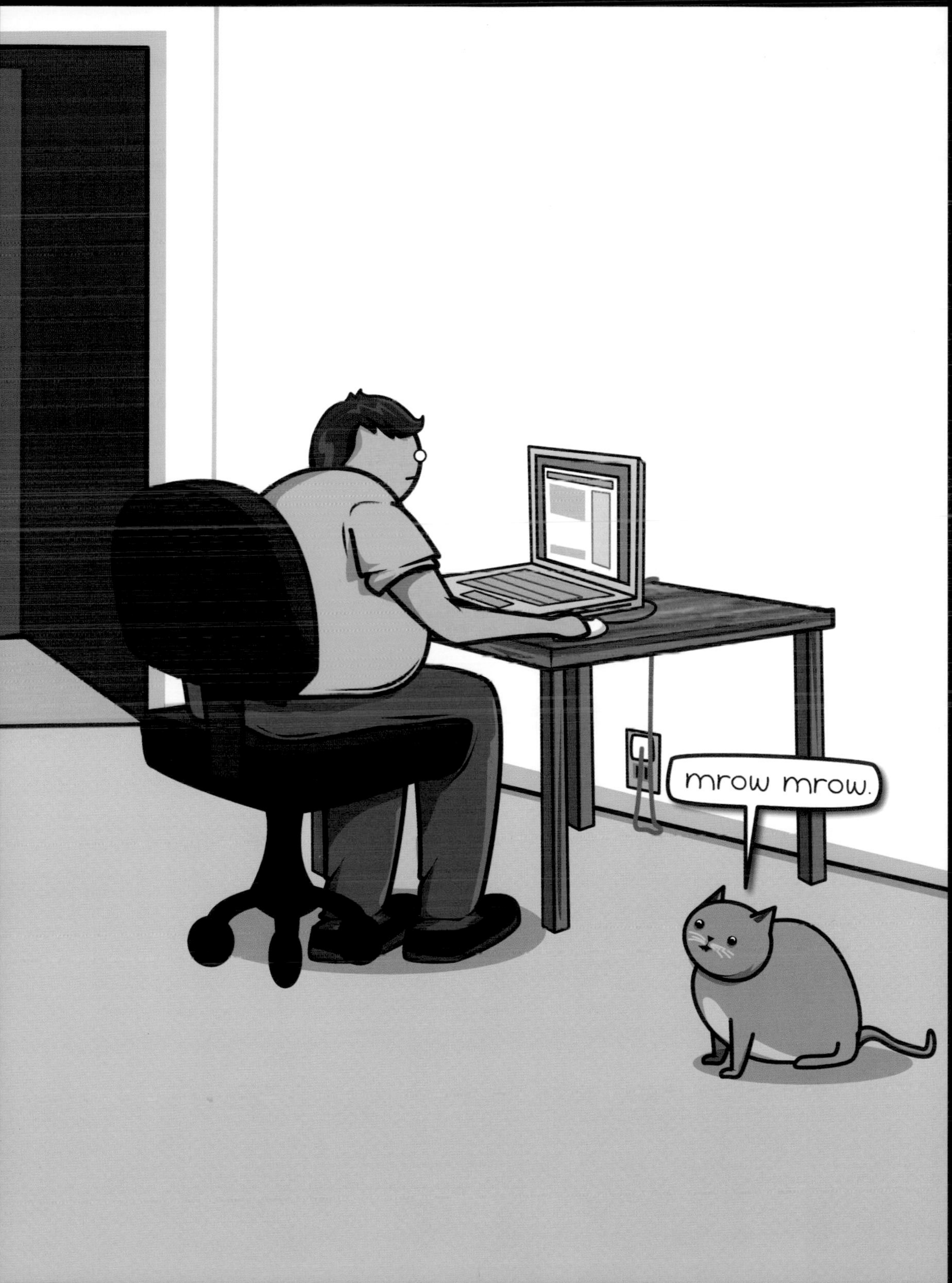
mrow mrow.

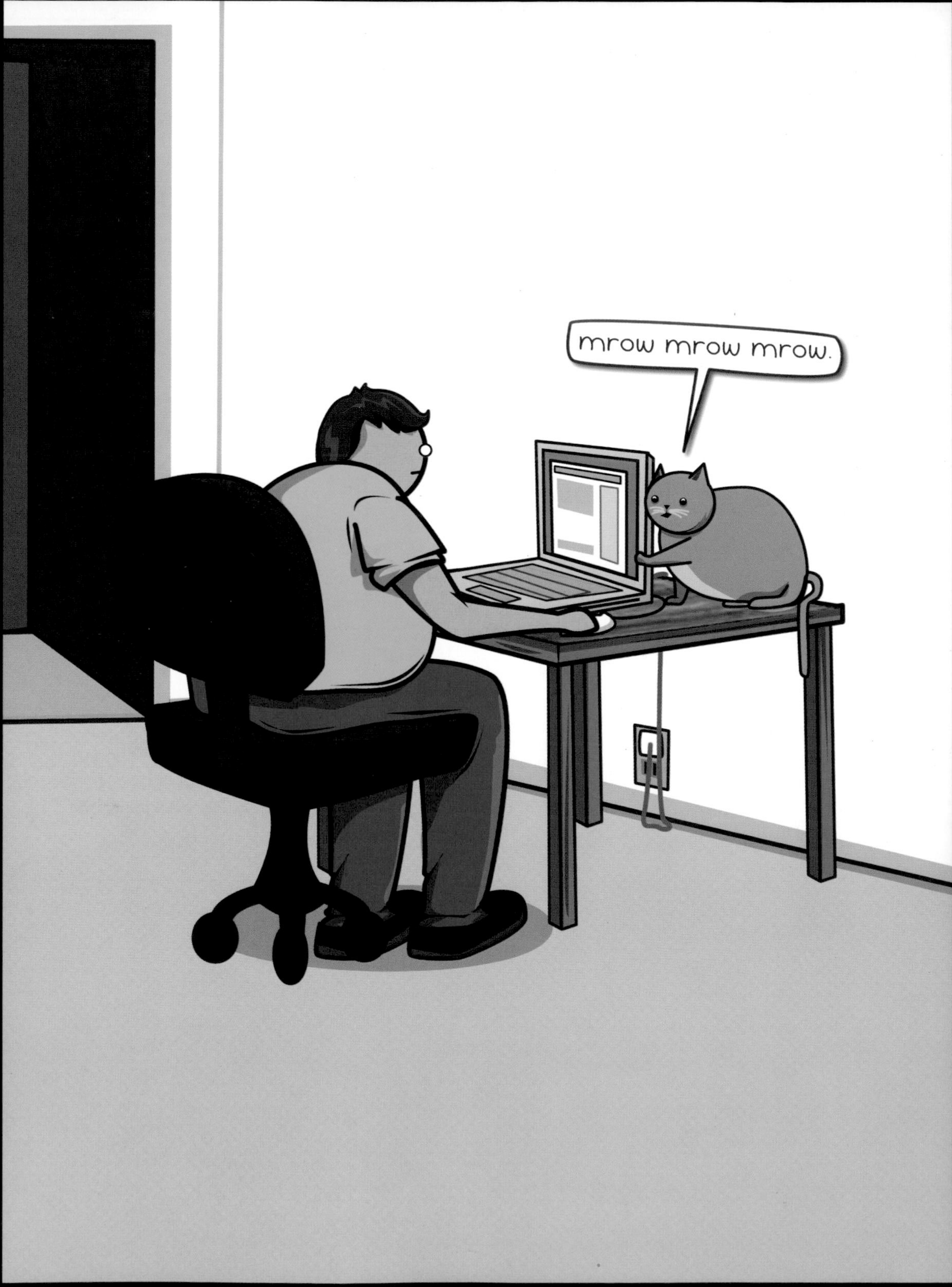
mrow mrow mrow.

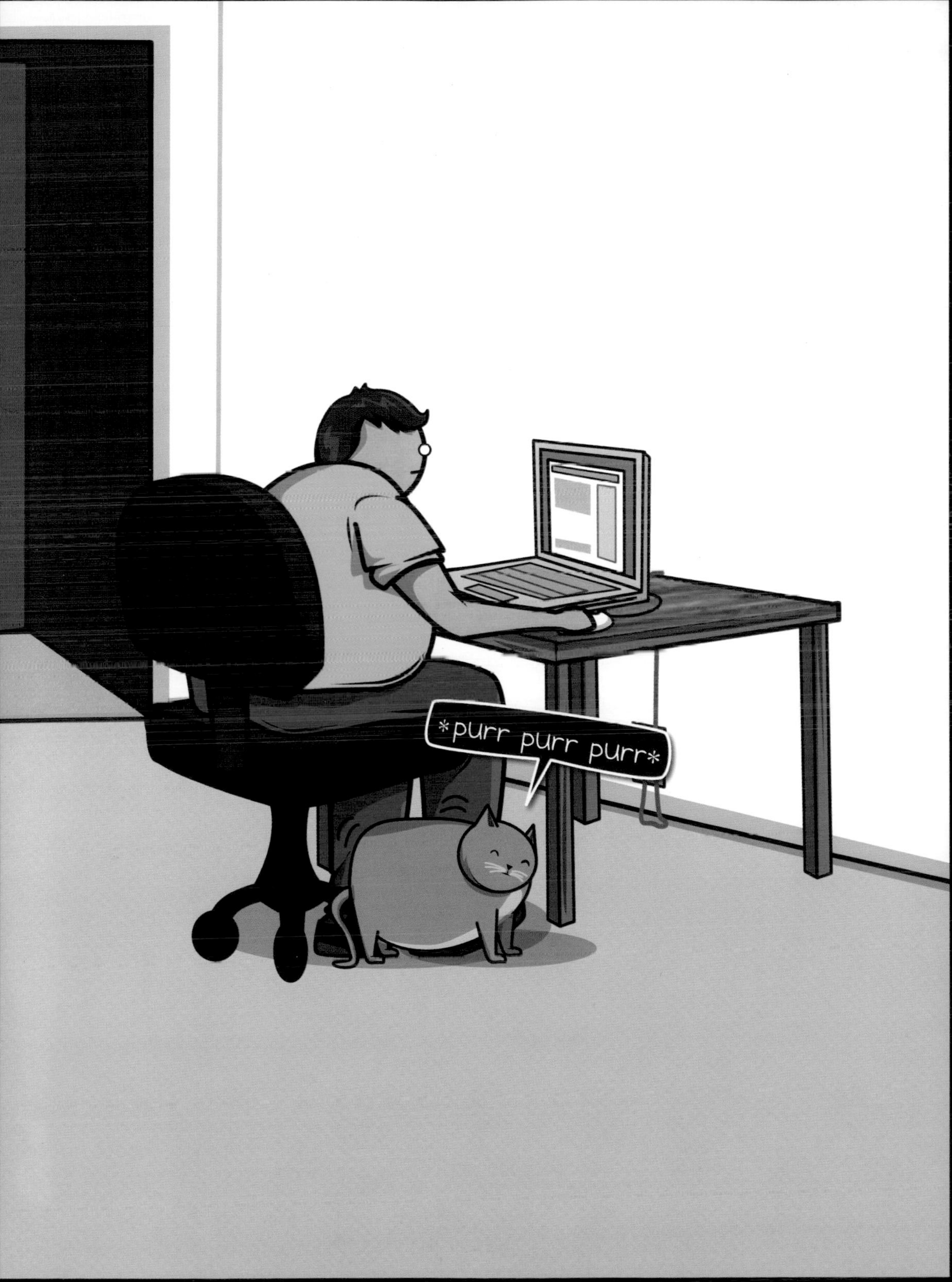
purr purr purr

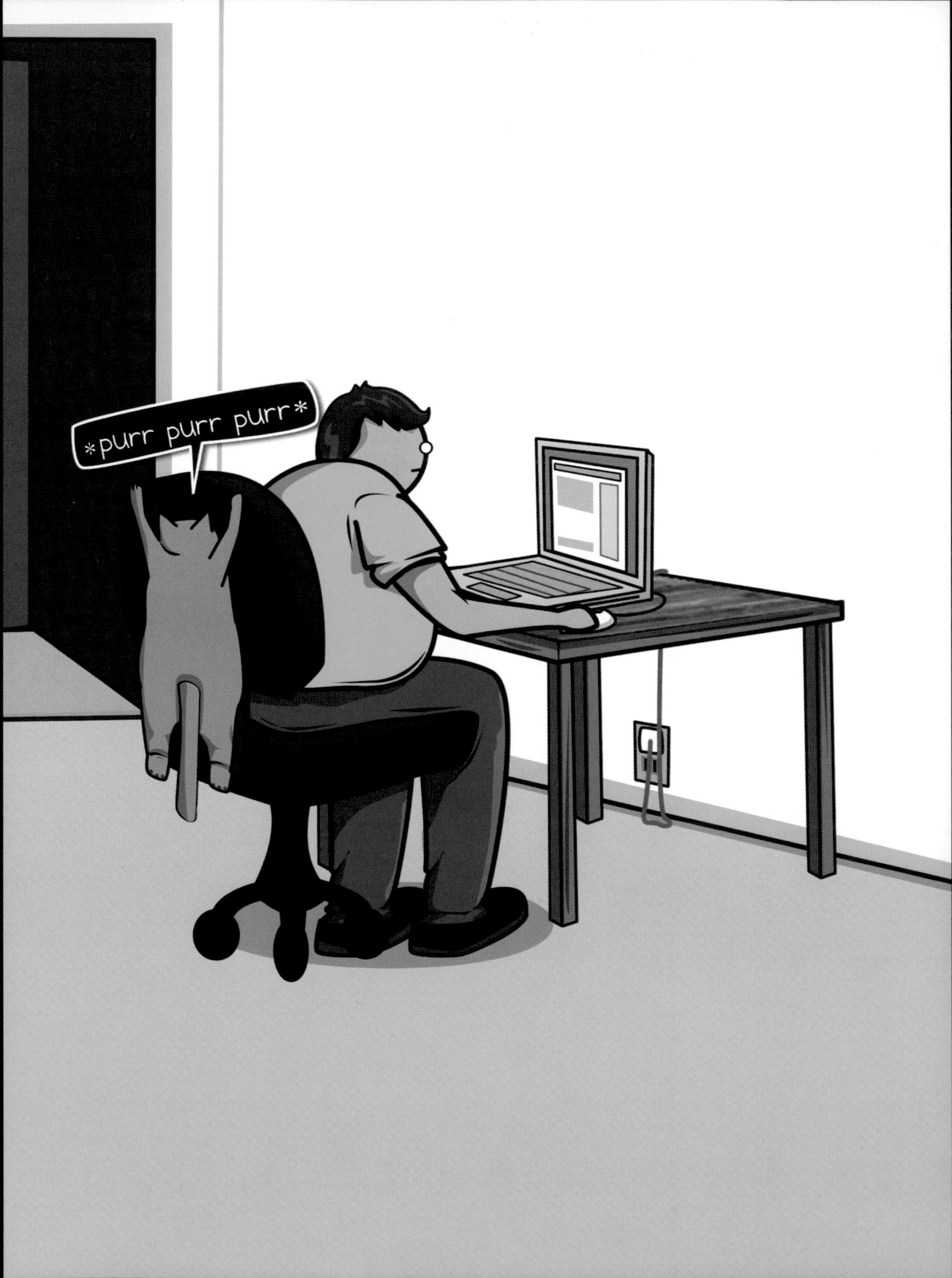
purr purr purr

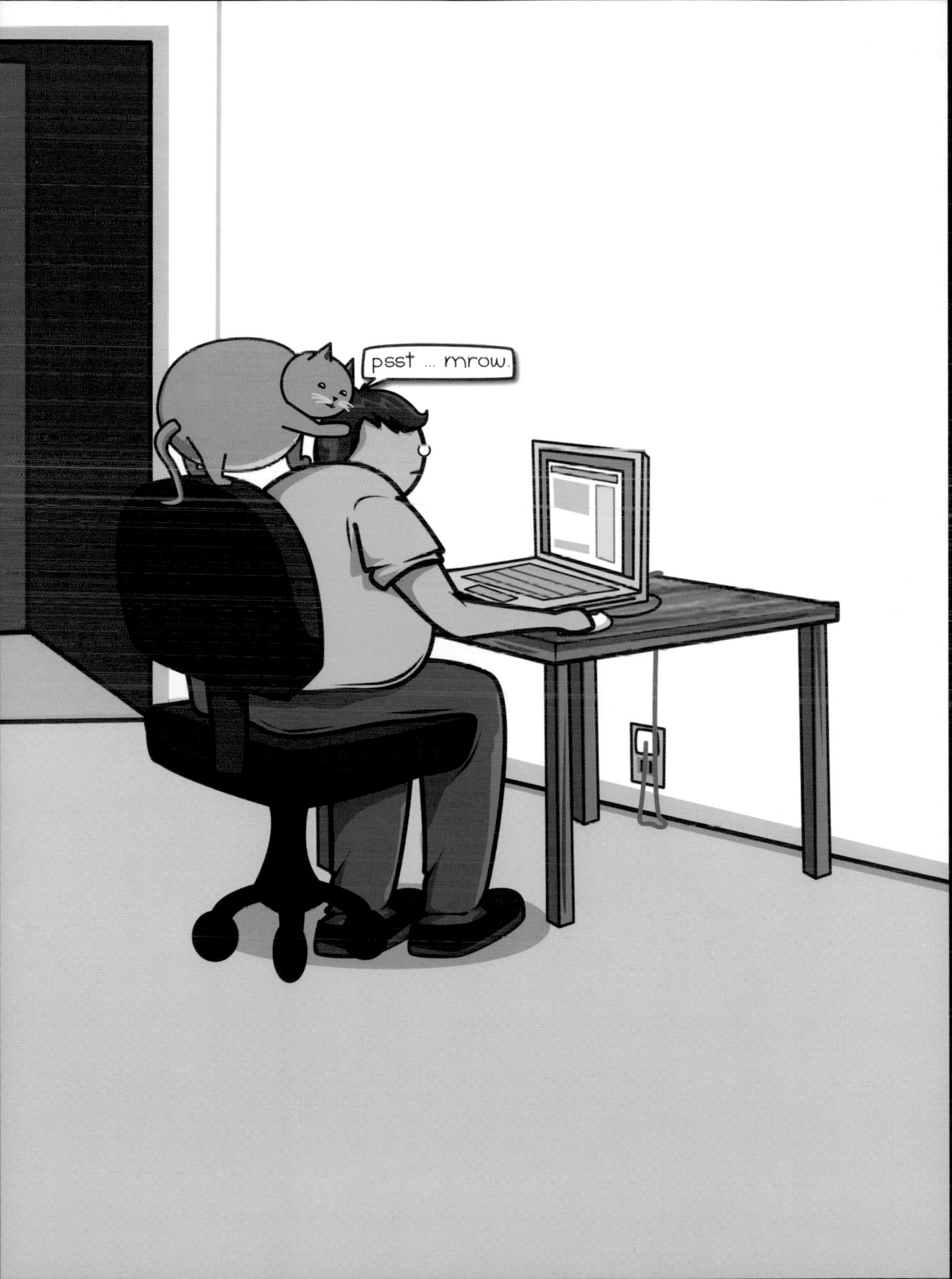
psst ... mrow.

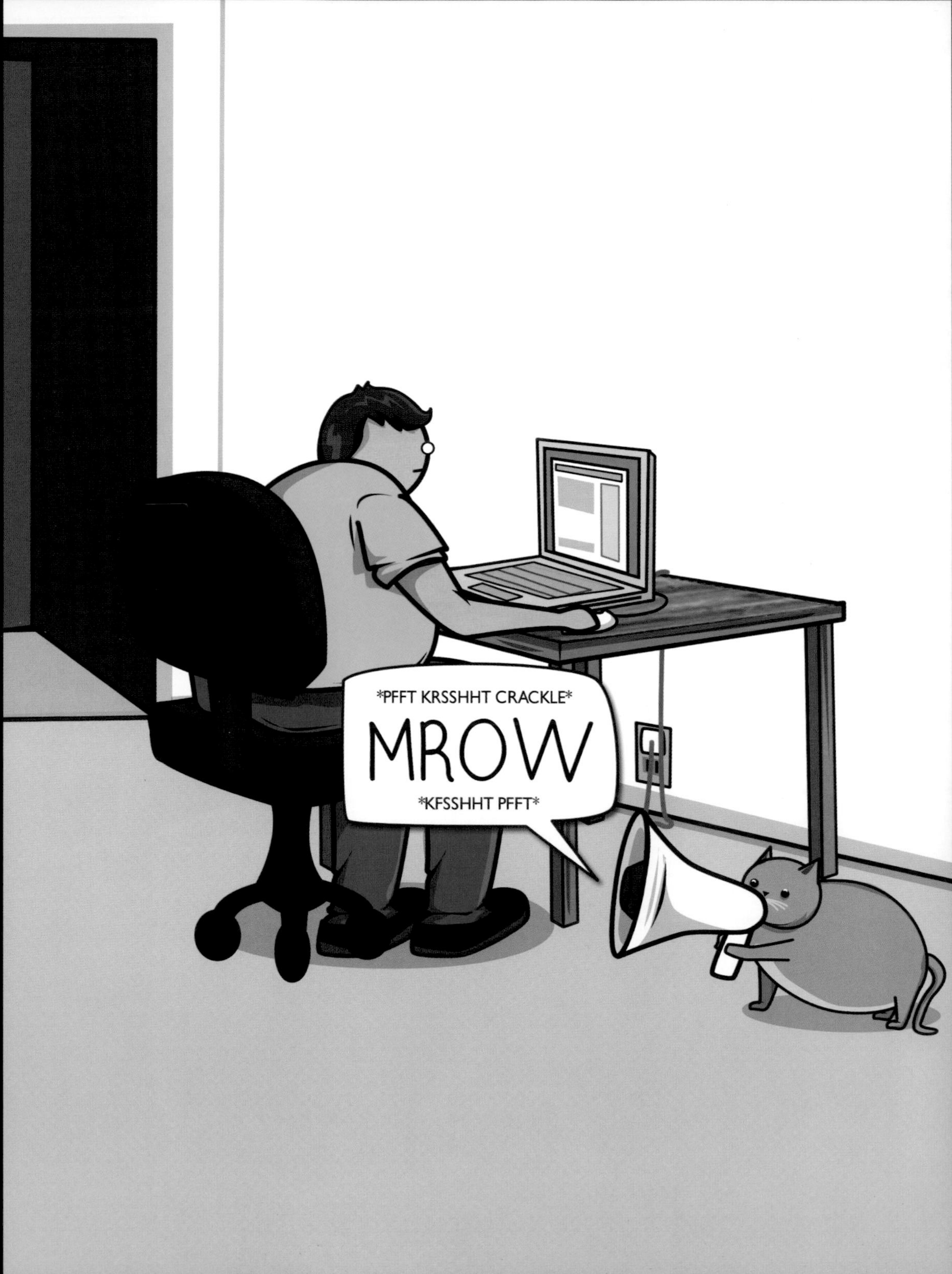
PFFT KRSSHHT CRACKLE
MROW
KFSSHHT PFFT

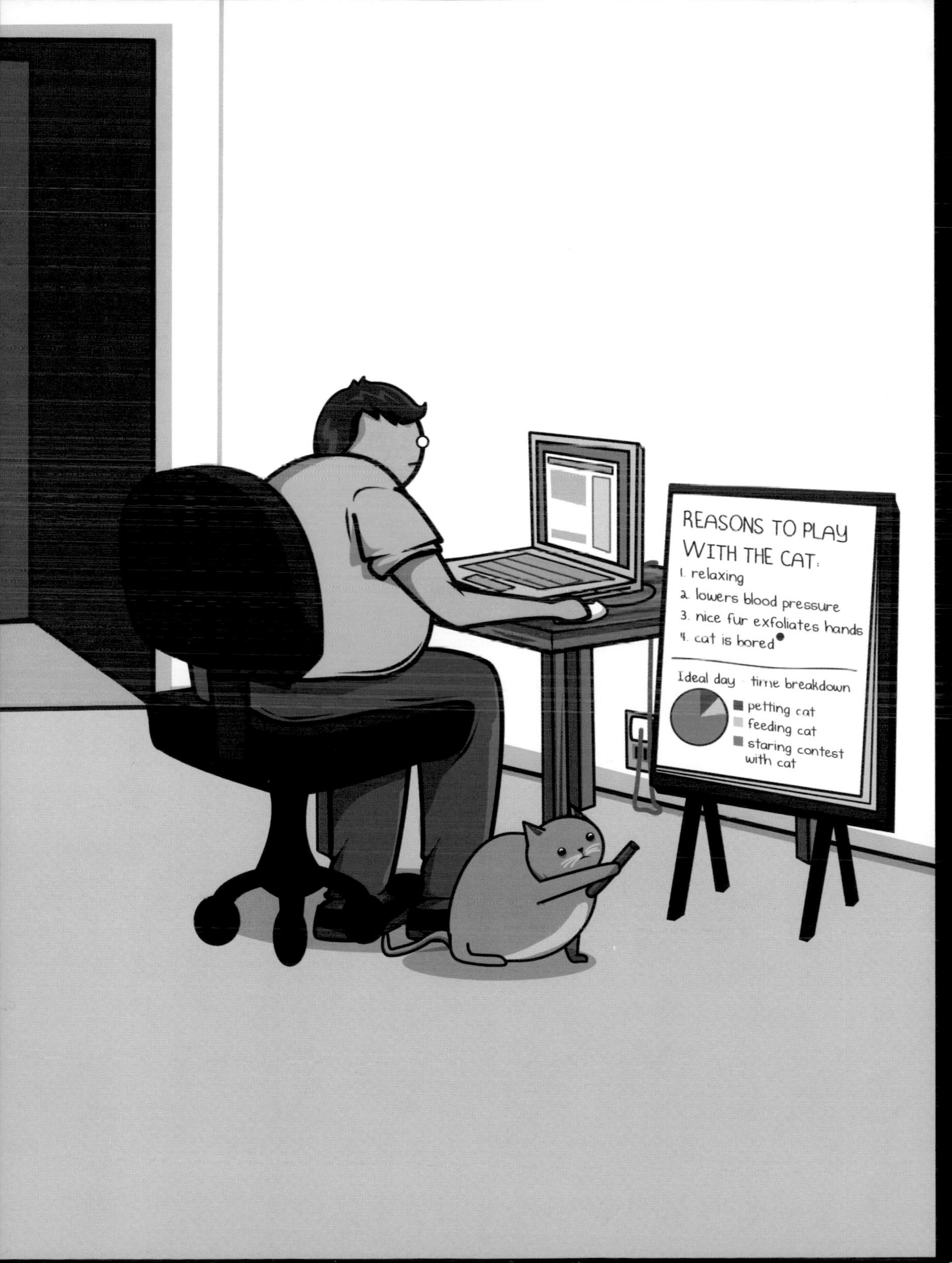
REASONS TO PLAY WITH THE CAT:
1. relaxing
2. lowers blood pressure
3. nice fur exfoliates hands
4. cat is bored
Ideal day - time breakdown
petting cat
feeding cat
staring contest with cat

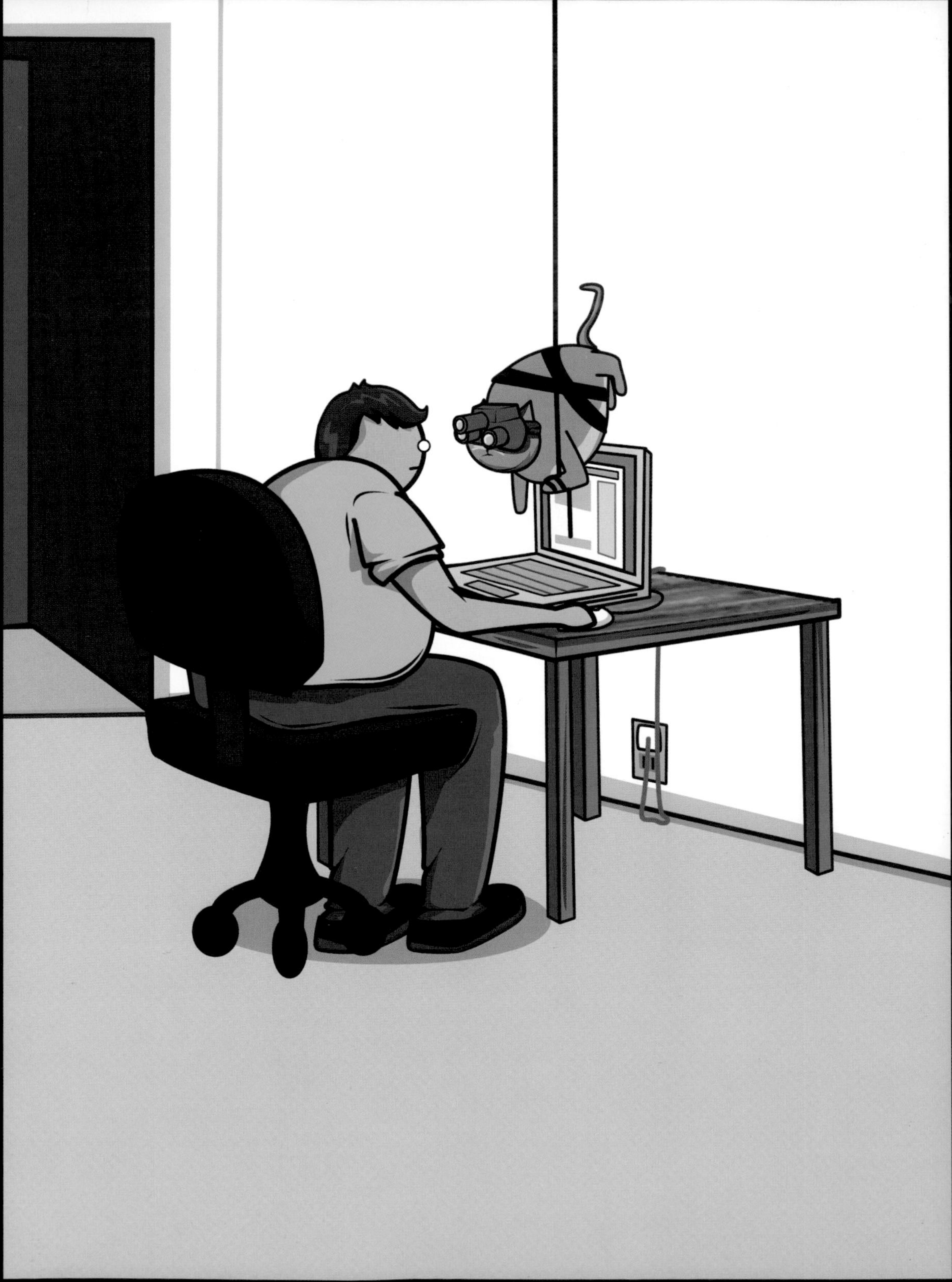

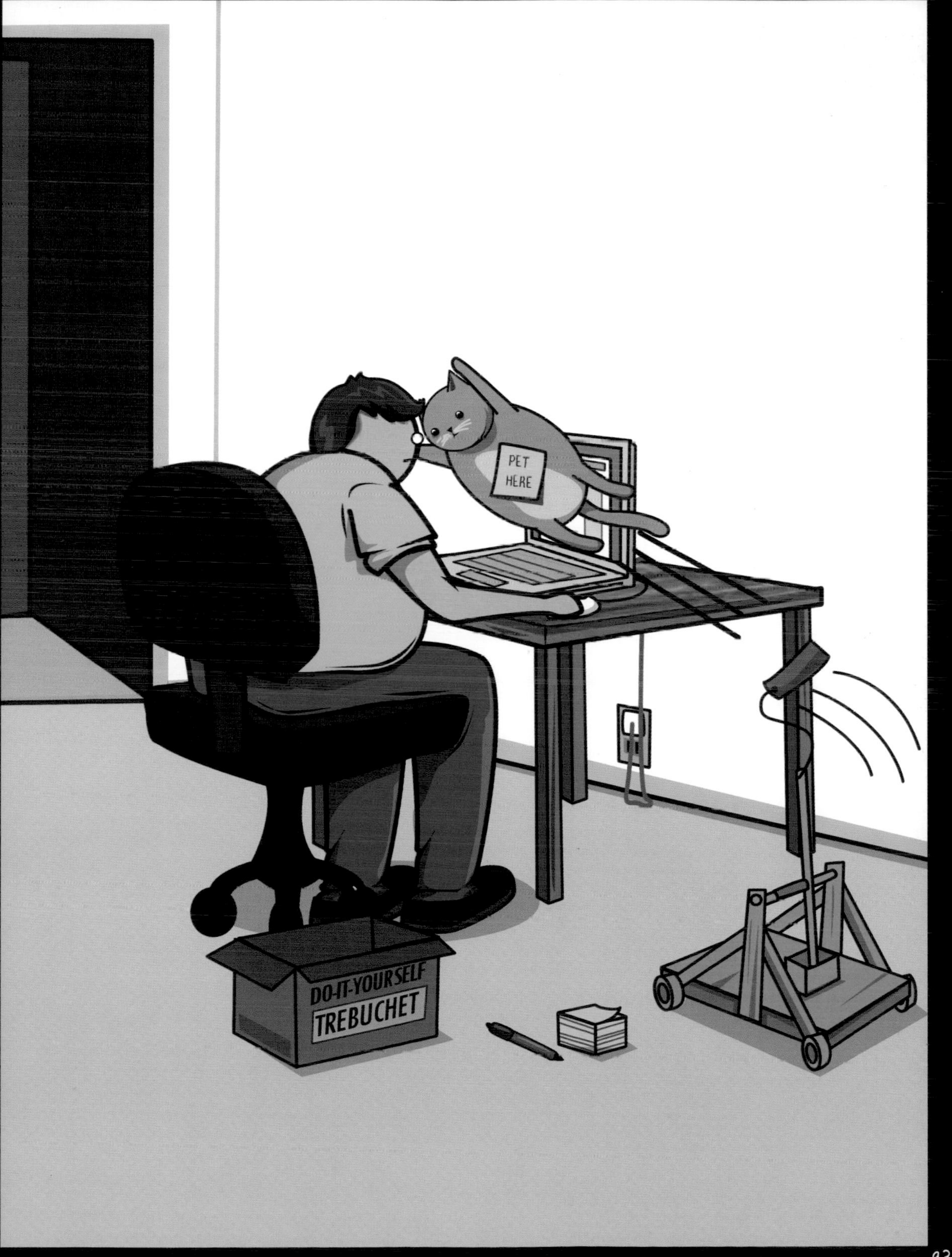
PET
HERE
DO-IT-YOURSELF
TREBUCHET

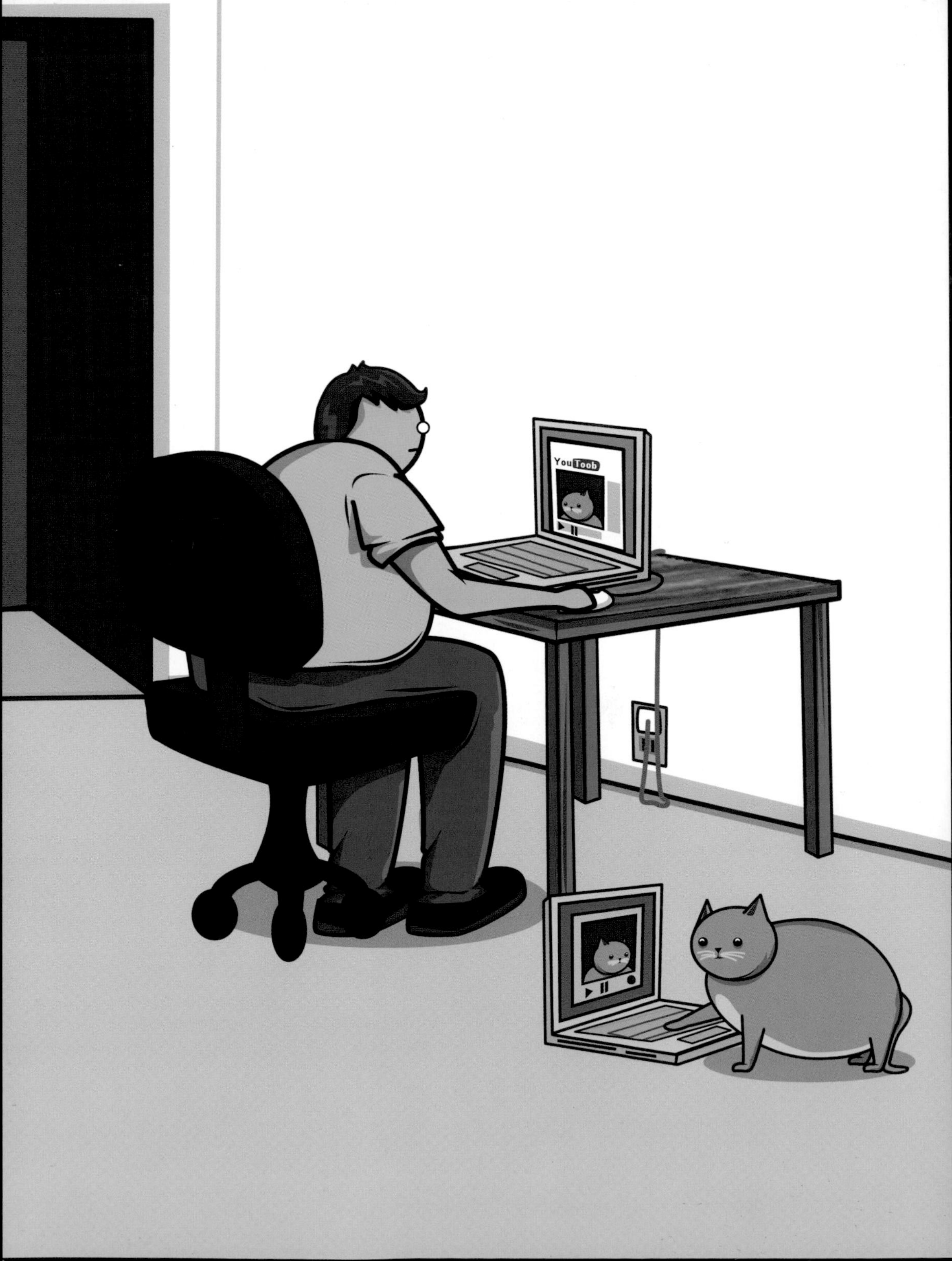
YouToob

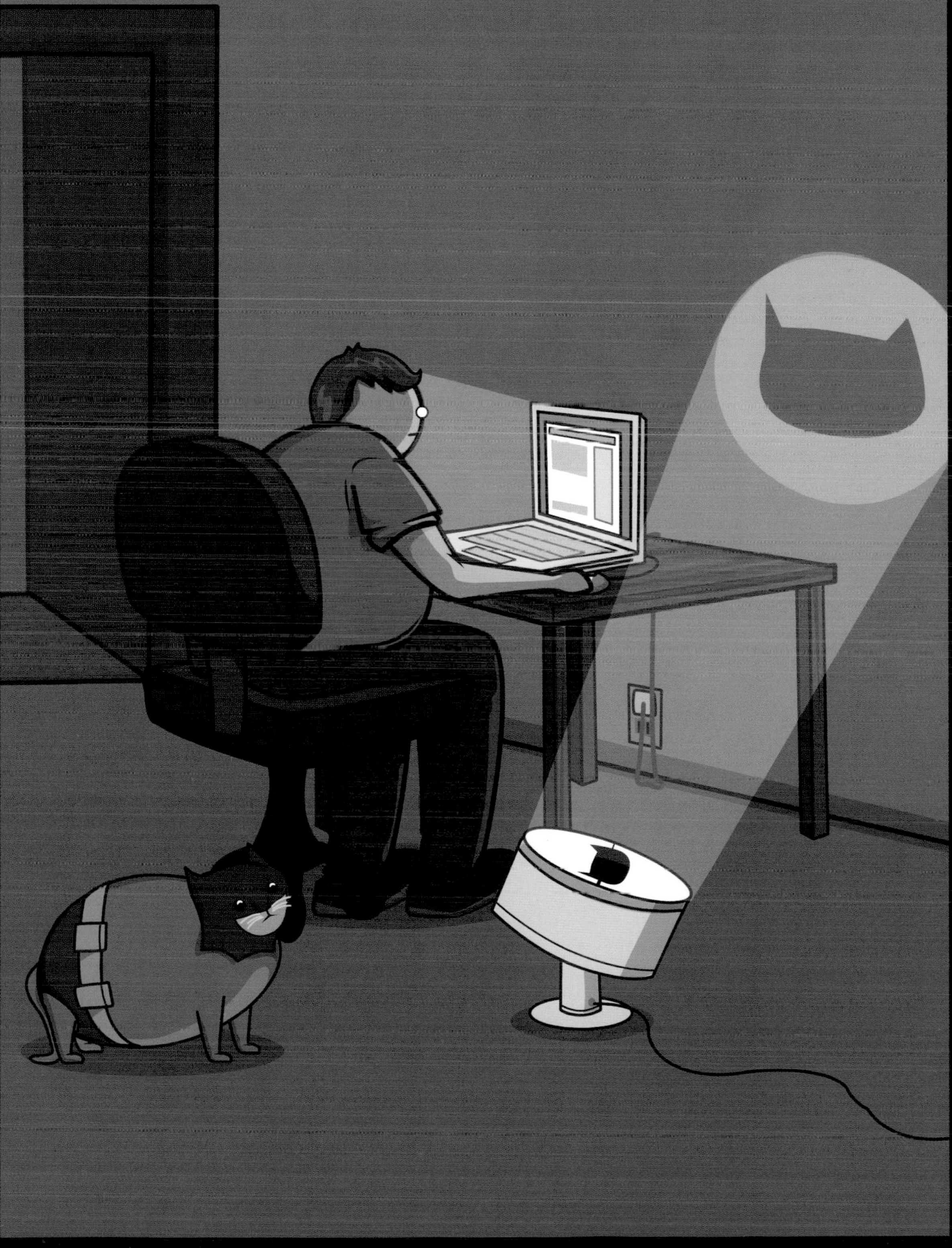

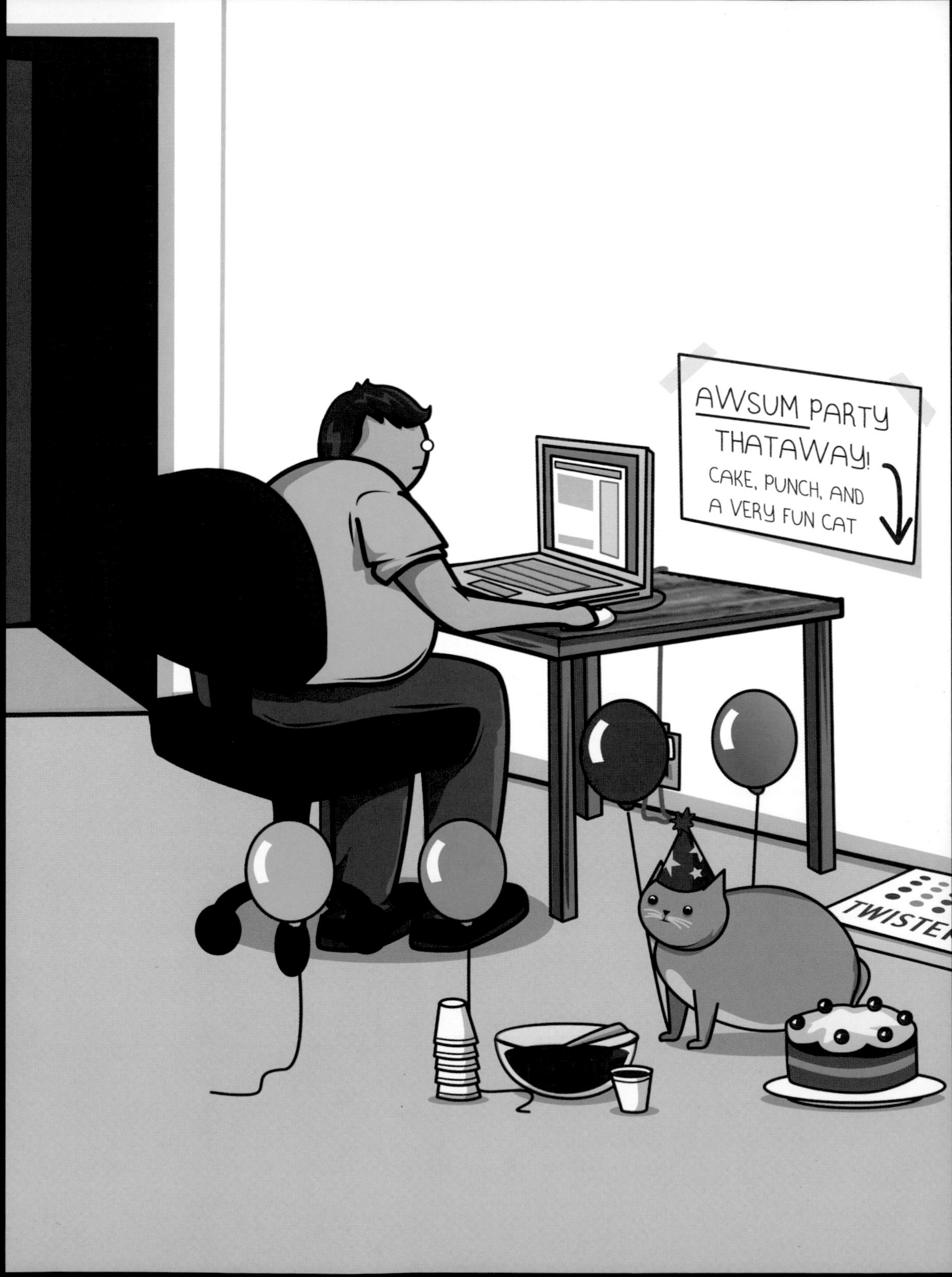
AWSUM PARTY
THATAWAY!
CAKE, PUNCH, AND
A VERY FUN CAT
TWISTER

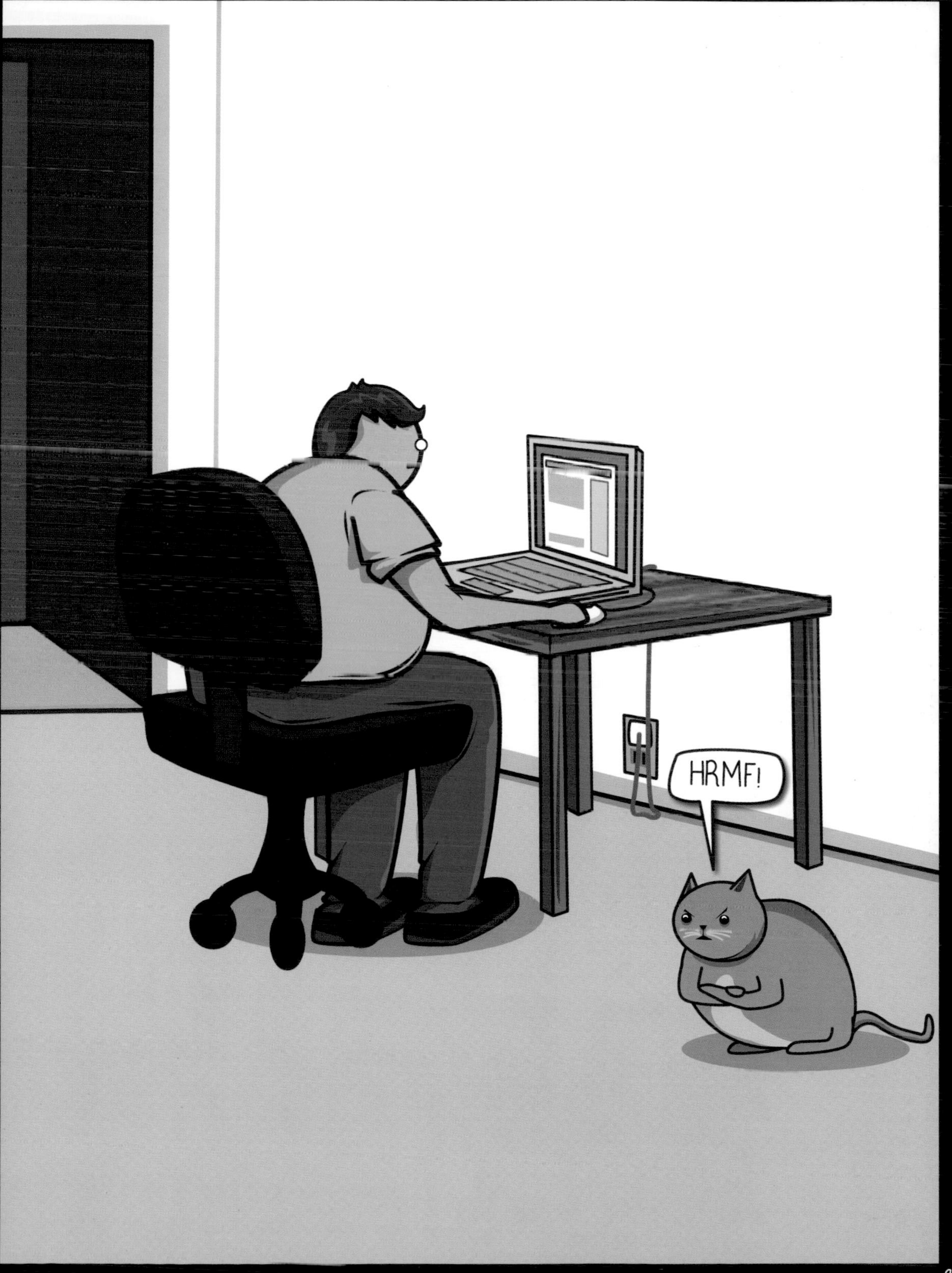
HRMF!

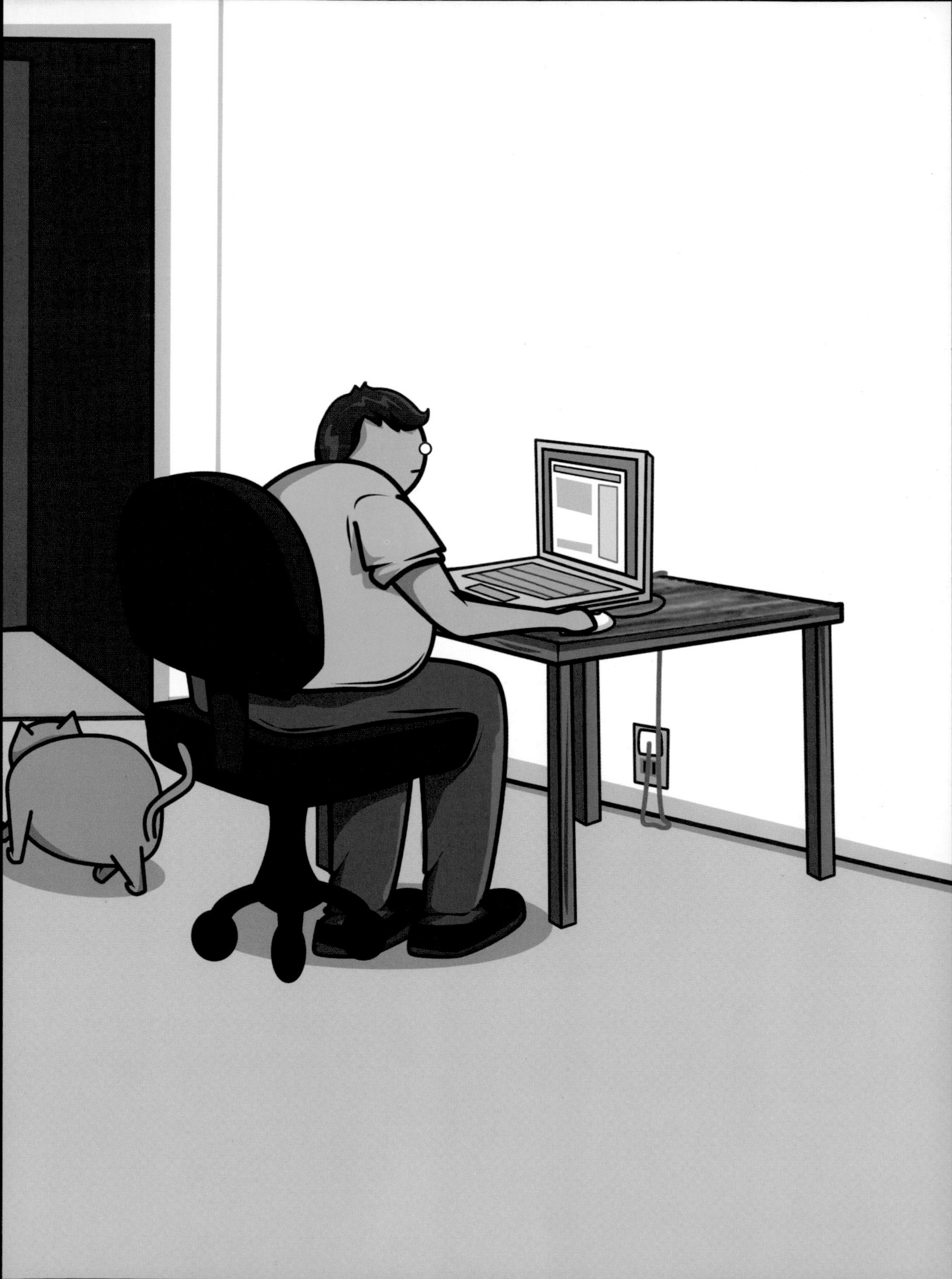

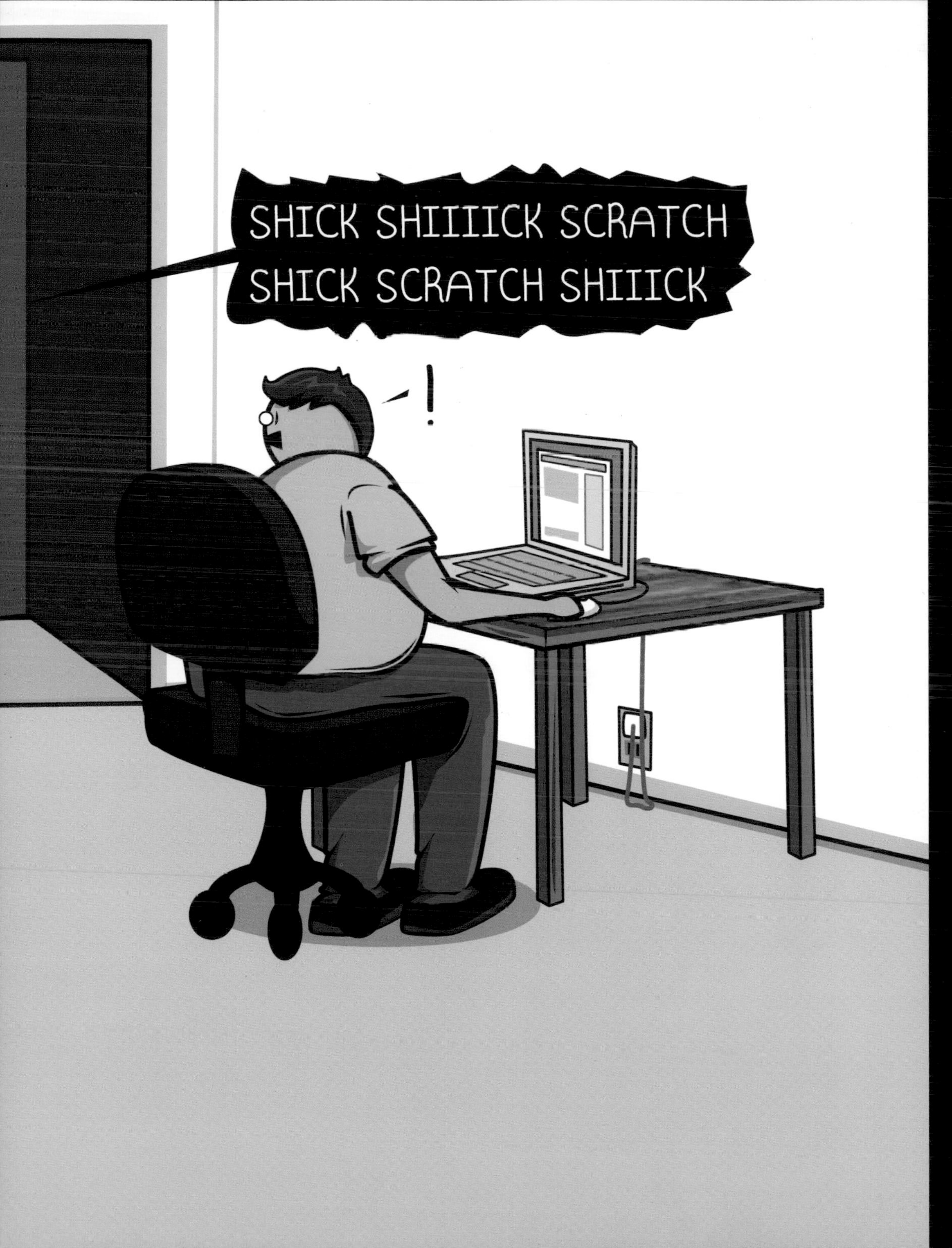
SHICK SHIIIICK SCRATCH
SHICK SCRATCH SHIIICK
!

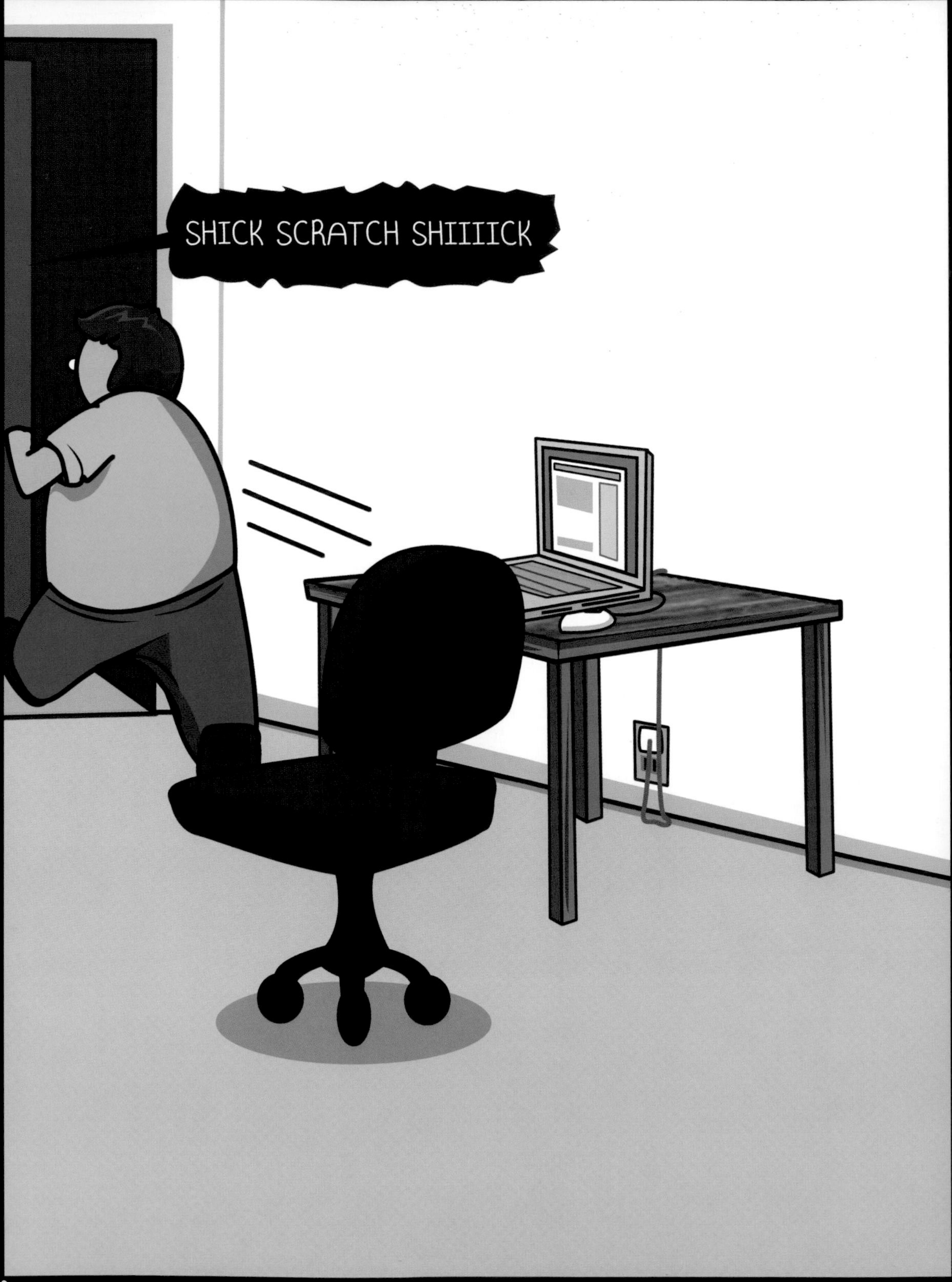
SHICK SCRATCH SHIIIICK

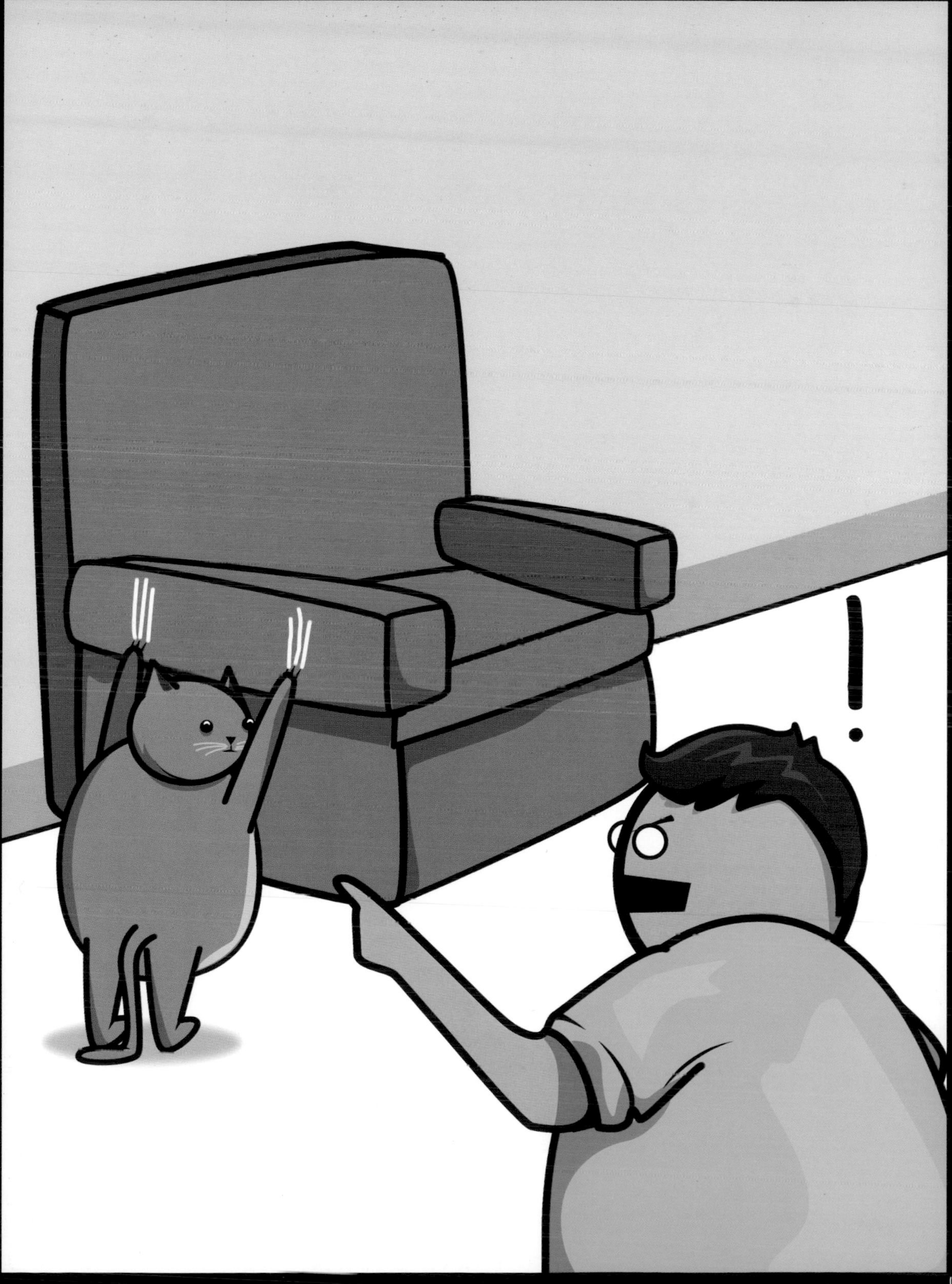
!

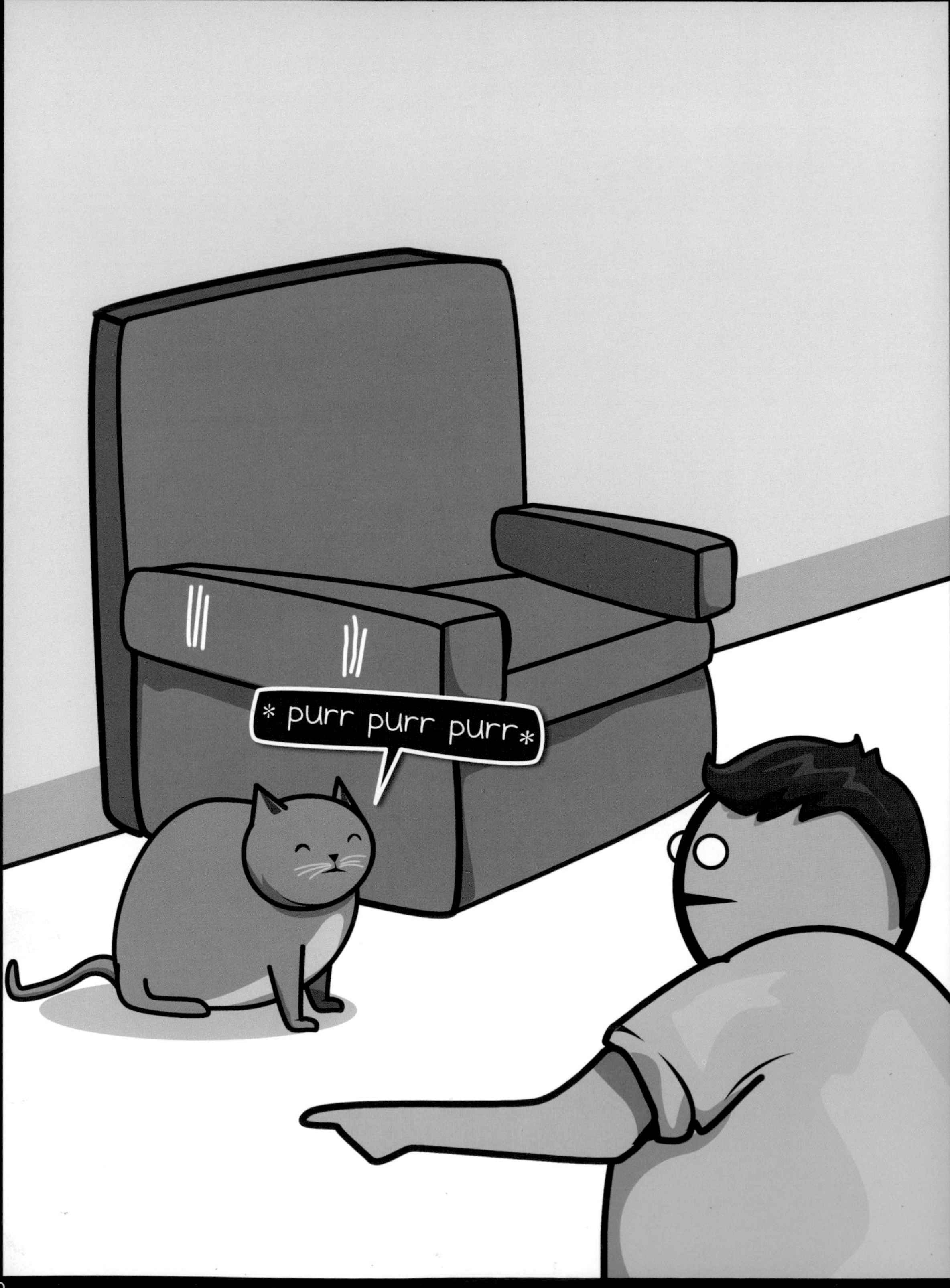
* purr purr purr*

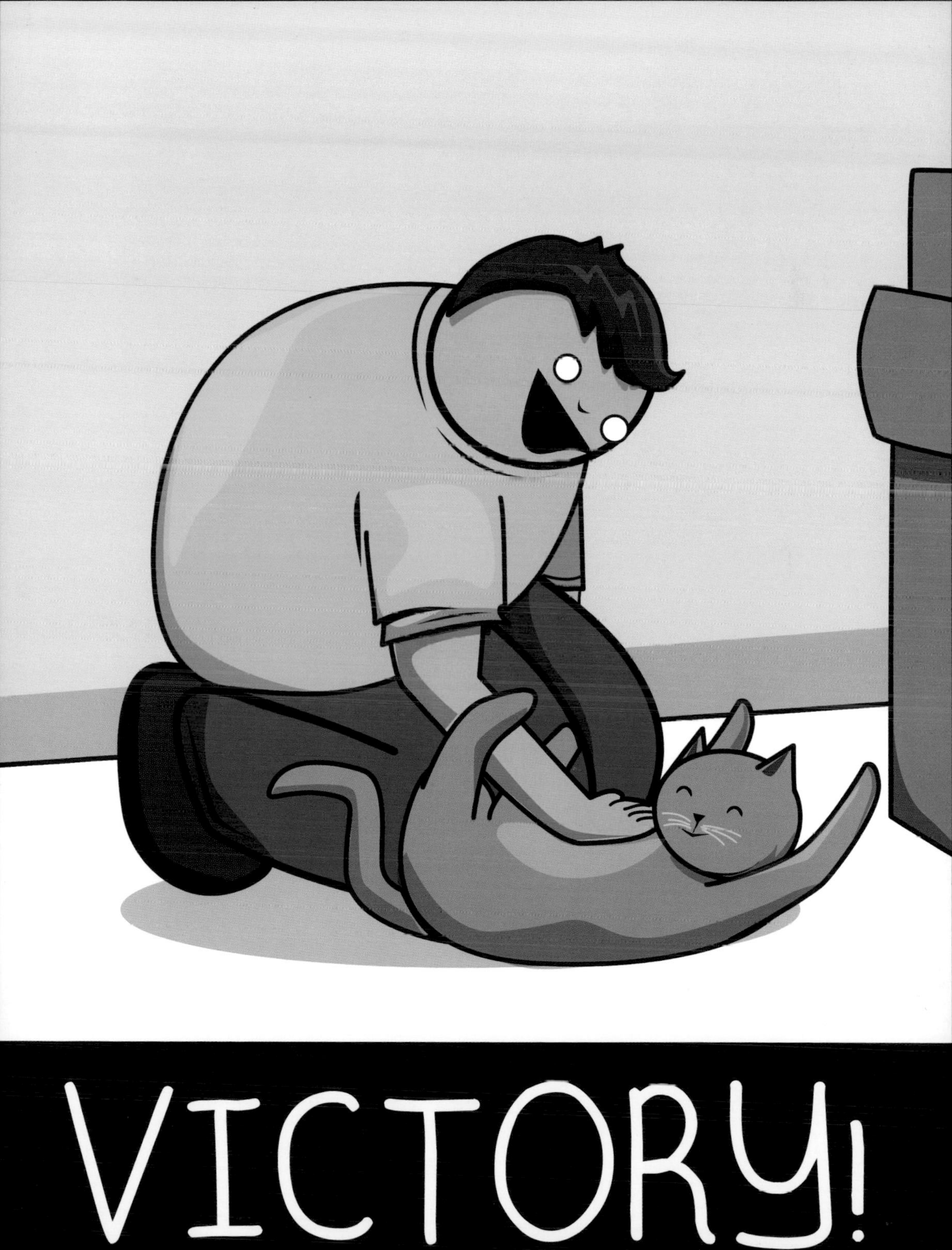
VICTORY!

The 3 ways of dealing with cat litter

The good way

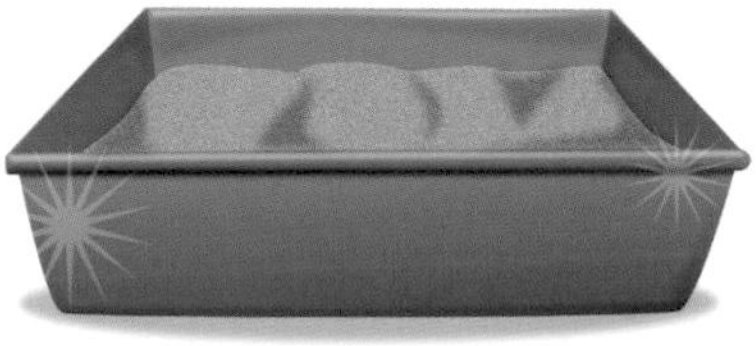

Scoop out all the poop and pee clumps.
Periodically rinse the box out and replace all the litter.

Try not to get upset when ten seconds after making it spotless your cat strolls in and takes a dump the size of Jupiter.

The bad way

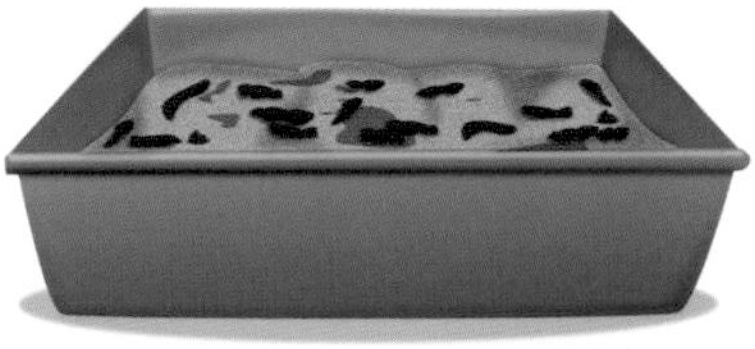

Let the waste pile up until the stench rivals that of the blackened, scorched rectum of Satan himself.

Permanently avoid that part of the house; it's dead to you.

The BEST way

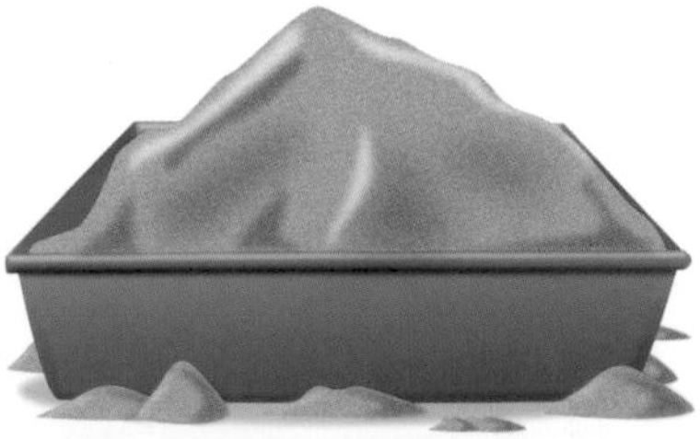

Just keep pouring new sand on top until your spouse/roommate/whoever has to deal with it.

You're not procrastinating, you're delegating!

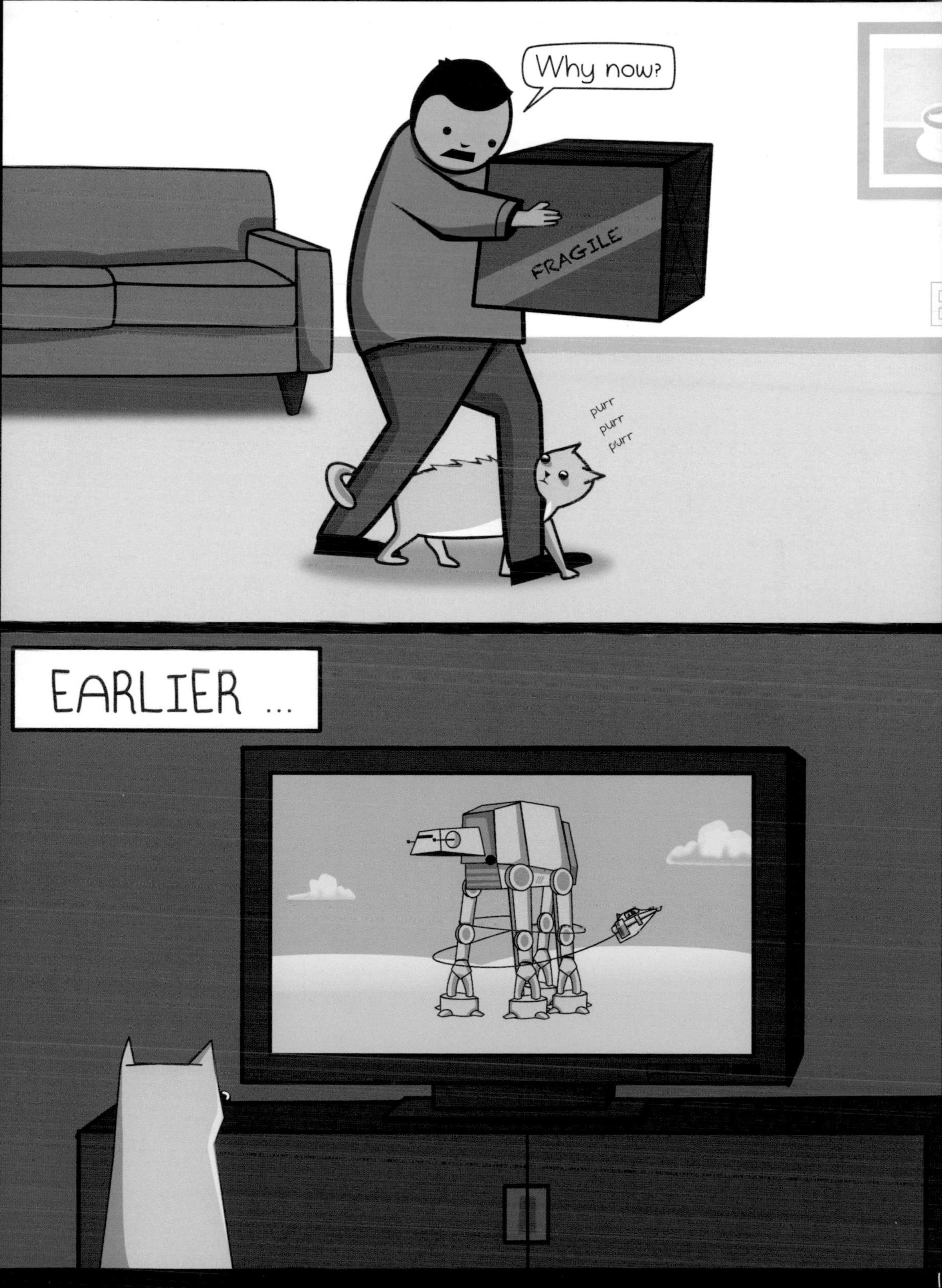
Why now?
FRAGILE
purr
purr
purr
EARLIER ...

How to tell if your cat is a
raging homosexual

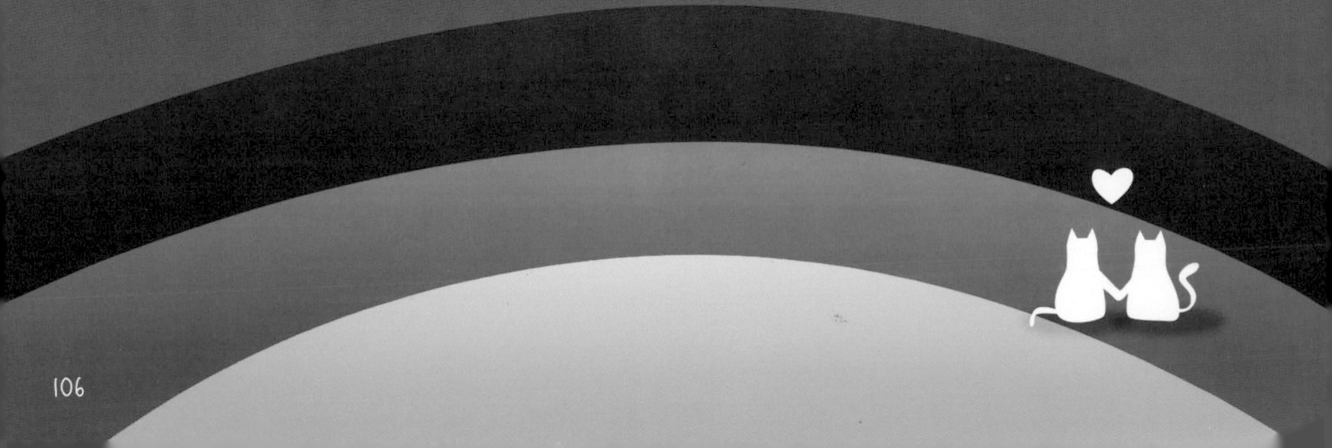

When your cat is around other cats of the same gender, keep an eye out for excessive touching.

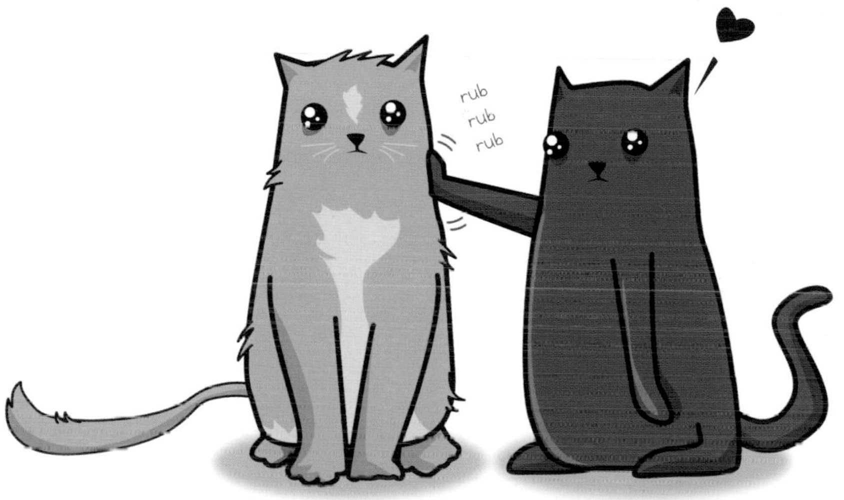
rub
rub
rub

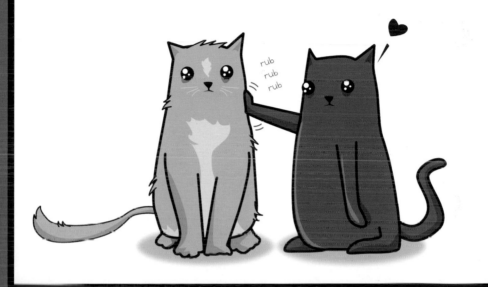

As well as excessive frolicking.

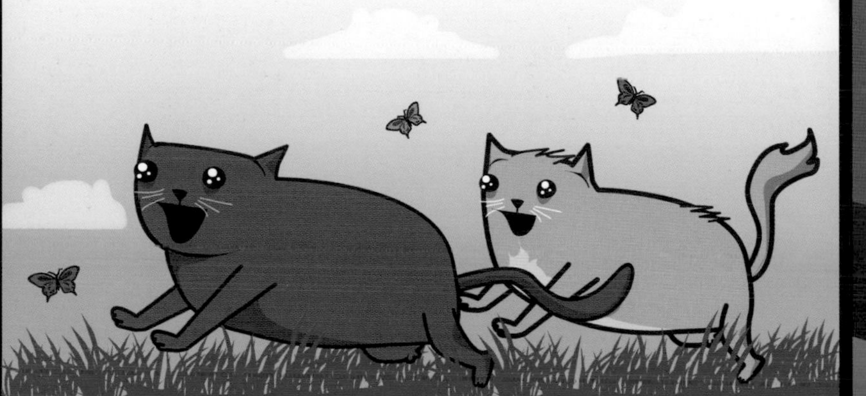

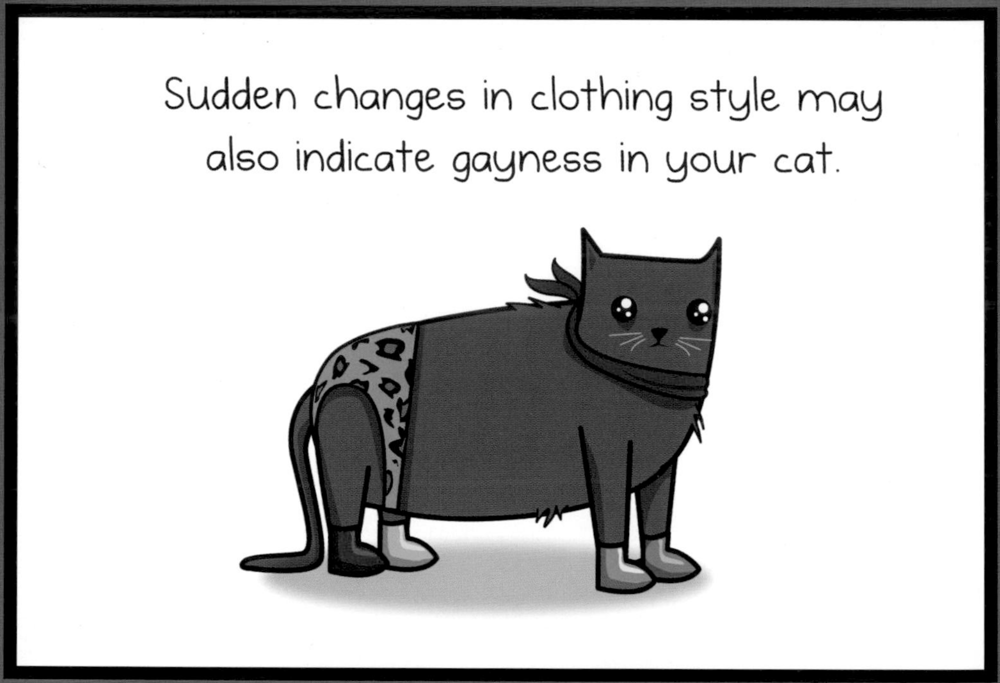
Sudden changes in clothing style may also indicate gayness in your cat.

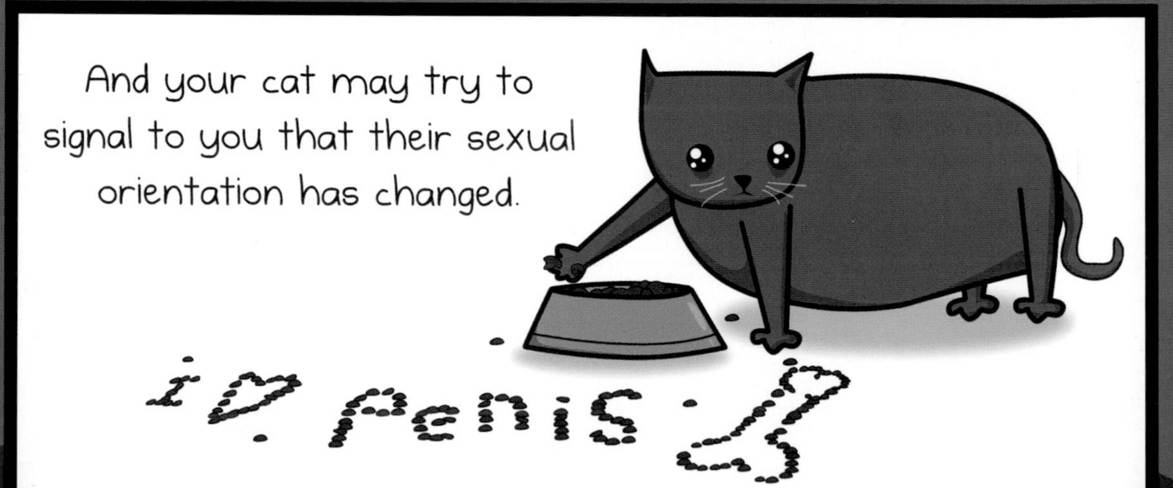
And your cat may try to signal to you that their sexual orientation has changed.
i ♡ penis

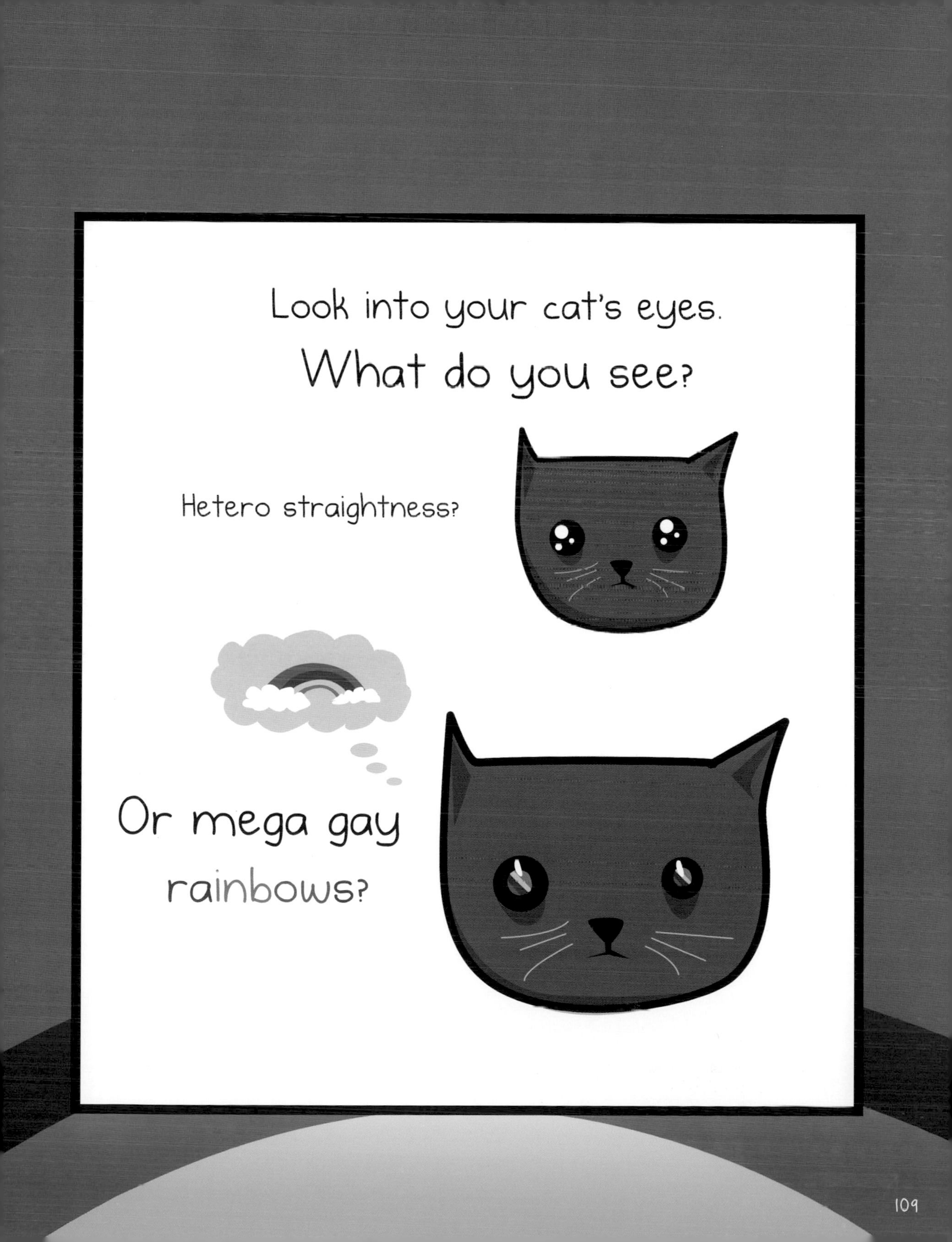
Look into your cat's eyes.
What do you see?
Hetero straightness?
Or mega gay rainbows?

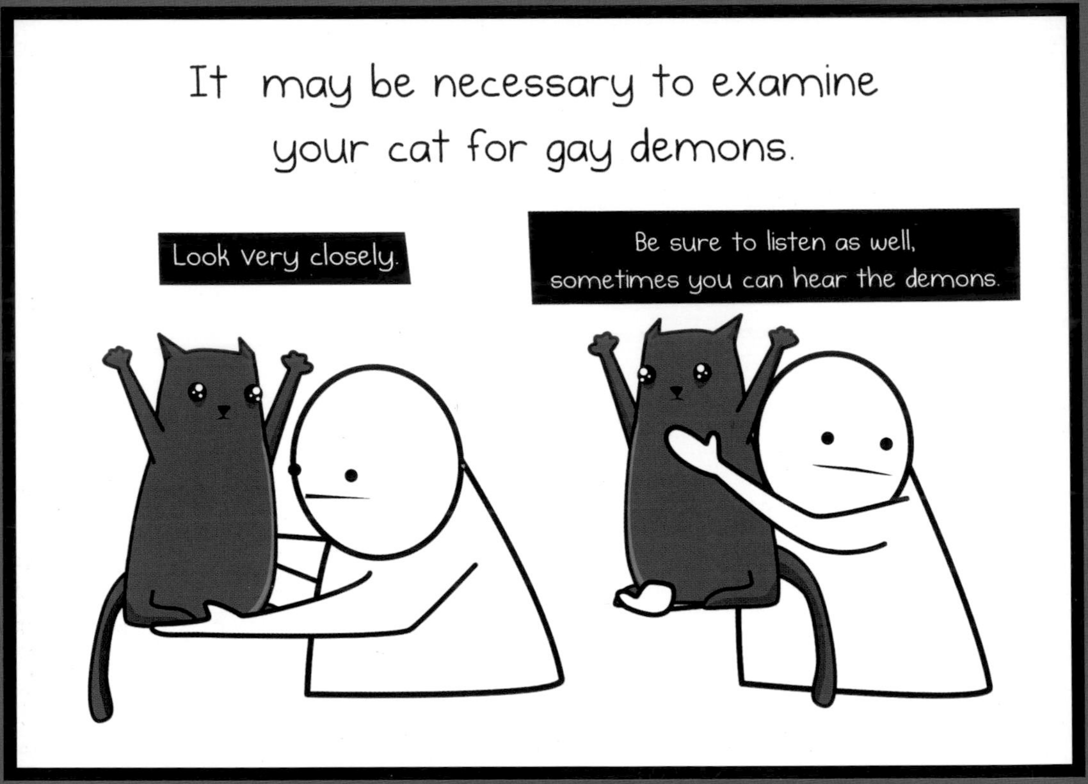
It may be necessary to examine your cat for gay demons.
Look very closely.
Be sure to listen as well, sometimes you can hear the demons.

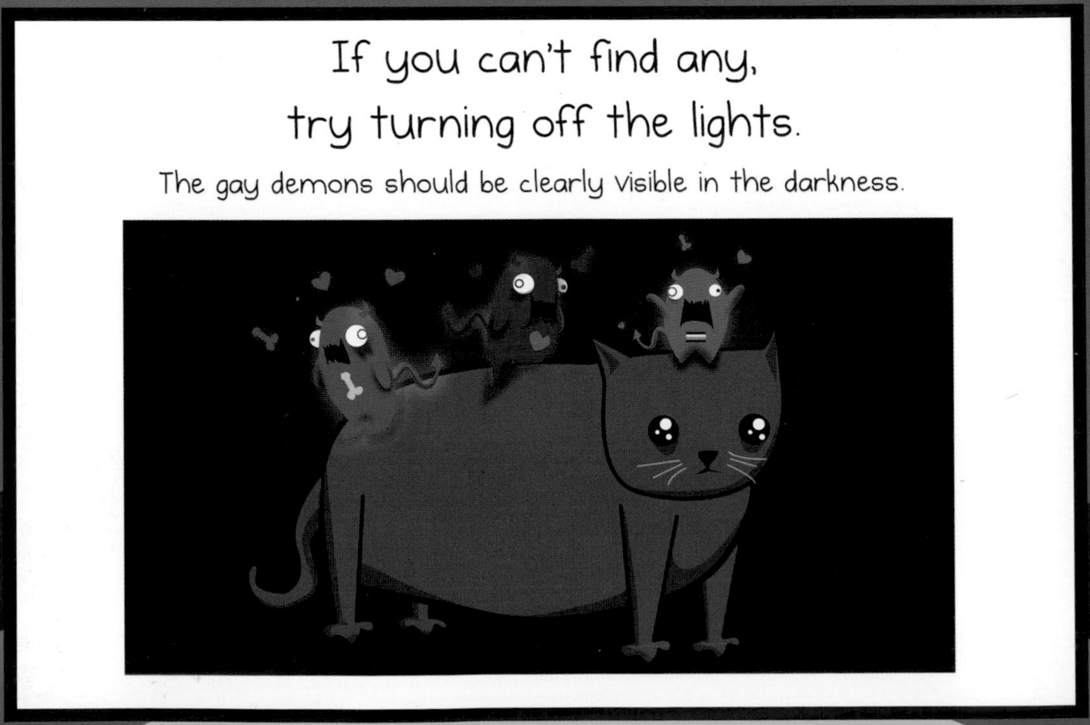
If you can't find any, try turning off the lights.
The gay demons should be clearly visible in the darkness.

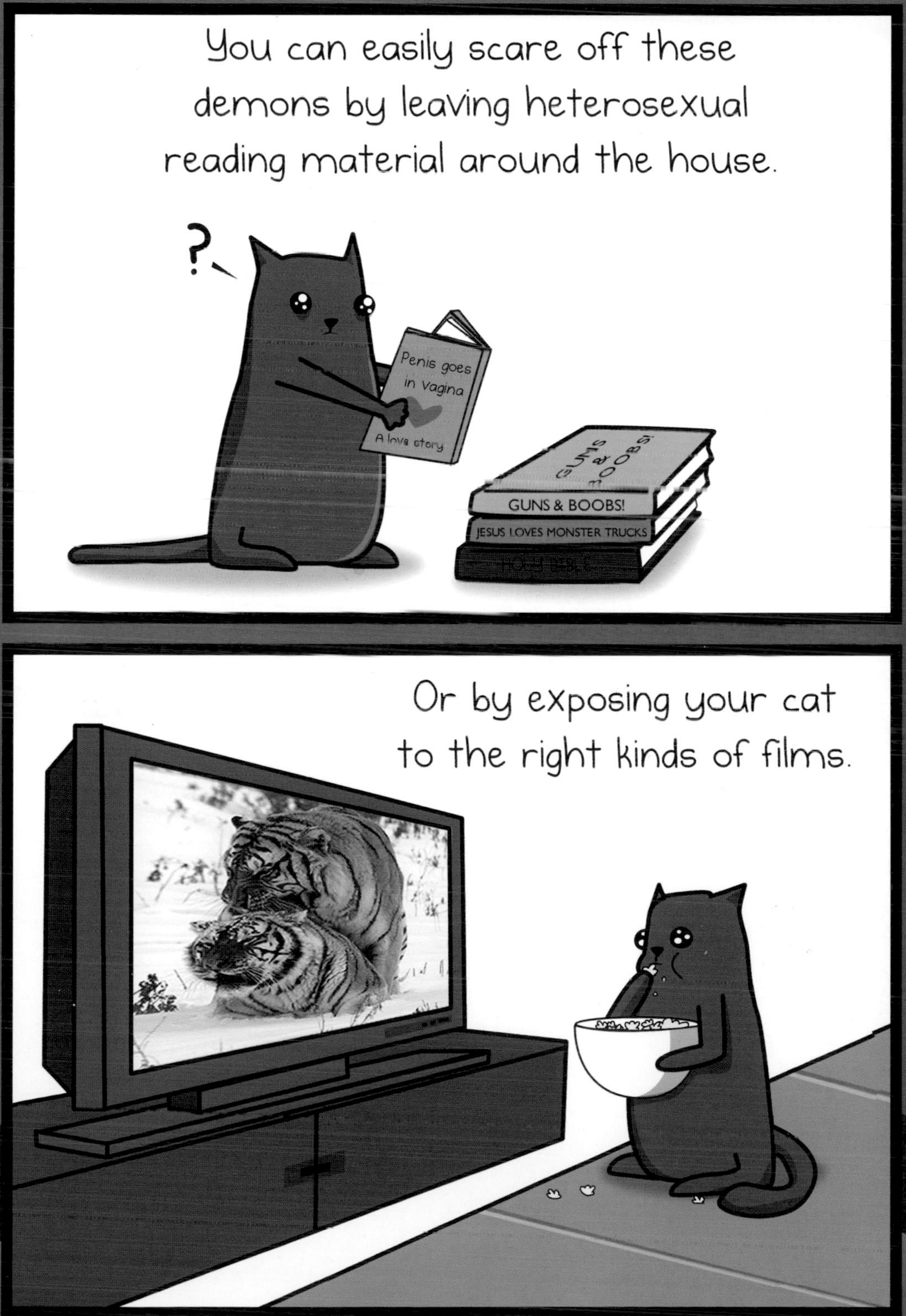
You can easily scare off these demons by leaving heterosexual reading material around the house.
?
Penis goes in Vagina
A love story
GUNS & BOOBS!
GUNS & BOOBS!
JESUS LOVES MONSTER TRUCKS
Or by exposing your cat to the right kinds of films.

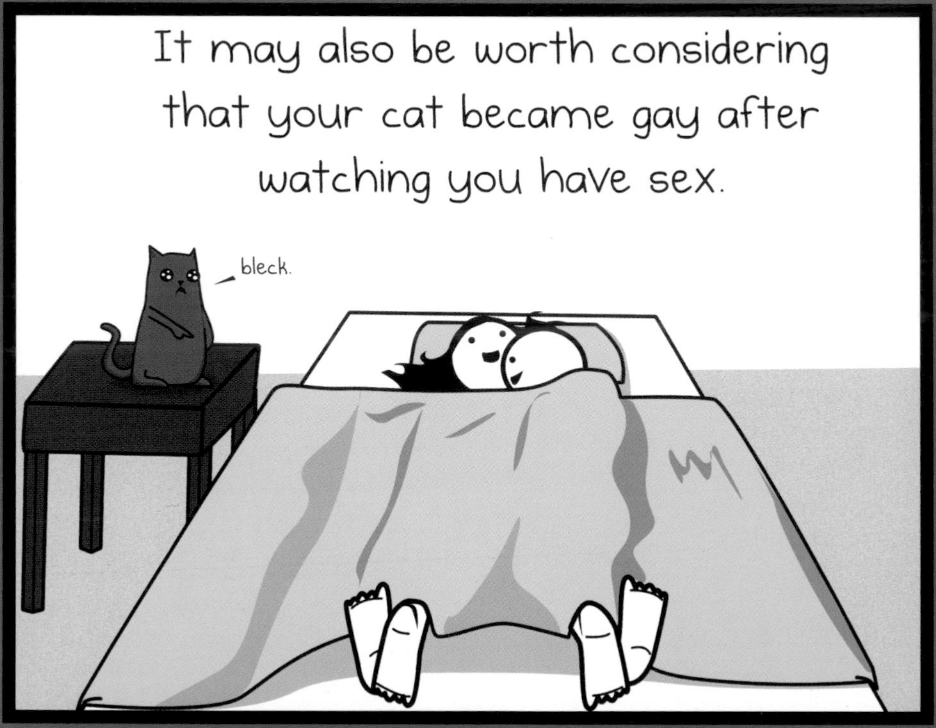
It may also be worth considering that your cat became gay after watching you have sex.
bleck.

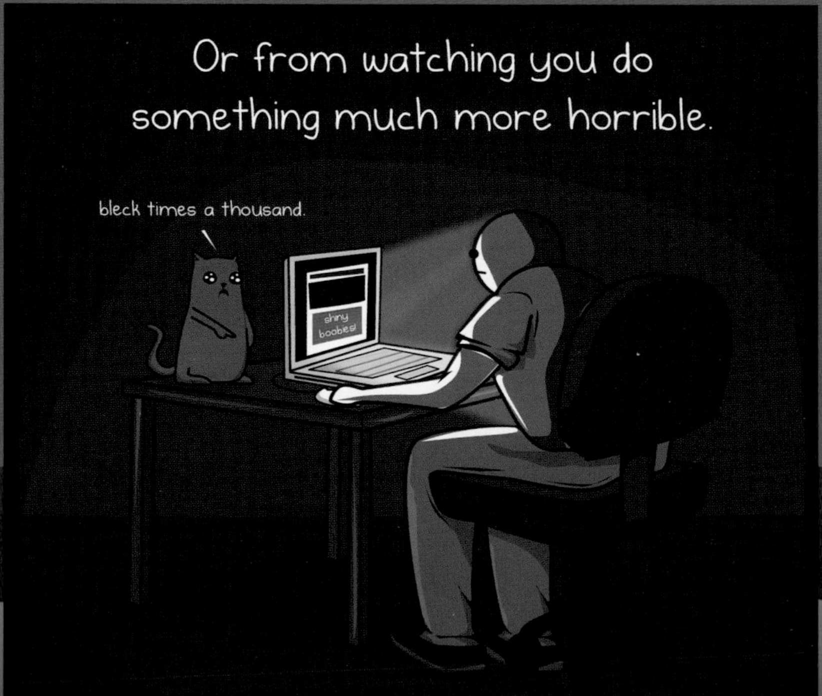
Or from watching you do something much more horrible.
bleck times a thousand.
shiny boobies!

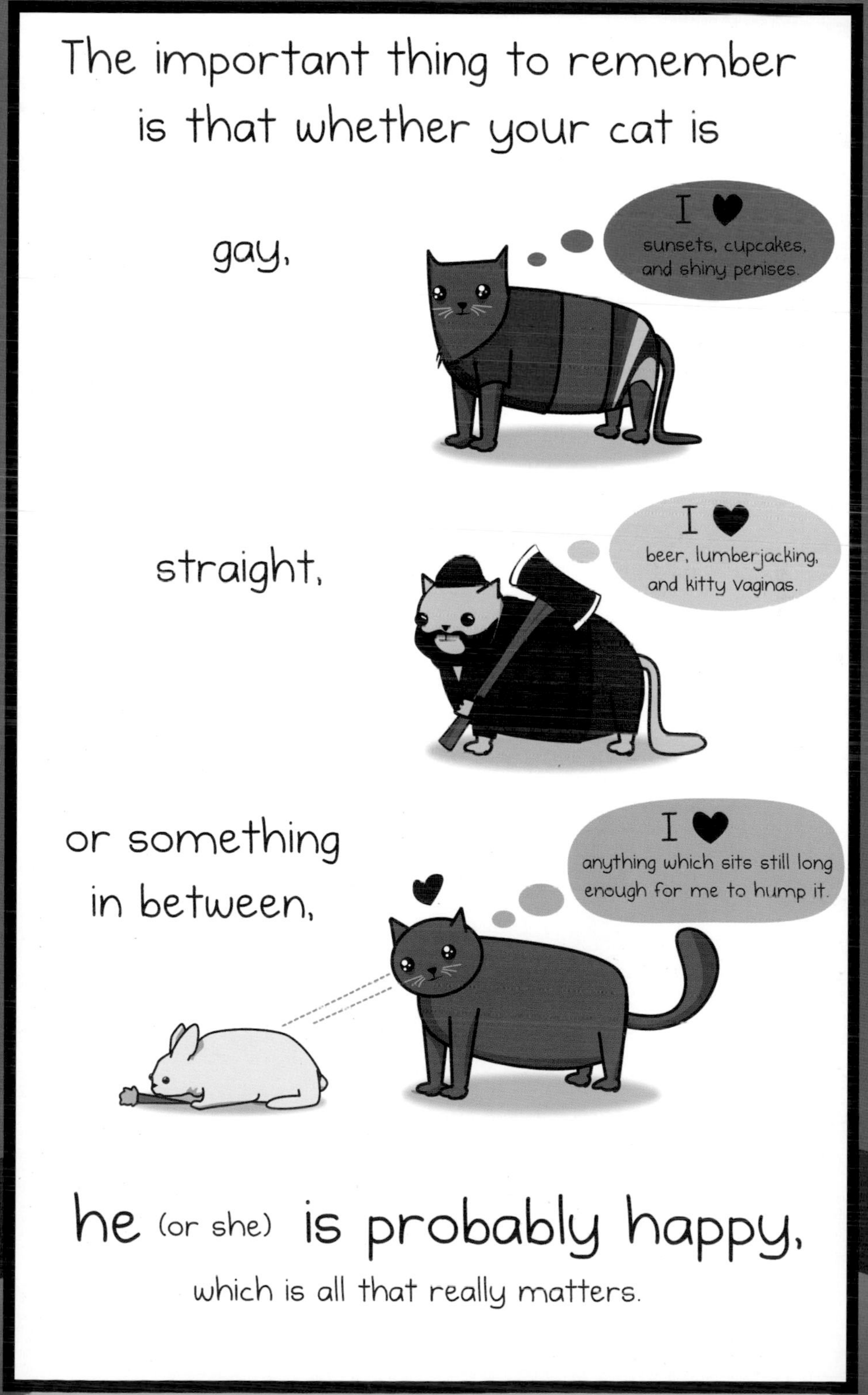
The important thing to remember
is that whether your cat is
gay,
I ♥ sunsets, cupcakes, and shiny penises.
straight,
I ♥ beer, lumberjacking, and kitty vaginas.
or something
in between,
I ♥ anything which sits still long enough for me to hump it.
he (or she) is probably happy,
which is all that really matters.

How kittens are plotting to take over the world

Shadowboxing the air

What appears
to be going on:

Harmless play

↓

What's *really*
going on:

**Drawing & Rehearsing
BATTLE
FORMATIONS**

Watching TV

What appears to be going on:

Kittens are amused by nature programs

↓

What's *really* going on:

[redacted]

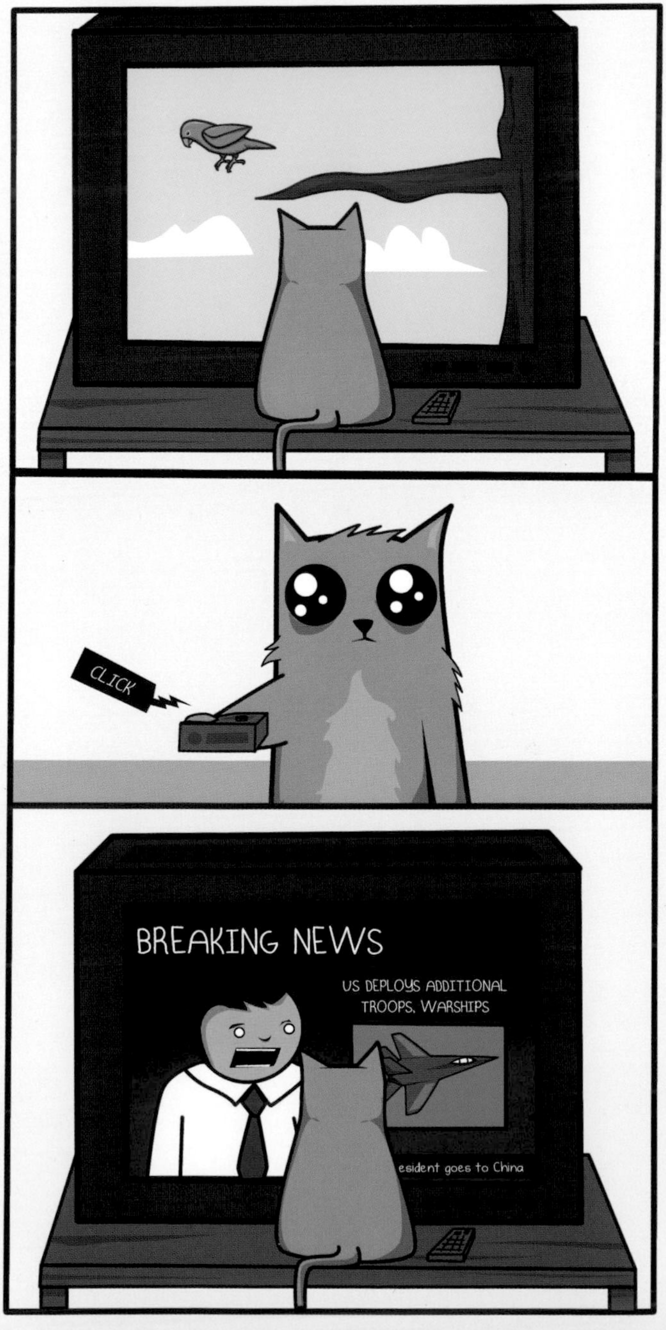
CLICK
BREAKING NEWS
US DEPLOYS ADDITIONAL TROOPS, WARSHIPS
esident goes to China

Excessive ear flicking

What appears to be going on:

Kittens have twitchy ears

What's really going on:

Kittens are sending and receiving messages of doom across the globe

Jumping from high places

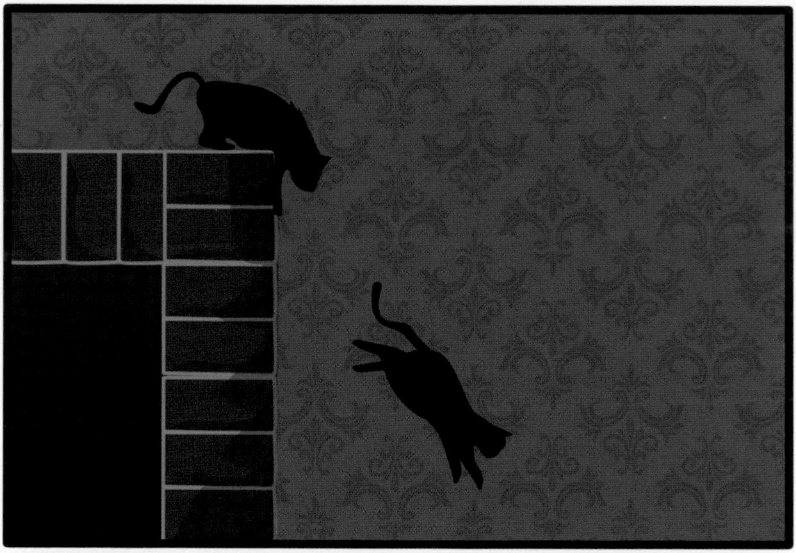

What appears to be going on:

Kittens are fearless when playing

What's *really* going on:

Kittens are training for high altitude drops

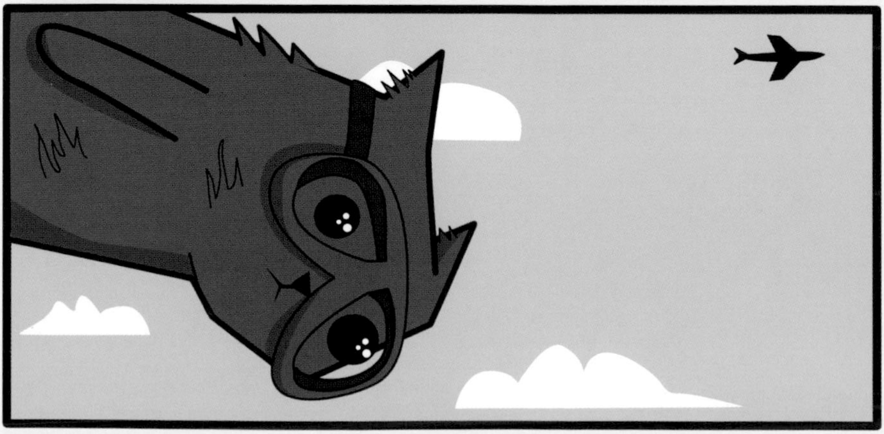

Sleeping in packs

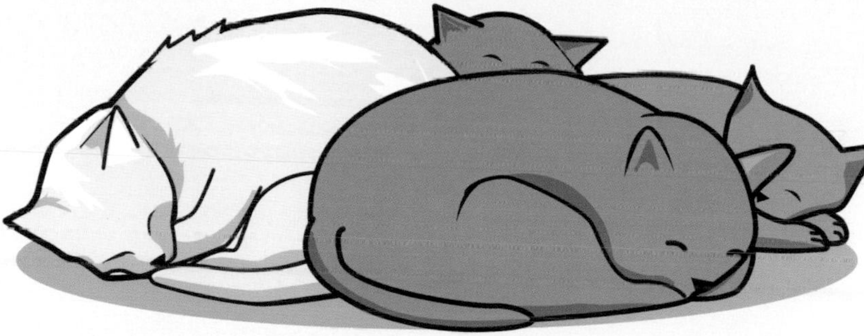

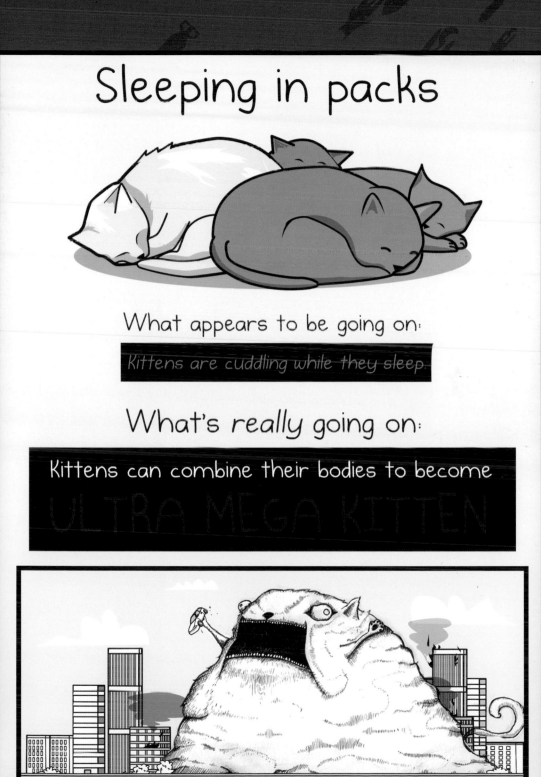

What appears to be going on:

Kittens are cuddling while they sleep.

What's *really* going on:

Kittens can combine their bodies to become

ULTRA MEGA KITTEN

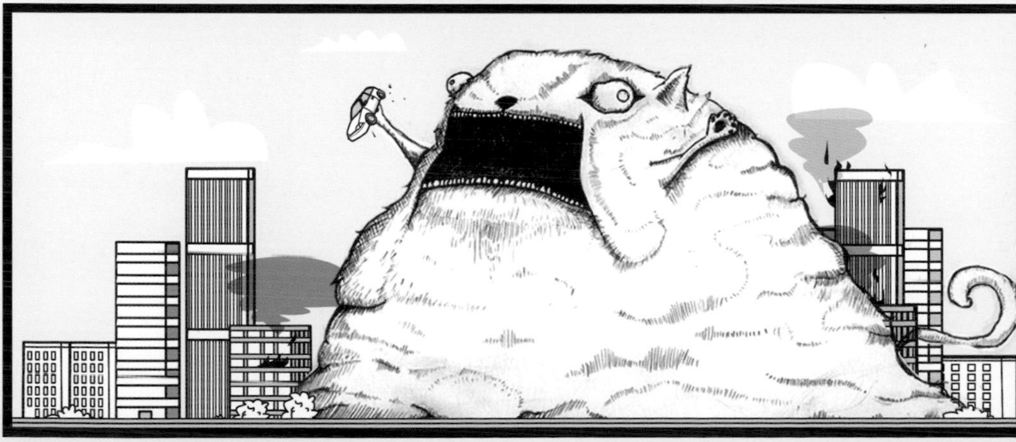

If we treated our cats
like they treat us

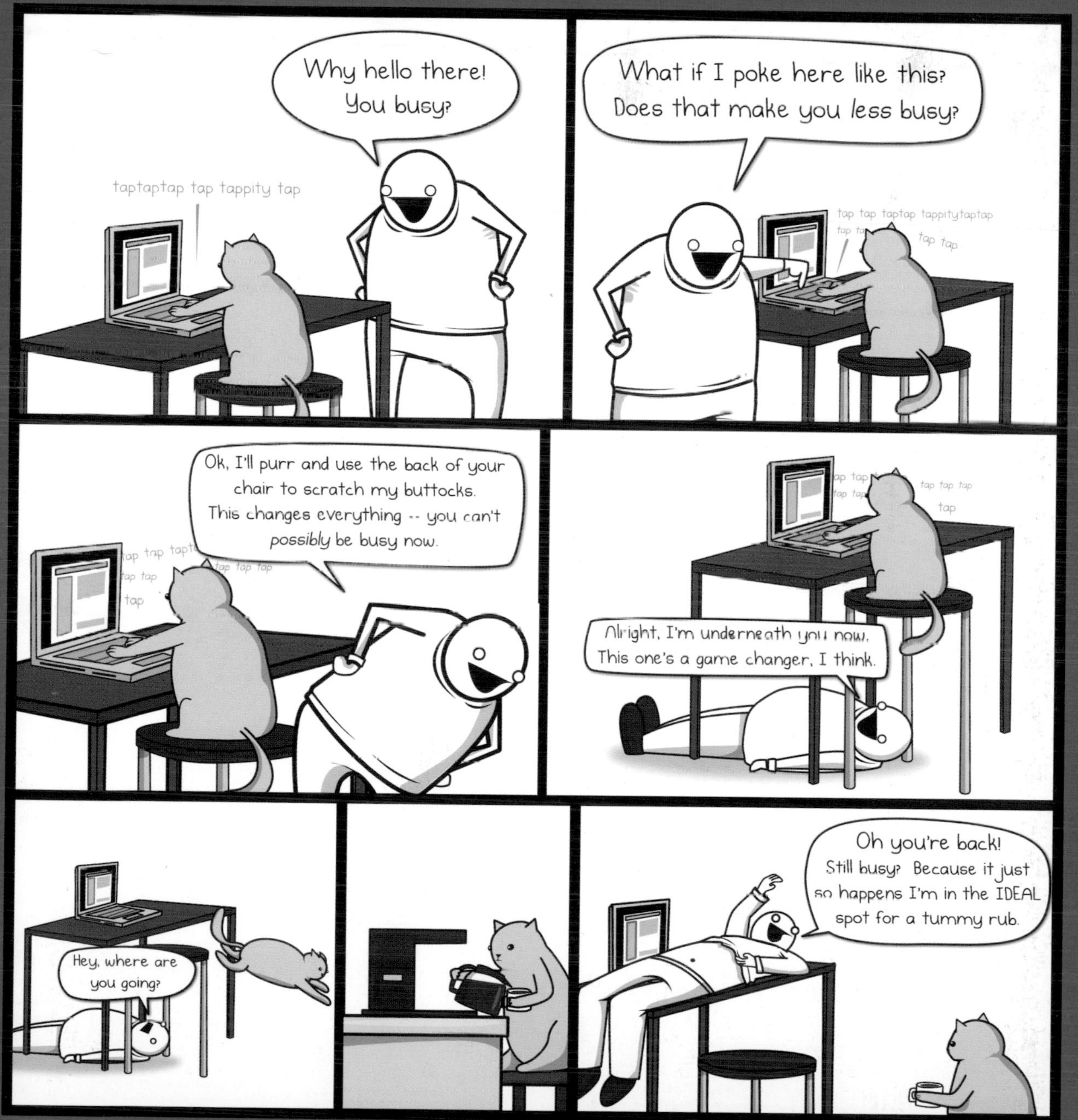
Why hello there! You busy?
taptaptap tap tappity tap
What if I poke here like this? Does that make you *less* busy?
tap tap taptap tappitytaptap
tap tap
Ok, I'll purr and use the back of your chair to scratch my buttocks. This changes everything -- you can't *possibly* be busy now.
tap
tap tap tap
tap
Alright, I'm underneath you now. This one's a game changer, I think.
Hey, where are you going?
Oh you're back! Still busy? Because it just so happens I'm in the IDEAL spot for a tummy rub.

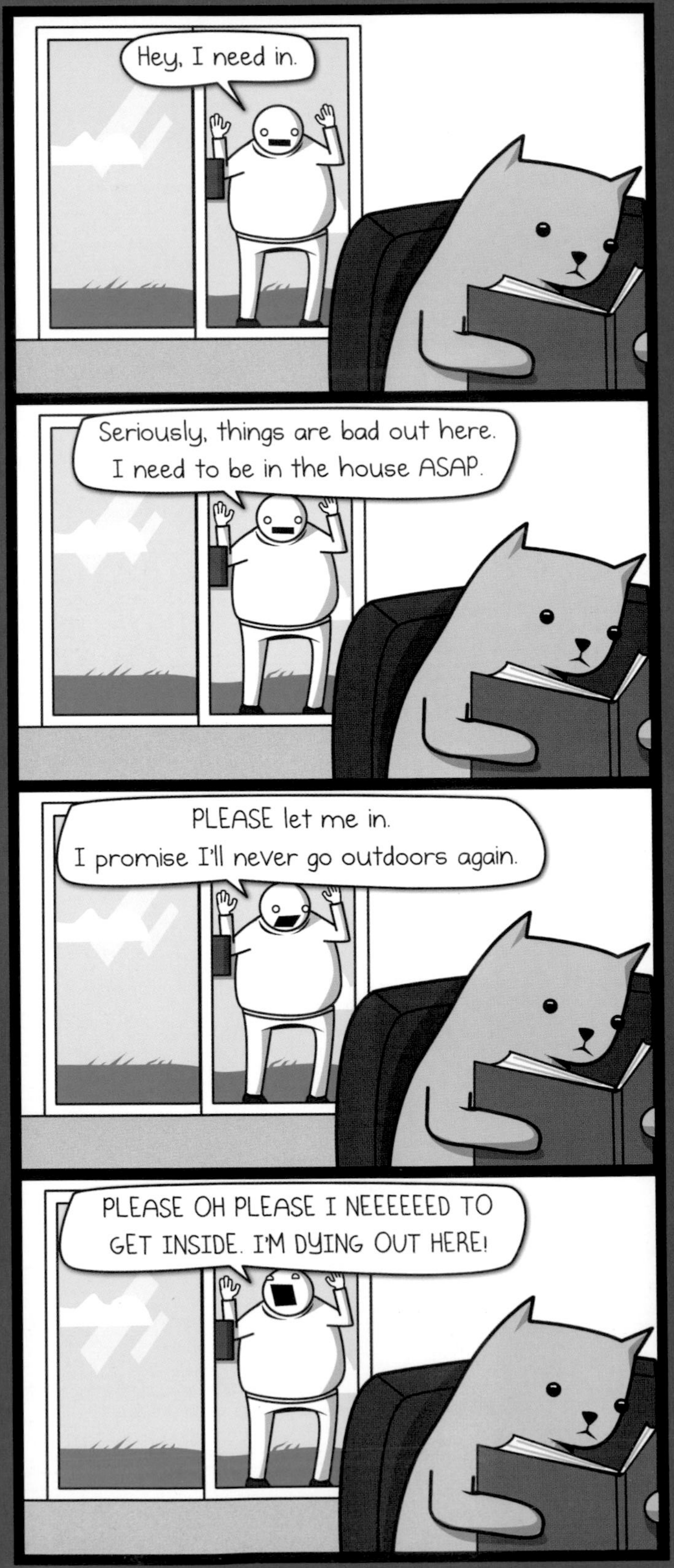
Hey, I need in.
Seriously, things are bad out here. I need to be in the house ASAP.
PLEASE let me in. I promise I'll never go outdoors again.
PLEASE OH PLEASE I NEEEEEED TO GET INSIDE. I'M DYING OUT HERE!

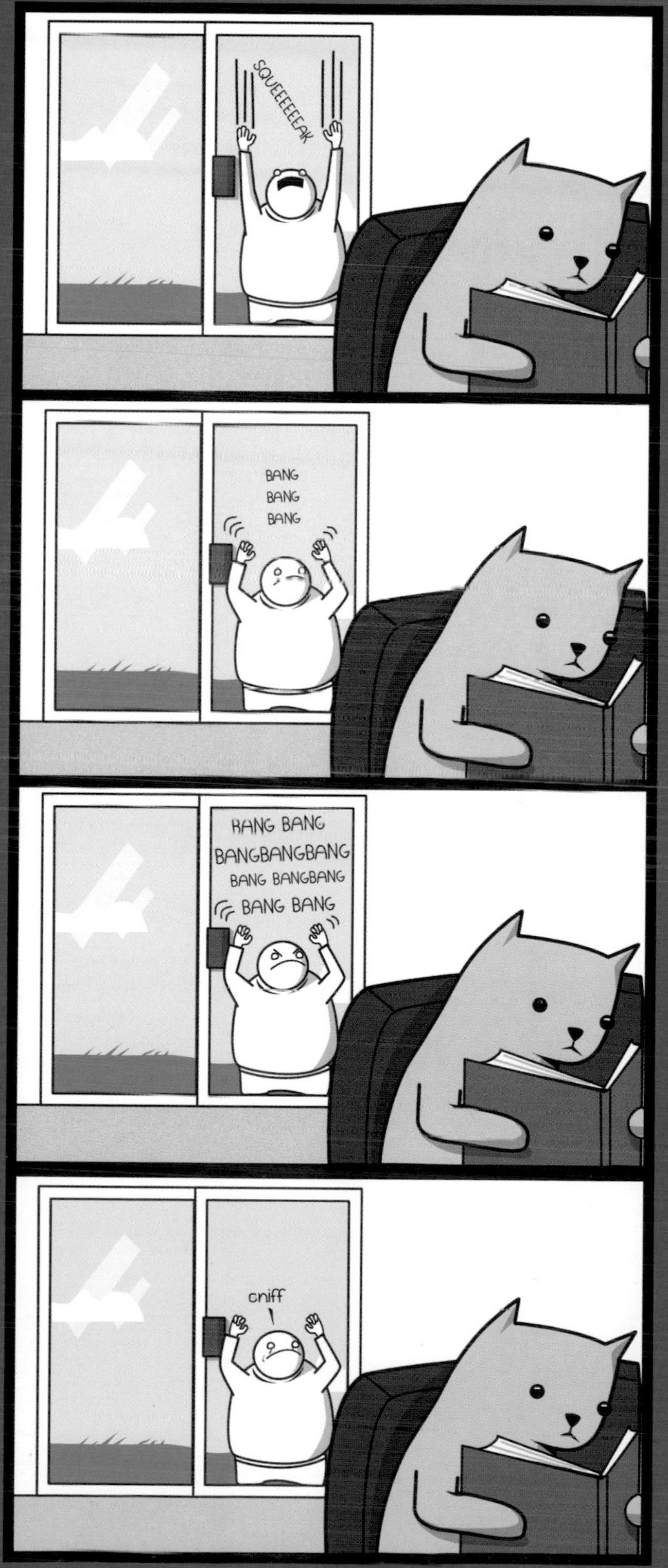
SQUEEEEEEEEAK
BANG
BANG
BANG
BANG BANG
BANGBANGBANG
BANG BANGBANG
BANG BANG
sniff

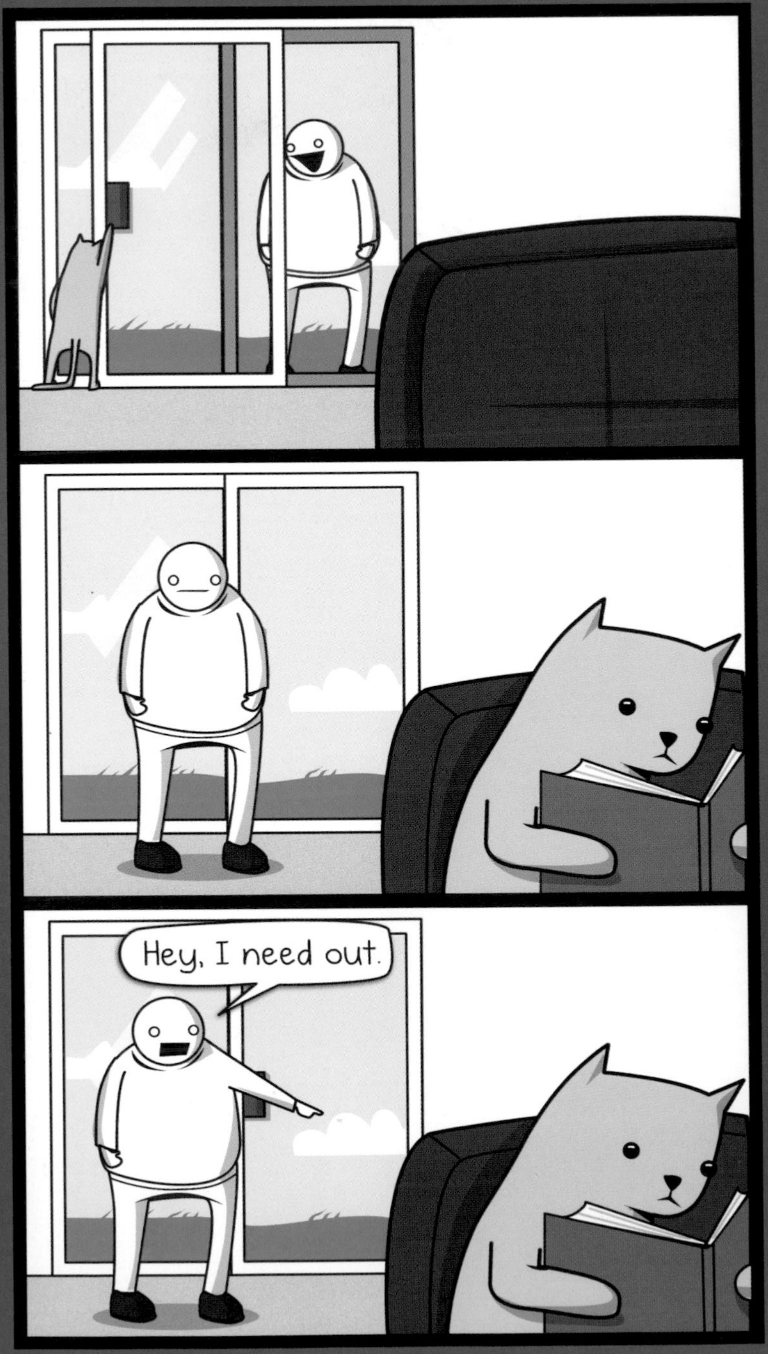
Hey, I need out.

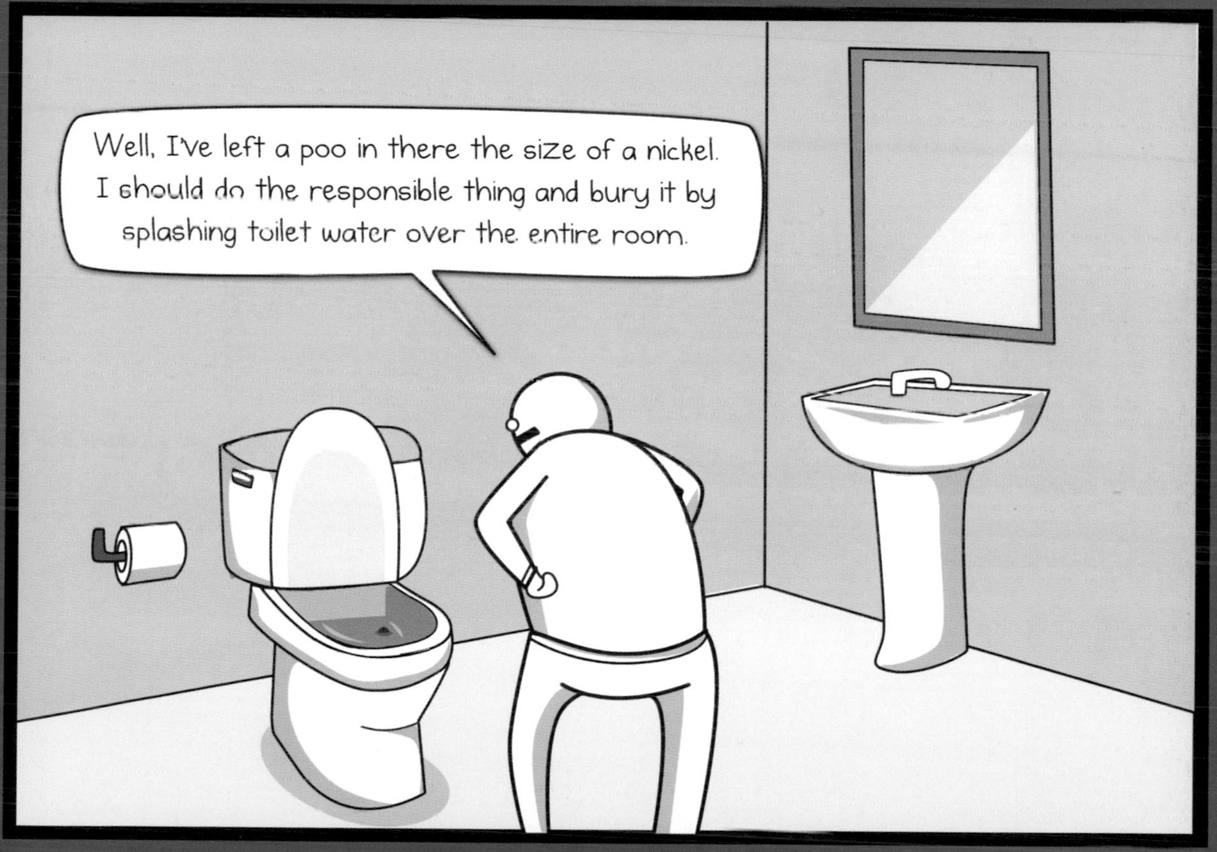
Well, I've left a poo in there the size of a nickel. I should do the responsible thing and bury it by splashing toilet water over the entire room.

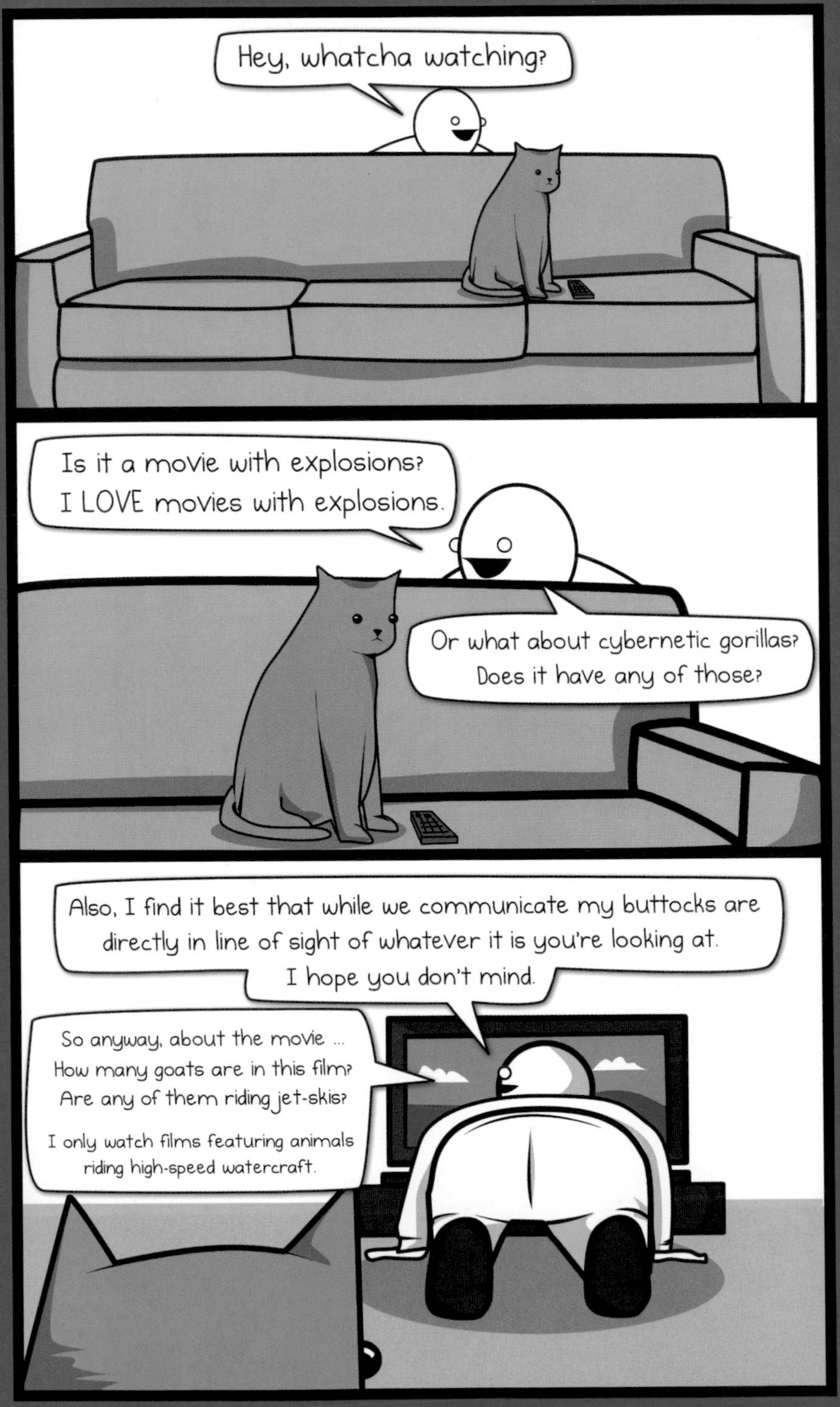
Hey, whatcha watching?
Is it a movie with explosions? I LOVE movies with explosions.
Or what about cybernetic gorillas? Does it have any of those?
Also, I find it best that while we communicate my buttocks are directly in line of sight of whatever it is you're looking at. I hope you don't mind.
So anyway, about the movie ... How many goats are in this film? Are any of them riding jet-skis?
I only watch films featuring animals riding high-speed watercraft.

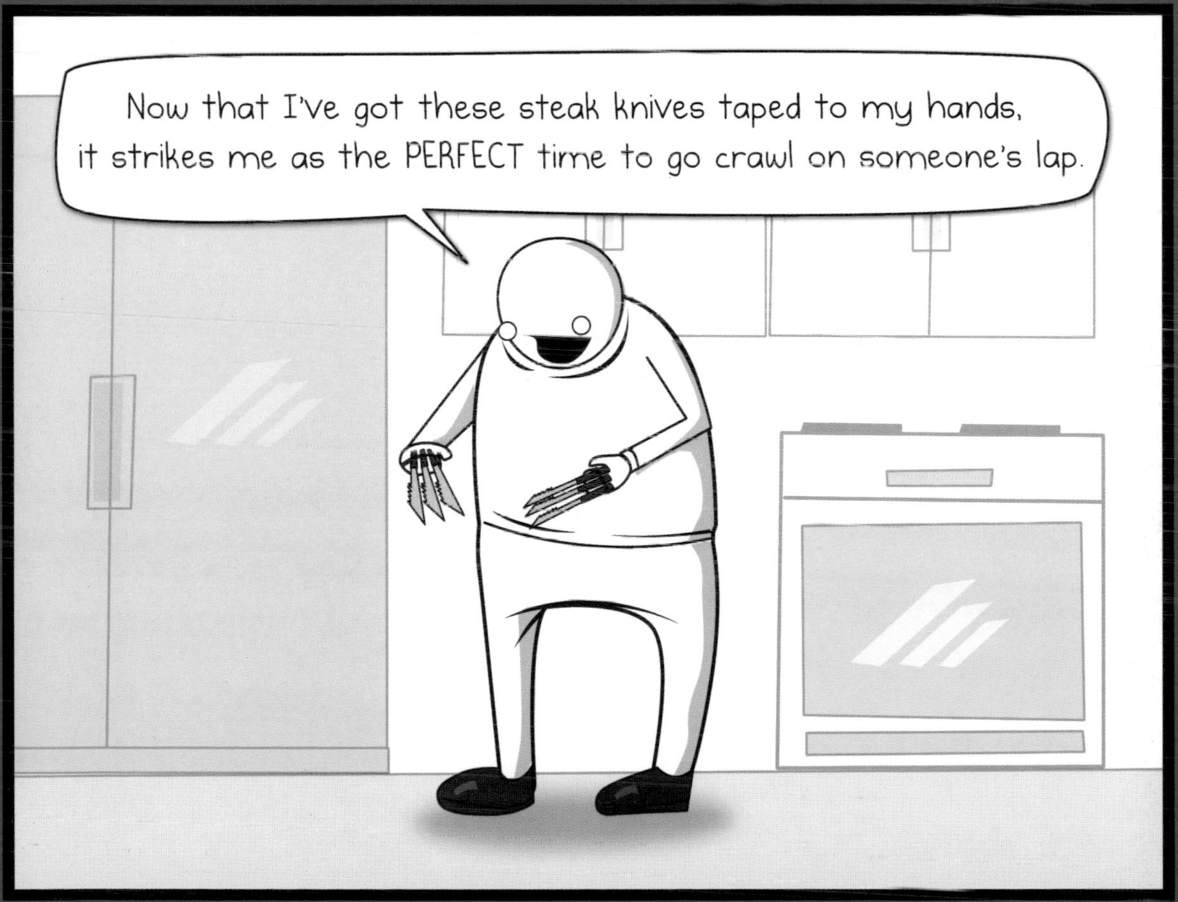
Now that I've got these steak knives taped to my hands, it strikes me as the PERFECT time to go crawl on someone's lap.

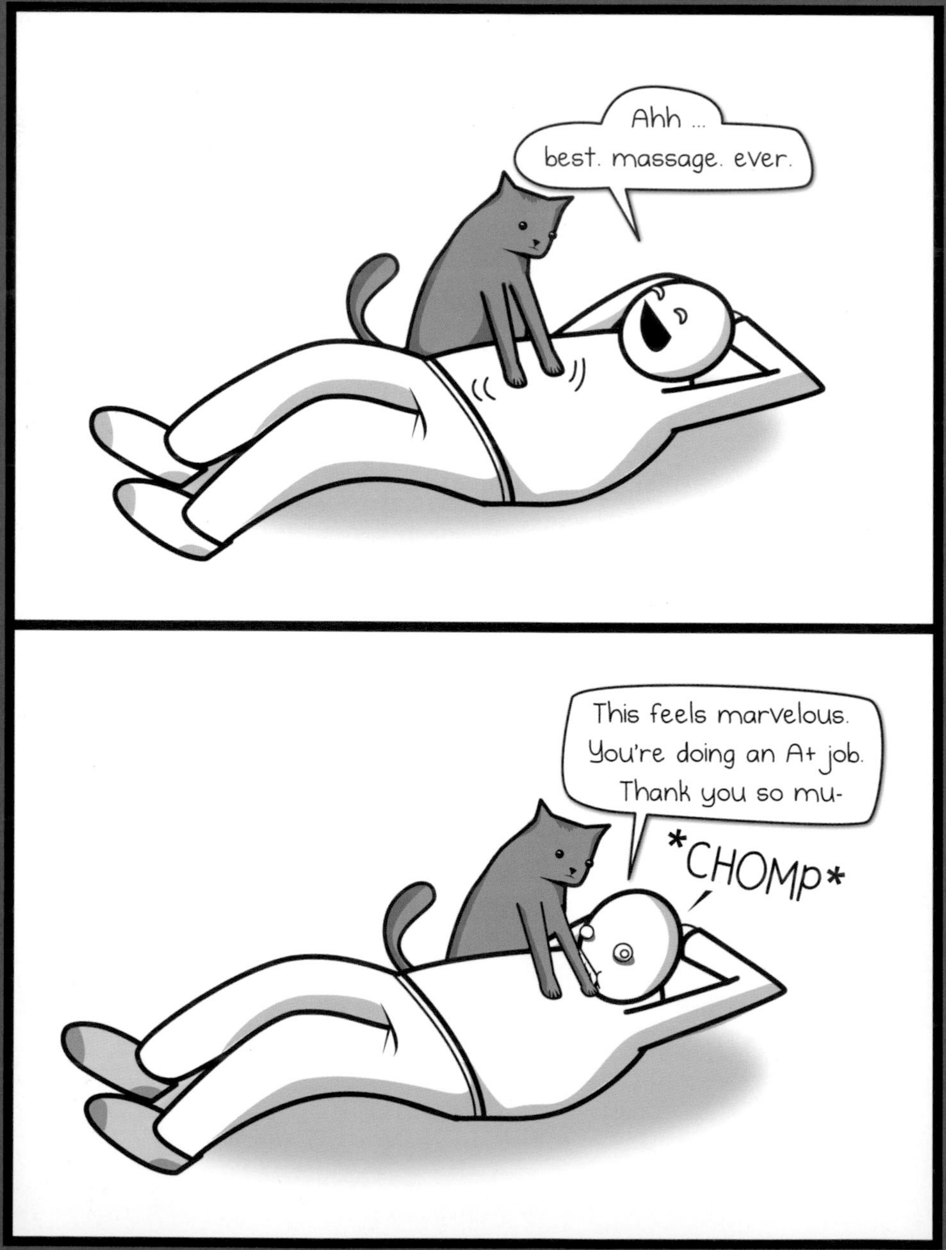

Ahh ... best. massage. ever.
This feels marvelous. You're doing an A+ job. Thank you so mu-
CHOMP

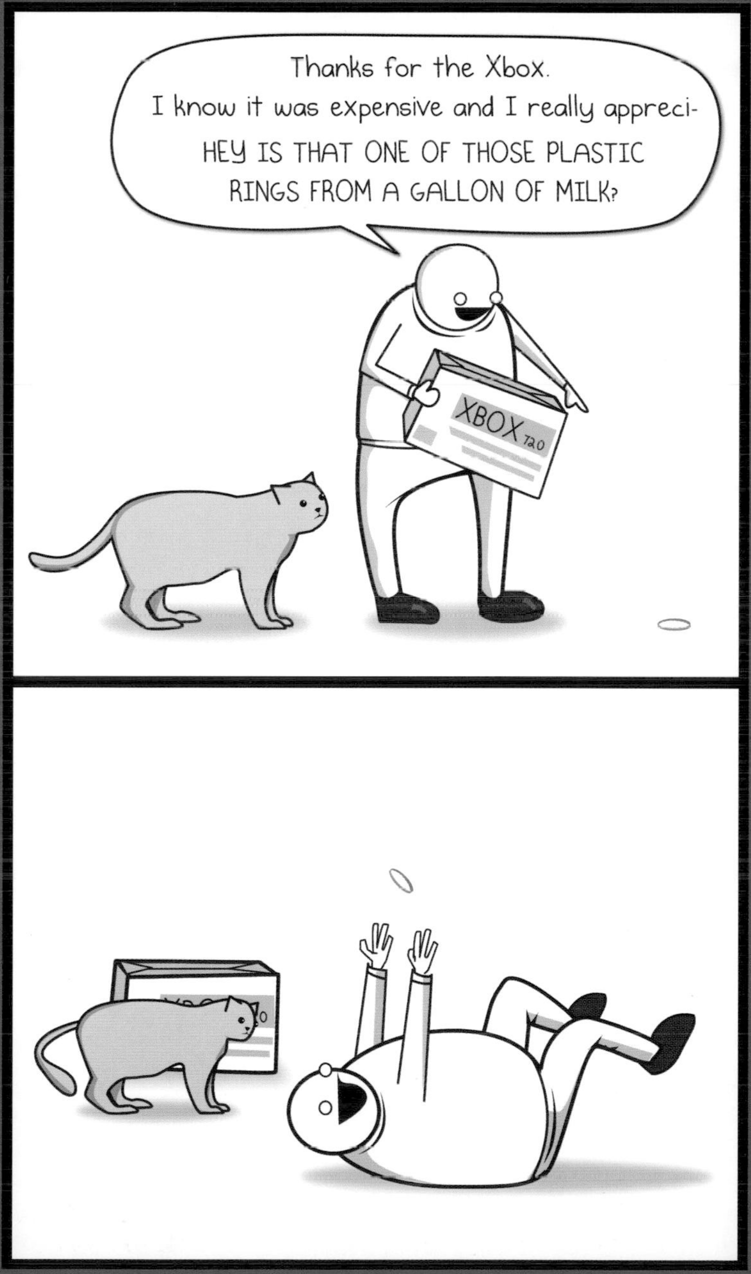
Thanks for the Xbox.
I know it was expensive and I really appreci-
HEY IS THAT ONE OF THOSE PLASTIC
RINGS FROM A GALLON OF MILK?
XBOX 720

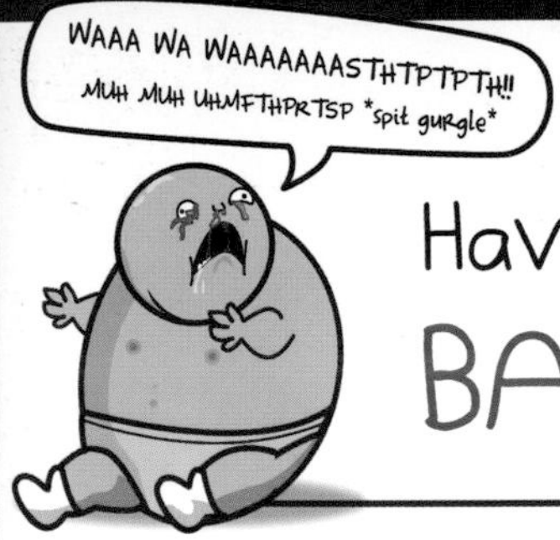
WAAA WA WAAAAAAAASTHTPTPTH!!
MUH MUH UHMFTHPRTSP *spit gurgle*

Having a BABY VS Having a CAT

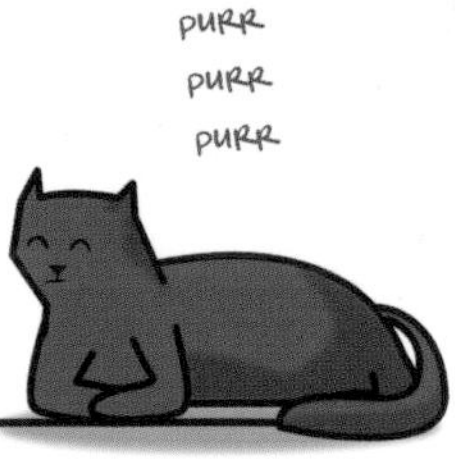
PURR
PURR
PURR

Having a BABY	Having a CAT
Comes shrieking out of a vagina like some kind of jam-covered goblin.	Comes from a pet store or some other mommy cat. Either way it's cute within ten seconds of being yours.
Infants crap in plastic underwear; children crap on your dreams.	Cats just crap in a box.
When upset, babies moan like overweight, needy vultures.	When upset, cats go kill something in the yard and then take a six-hour power nap. Cats handle pain like champs.
If you spoil your kids, they might not grow up to be responsible career-driven individuals.	Cats don't have careers other than being lovable, entertaining, and hairy. Spoil away.
Babies have no special powers other than making you lose your hair and grow love handles.	Cats see in the dark, have glowing eyes, and can perform amazing acrobatic feats. It's like having your own private Batman running around the house.
When they reach the age of 15, they get hormonal, pimply, and start blaring crappy music to cope with their "pain."	When they reach the age of 15, they die of old age. This sounds terrible but it immortalizes them as being perfect. The flame of a cat's life burns fast and bright—they're like furry little cruise missiles.

The Oatmeal

This book was written and drawn by
Matthew Inman.

MAYONNAISE
4 EVER!

The Oatmeal always wears a party hat,
because he's always in the mood to party.

The Oatmeal's real name is Matthew
and he lives in Seattle, Washington.

His favorite activities include
rollerblading in the nude, watching
The Little Mermaid while drunk,
and shampooing his chest hair.

Visit www.theoatmeal.com for
more of Matthew's comics, or
check out his other book:

↳ 5 *Very Good Reasons to
Punch a Dolphin in the Mouth
(and Other Useful Guides)*

www.theoatmeal.com

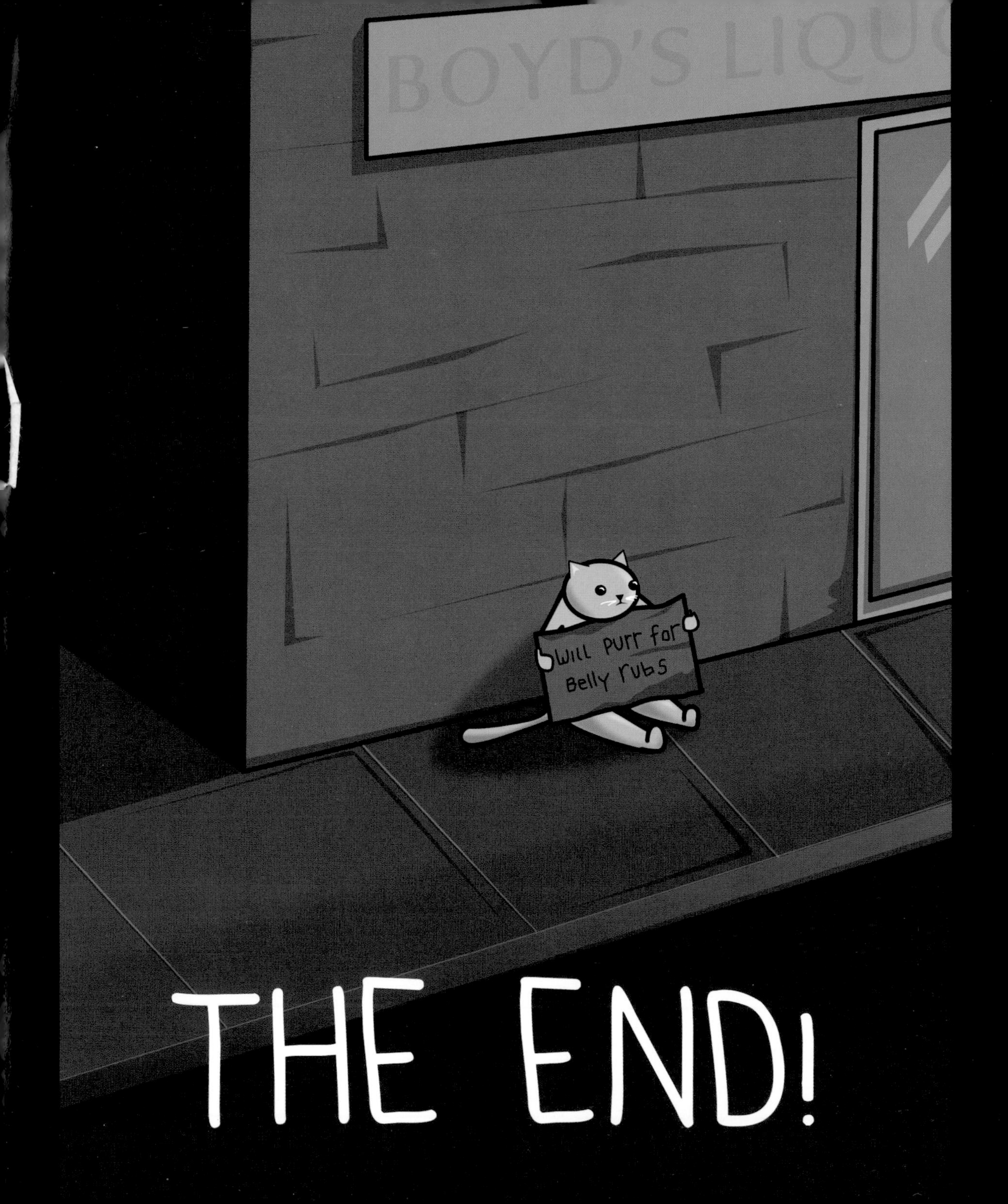
BOYD'S LIQU
Will purr for
Belly rubs
THE END!